THE
MOTHER'S
TOPICAL BIBLE

NEW INTERNATIONAL
VERSION

HONOR

Tulsa, Oklahoma

Presented By:
Wisdom International
P. O. Box 747
Dallas, Texas 75221
214/518-1833

Published by
Honor Books
P. O. Box 55388
Tulsa, Oklahoma 74155

4th Printing
Over 55,000 in Print

ISBN 1-56292-015-4

Presented

to

_____

by

_____

_____

Date

Additional copies of
The Mother's Topical Bible
are available from your local bookstore
or by writing:

Honor Books
P. O. Box 35035 • Tulsa, OK 74153

Contents

A Virtuous Woman
The Salvation Experience
Your Relationship With God

When You Want To Be . . .

When Your Child . . .

When Your Husband . . .

Your Work

Your Daily Schedule

Your Finances

Your Role in the Church

Your Personal Needs

Great Mothers of the Bible

A Virtuous Woman

A wife of noble character who can find? She is worth far more than rubies.

Her husband has full confidence in her and lacks nothing of value. She brings him good, not harm, all the days of her life.

She selects wool and flax and works with eager hands.

She is like the merchant ships, bringing her food from afar.

She gets up while it is still dark; she provides food for her family and portions for her servant girls.

She considers a field and buys it; out of her earnings she plants a vineyard.

She sets about her work vigorously; her arms are strong for her tasks.

She sees that her trading is profitable, and her lamp does not go out at night.

In her hand she holds the distaff and grasps the spindle with her fingers.

She opens her arms to the poor and extends her hands to the needy.

When it snows, she has no fear for her household; for all of them are clothed in scarlet.

She makes coverings for her bed; she is clothed in fine linen and purple.

Her husband is respected at the city gate, where he takes his seat among the elders of the land.

She makes linen garments and sells them, and supplies the merchants with sashes.

She is clothed with strength and dignity; she can laugh at the days to come.

She speaks with wisdom, and faithful instruction is on her tongue.

She watches over the affairs of her household and does not eat the bread of idleness.

Her children arise and call her blessed; her husband also, and he praises her:

"Many women do noble things, but you surpass them all."

Charm is deceptive, and beauty is fleeting; but a woman who fears the LORD is to be praised.

Give her the reward she has earned, and let her works bring her praise at the city gate.

Proverbs 31:10-31

The Salvation Experience

**There Are Three Basic Reasons
To Believe the Bible Is
the Infallible and Pure Word of God**

1. *No human would have written a standard this high.* Think of the best person you know. You must admit he would have left certain scriptures out had he written the Bible. So the Bible projects an inhuman standard and way of life. It has to be God because no man you know would have ever written a standard that high.

2. *There is an aura, a climate, a charisma, a presence the Bible generates which no other book in the world creates.* Lay an encyclopedia on your table at the restaurant, nobody will look at you twice. But when you lay your Bible on the table, they will stare at you, watch you chew your food, and even read your license plate when you get in your car! Why? The Bible creates the presence of God and forces a reaction in the hearts of men.

3. *The nature of man is changed when he reads the Bible.* Men change. *Peace* enters into their spirits. Joy wells up within their lives. Men like what they become when they read this book. Men accept Christ, because this Bible says Jesus Christ is the Son of God and that all have sinned and the wages of sin will bring death; and the only

forgiveness that they can find is through Jesus, the Son of God.

Three Basic Reasons for Accepting Christ

1. *You needed forgiveness.* At some point in your life, you will want to be clean. You will hate guilt; you will crave purity. You have a built-in desire toward God, and you will have to address that appetite at some point in your life.

2. *You need a friend.* You may be sitting there saying, "But, don't I have friends?" Yes, but you have never had a friend like Jesus. Nobody can handle the information about your life as well as He can. He is the most consistent relationship you will ever know. Human friends vacillate in their reaction, depending on your mood or theirs. Jesus Christ never changes his opinion of you. Nobody can tell Him anything which will change His mind about you. You cannot enjoy His world without His companionship.

3. *You needed a future.* All men have a built-in need for immortality, a craving for an eternity. God placed it within us. D.L. Moody once made a statement, "One of these days you are going to hear that I'm dead and gone. When you do, don't believe a word of it. I'll be more alive then, than at any other time in my life." Each of us wonders about eternity. What is death like? What happens when I die? Is there a hell? a heaven? a God? a

devil? What happens? Every man wants to be around tomorrow. The only guarantee you will have of a future is to have the Eternal One on the inside of you. *He is Jesus Christ, the Son of God!*

The Gospel means Good News, you can change; your sins can be forgiven; your guilt can be dissolved; God loves *you*! He wants to be the difference in your life. All have sinned and come short of the glory of God.'' Romans 3:23. ''The wages of sin is death.'' Romans 6:23. You might say, what does that mean? It means that all unconfessed sin will be judged and penalized, but that is not the end of the story. The second part of verse 23 says ''but the gift of God is eternal life through Jesus Christ our Lord.'' What does that mean? It means that between the wrath and judgment of God upon your sin, Jesus Christ the Son of God stepped in and absorbed your judgment and your penalty for you. God says if you recognize and respect Him and His worth as the Son of God, judgment will be withheld, and you will receive a pardon, forgiveness of all your mistakes.

What do you have to do? ''If you believe in your heart that Jesus is the Son of God and that God raised him from the dead on the third day, and confess that with your mouth, then you will be saved.'' Romans 10:9-10. What does the word ''saved'' mean? *Removed from danger*. It simply means if you respect and recognize the worth of Jesus Christ, God will take you out of the danger zone and receive you as a child of the Most High

God. What is His gift that you are to receive? His Son. "For God so loved the world that he gave his only begotten Son, that whosoever believeth in Him should not perish but have everlasting life." John 3:16. How do you accept His Son? Accept His mercy. How do you reject your sins? Confess them and turn away from them. "If I confess my sins he is faithful and just to forgive me my sins and to cleanse me from all unrighteousness." 1 John 1:9. That is the Gospel.

Your Relationship With God

Your Prayer Life

If my people, who are called by my name, will humble themselves and pray and seek my face and turn from their wicked ways, then will I hear from heaven and will forgive their sin and will heal their land.

2 Chronicles 7:14

My heart says of you, "Seek his face!" Your face, LORD, I will seek.

Psalm 27:8

But I call to God, and the LORD saves me. Evening, morning and noon I cry out in distress, and he hears my voice.

Psalm 55:16,17

Glory in his holy name; let the hearts of those who seek the LORD rejoice.
Look to the LORD and his strength; seek his face always.

Psalm 105:3,4

The LORD is near to all who call on him, to all who call on him in truth.

Psalm 145:18

Seek the LORD while he may be found; call on him while he is near.

Isaiah 55:6

But when you pray, go into your room, close the door and pray to your Father, who is unseen. Then your Father, who sees what is done in secret, will reward you.

Matthew 6:6

Then Jesus told his disciples a parable to show them that they should always pray and not give up.

Luke 18:1

In the same way, the Spirit helps us in our weakness. We do not know what we ought to pray for, but the Spirit himself intercedes for us with groans that words cannot express.

Romans 8:26

And pray in the Spirit on all occasions with all kinds of prayers and requests. With this in mind, be alert and always keep on praying for all the saints.

Ephesians 6:18

Do not be anxious about anything, but in everything, by prayer and petition, with thanksgiving, present your requests to God.

Philippians 4:6

Devote yourselves to prayer, being watchful and thankful.

Colossians 4:2

Pray continually.

1 Thessalonians 5:17

I want men everywhere to lift up holy hands in prayer, without anger or disputing.
1 Timothy 2:8

Let us then approach the throne of grace with confidence, so that we may receive mercy and find grace to help us in our time of need.
Hebrews 4:16

For the eyes of the Lord are on the righteous and his ears are attentive to their prayer, but the face of the Lord is against those who do evil.
1 Peter 3:12

But you, dear friends, build yourselves up in your most holy faith and pray in the Holy Spirit.
Jude 1:20

Your Study of God's Word

When Moses went and told the people all the LORD's words and laws, they responded with one voice, "Everything the LORD has said we will do."
Exodus 24:3

Do not add to what I command you and do not subtract from it, but keep the commands of the LORD your God that I give you.
Deuteronomy 4:2

These commandments that I give you today are to be upon your hearts.
Deuteronomy 6:6

He humbled you, causing you to hunger and then feeding you with manna, which neither you nor your fathers had known, to teach you that man does not live on bread alone but on every word that comes from the mouth of the LORD.

Deuteronomy 8:3

No, the word is very near you; it is in your mouth and in your heart so you may obey it.

Deuteronomy 30:14

Do not let this Book of the Law depart from your mouth; meditate on it day and night, so that you may be careful to do everything written in it. Then you will be prosperous and successful.

Joshua 1:8

He remembers his covenant forever, the word he commanded, for a thousand generations.

1 Chronicles 16:15

Accept instruction from his mouth and lay up his words in your heart.

Job 22:22

I have not departed from the commands of his lips; I have treasured the words of his mouth more than my daily bread.

Job 23:12

But his delight is in the law of the LORD, and on his law he meditates day and night.

Psalm 1:2

The law of the LORD is perfect, reviving the soul. The statutes of the LORD are trustworthy, making wise the simple.

Psalm 19:7

I will instruct you and teach you in the way you should go; I will counsel you and watch over you.

Psalm 32:8

The law of his God is in his heart; his feet do not slip.

Psalm 37:31

I have hidden your word in my heart that I might not sin against you.

Your word is a lamp to my feet and a light for my path.

Psalm 119:11,105

When you walk, they will guide you; when you sleep, they will watch over you; when you awake, they will speak to you.

For these commands are a lamp, this teaching is a light, and the corrections of discipline are the way to life.

Proverbs 6:22,23

Therefore everyone who hears these words of mine and puts them into practice is like a wise man who built his house on the rock.

Matthew 7:24

Jesus replied, ''You are in error because you do not know the Scriptures or the power of God.''

Matthew 22:29

Heaven and earth will pass away, but my words will never pass away.

Mark 13:31

To the Jews who had believed him, Jesus said, ''If you hold to my teaching, you are really my disciples.
Then you will know the truth, and the truth will set you free.''

John 8:31,32

Consequently, faith comes from hearing the message, and the message is heard through the word of Christ.

Romans 10:17

All Scripture is God-breathed and is useful for teaching, rebuking, correcting and training in righteousness, so that the man of God may be thoroughly equipped for every good work.

2 Timothy 3:16,17

Your Attitude Toward Praise and Worship

I call to the LORD, who is worthy of praise, and I am saved from my enemies.

2 Samuel 22:4

Ascribe to the LORD the glory due his name. Bring an offering and come before him; worship the LORD in the splendor of his holiness.

1 Chronicles 16:29

The trumpeters and singers joined in unison, as with one voice, to give praise and thanks to the LORD. Accompanied by trumpets, cymbals and other instruments, they raised their voices in praise to the LORD and sang: "He is good; his love endures forever." Then the temple of the LORD was filled with a cloud.

2 Chronicles 5:13

I will give you thanks in the great assembly; among throngs of people I will praise you.

Psalm 35:18

Blessed are those who dwell in your house; they are ever praising you. Selah.

Psalm 84:4

It is good to praise the LORD and make music to your name, O Most High.

Psalm 92:1

Come, let us bow down in worship, let us kneel before the LORD our Maker.

Psalm 95:6

Shout for joy to the LORD, all the earth.
Worship the LORD with gladness; come before him with joyful songs.

Know that the LORD is God. It is he who made us, and we are his; we are his people, the sheep of his pasture.

Enter his gates with thanksgiving and his courts with praise; give thanks to him and praise his name.

Psalm 100:1-4

Let them give thanks to the LORD for his unfailing love and his wonderful deeds for men.

Let them exalt him in the assembly of the people and praise him in the council of the elders.

Psalm 107:8,32

I will bow down toward your holy temple and will praise your name for your love and your faithfulness, for you have exalted above all things your name and your word.

Psalm 138:2

Praise the LORD. Praise God in his sanctuary; praise him in his mighty heavens.

Praise him for his acts of power; praise him for his surpassing greatness.

Praise him with the sounding of the trumpet, praise him with the harp and lyre, praise him with the clash of cymbals, praise him with resounding cymbals.

Let everything that has breath praise the LORD. Praise the LORD.

Psalm 150:1-3,5,6

Yet a time is coming and has now come when the true worshipers will worship the Father in spirit and truth, for they are the kind of worshipers the Father seeks.

God is spirit, and his worshipers must worship in spirit and in truth.

John 4:23,24

So what shall I do? I will pray with my spirit, but I will also pray with my mind; I will sing with my spirit, but I will also sing with my mind.

1 Corinthians 14:15

I want men everywhere to lift up holy hands in prayer, without anger or disputing.

1 Timothy 2:8

You also, like living stones, are being built into a spiritual house to be a holy priesthood, offering spiritual sacrifices acceptable to God through Jesus Christ.

1 Peter 2:5

Your Hourly Obedience to God

Now if you obey me fully and keep my covenant, then out of all nations you will be my treasured possession. Although the whole earth is mine.

Exodus 19:5

And if you walk in my ways and obey my statutes and commands as David your father did, I will give you a long life.

1 Kings 3:14

Blessed is the man who does not walk in the counsel of the wicked or stand in the way of sinners or sit in the seat of mockers.

But his delight is in the law of the LORD, and on his law he meditates day and night.

Psalm 1:1,2

All the ways of the LORD are loving and faithful for those who keep the demands of his covenant.

Psalm 25:10

The fear of the LORD is the beginning of wisdom; all who follow his precepts have good understanding. To him belongs eternal praise.

Psalm 111:10

If you are willing and obedient, you will eat the best from the land.

Isaiah 1:19

Anyone who breaks one of the least of these commandments and teaches others to do the same will be called least in the kingdom of heaven, but whoever practices and teaches these commands will be called great in the kingdom of heaven.

Matthew 5:19

For whoever does the will of my Father in heaven is my brother and sister and mother.
Matthew 12:50

If you love me, you will obey what I command.
Jesus replied, ''If anyone loves me, he will obey my teaching. My Father will love him, and we will come to him and make our home with him.
John 14:15,23

If you obey my commands, you will remain in my love, just as I have obeyed my Father's commands and remain in his love.
You are my friends if you do what I command.
John 15:10,14

And receive from him anything we ask, because we obey his commands and do what pleases him.
1 John 3:22

When You Want To Be...

A Patient Mother

Be still before the LORD and wait patiently for him; do not fret when men succeed in their ways, when they carry out their wicked schemes.

Psalm 37:7

I waited patiently for the LORD; he turned to me and heard my cry.

Psalm 40:1

For you have been my hope, O Sovereign LORD, my confidence since my youth.

Psalm 71:5

The end of a matter is better than its beginning, and patience is better than pride.

Do not be quickly provoked in your spirit, for anger resides in the lap of fools.

Ecclesiastes 7:8,9

But those who hope in the LORD will renew their strength. They will soar on wings like eagles; they will run and not grow weary, they will walk and not be faint.

Isaiah 40:31

But blessed is the man who trusts in the LORD, whose confidence is in him.

Jeremiah 17:7

By standing firm you will gain life.

Luke 21:19

Not only so, but we also rejoice in our sufferings, because we know that suffering produces perseverance; perseverance, character; and character, hope.

And hope does not disappoint us, because God has poured out his love into our hearts by the Holy Spirit, whom he has given us.

Romans 5:3-5

But if we hope for what we do not yet have, we wait for it patiently.

Romans 8:25

For everything that was written in the past was written to teach us, so that through endurance and the encouragement of the Scriptures we might have hope.

May the God who gives endurance and encouragement give you a spirit of unity among yourselves as you follow Christ Jesus,

May the God of hope fill you with all joy and peace as you trust in him, so that you may overflow with hope by the power of the Holy Spirit.

Romans 15:4,5,13

But the fruit of the Spirit is love, joy, peace, patience, kindness, goodness, faithfulness.

Galatians 5:22

I can do everything through him who gives me strength.

Philippians 4:13

We do not want you to become lazy, but to imitate those who through faith and patience inherit what has been promised.

Hebrews 6:12

So do not throw away your confidence; it will be richly rewarded.

You need to persevere so that when you have done the will of God, you will receive what he has promised.

For in just a very little while, "He who is coming will come and will not delay."

Hebrews 10:35-37

Because you know that the testing of your faith develops perseverance.

Perseverance must finish its work so that you may be mature and complete, not lacking anything.

James 1:3,4

Be patient, then, brothers, until the Lord's coming. See how the farmer waits for the land to yield its valuable crop and how patient he is for the autumn and spring rains.

You too, be patient and stand firm, because the Lord's coming is near.

James 5:7,8

For this very reason, make every effort to add to your faith goodness; and to goodness, knowledge; and to knowledge, self-control; and to self-control, perseverance; and to perseverance, godliness.

2 Peter 1:5,6

A Loving Mother

Hatred stirs up dissension, but love covers over all wrongs.

Proverbs 10:12

Many waters cannot quench love; rivers cannot wash it away. If one were to give all the wealth of his house for love, it would be utterly scorned.

Song of Solomon 8:7

A new command I give you: Love one another. As I have loved you, so you must love one another.

By this all men will know that you are my disciples, if you love one another.

John 13:34,35

As the Father has loved me, so have I loved you. Now remain in my love.

If you obey my commands, you will remain in my love, just as I have obeyed my Father's commands and remain in his love.

My command is this: Love each other as I have loved you.

Greater love has no one than this, that he lay down his life for his friends.

You are my friends if you do what I command.

I no longer call you servants, because a servant does not know his master's business. Instead, I have called you friends, for everything that I learned from my Father I have made known to you.

You did not choose me, but I chose you and appointed you to go and bear fruit — fruit that will last. Then the Father will give you whatever you ask in my name.

This is my command: Love each other.

John 15:9,10,12-17

Let no debt remain outstanding, except the continuing debt to love one another, for he who loves his fellowman has fulfilled the law.

Love does no harm to its neighbor. Therefore love is the fulfillment of the law.

Romans 13:8,10

If I speak in the tongues of men and of angels, but have not love, I am only a resounding gong or a clanging cymbal.

If I have the gift of prophecy and can fathom all mysteries and all knowledge, and if I have a faith that can move mountains, but have not love, I am nothing.

If I give all I possess to the poor and surrender my body to the flames, but have not love, I gain nothing.

Love is patient, love is kind. It does not envy, it does not boast, it is not proud.

It is not rude, it is not self-seeking, it is not easily angered, it keeps no record of wrongs.

Love does not delight in evil but rejoices with the truth.

It always protects, always trusts, always hopes, always perseveres.

Love never fails.

1 Corinthians 13:1-8a

And now these three remain: faith, hope and love. But the greatest of these is love.

1 Corinthians 13:13

And live a life of love, just as Christ loved us and gave himself up for us as a fragrant offering and sacrifice to God.

Ephesians 5:2

May the Lord make your love increase and overflow for each other and for everyone else, just as ours does for you.

1 Thessalonians 3:12

God is not unjust; he will not forget your work and the love you have shown him as you have helped his people and continue to help them.

Hebrews 6:10

And let us consider how we may spur one another on toward love and good deeds.

Hebrews 10:24

If you really keep the royal law found in Scripture, "Love your neighbor as yourself," you are doing right.

James 2:8

This is the message you heard from the beginning: We should love one another.

1 John 3:11

We know that we have passed from death to life, because we love our brothers. Anyone who does not love remains in death.

1 John 3:14

Dear children, let us not love with words or tongue but with actions and in truth.

1 John 3:18

Dear friends, let us love one another, for love comes from God. Everyone who loves has been born of God and knows God.

Whoever does not love does not know God, because God is love.

1 John 4:7,8

Above all, love each other deeply, because love covers over a multitude of sins.

1 Peter 4:8

A Giving Mother

"Bring the whole tithe into the storehouse, that there may be food in my house. Test me in this," says the LORD Almighty, "and see if I will not throw open the floodgates of heaven and pour out so much blessing that you will not have room enough for it.

I will prevent pests from devouring your crops, and the vines in your fields will not cast their fruit," says the LORD Almighty.

"Then all the nations will call you blessed, for yours will be a delightful land," says the LORD Almighty.

Malachi 3:10-12

But as for you, be strong and do not give up, for your work will be rewarded.

2 Chronicles 15:7

Good will come to him who is generous and lends freely, who conducts his affairs with justice.

Psalm 112:5

Honor the LORD with your wealth, with the firstfruits of all your crops; then your barns will be filled to overflowing, and your vats will brim over with new wine.

Proverbs 3:9,10

He who is kind to the poor lends to the LORD, and he will reward him for what he has done.

Proverbs 19:17

A generous man will himself be blessed, for he shares his food with the poor.

Proverbs 22:9

He who gives to the poor will lack nothing, but he who closes his eyes to them receives many curses.

Proverbs 28:27

Cast your bread upon the waters, for after many days you will find it again.

Ecclesiastes 11:1

Heal the sick, raise the dead, cleanse those who have leprosy, drive out demons. Freely you have received, freely give.

Matthew 10:8

And everyone who has left houses or brothers or sisters or father or mother or children or fields for my sake will receive a hundred times as much and will inherit eternal life.

Matthew 19:29

Give, and it will be given to you. A good measure, pressed down, shaken together and running over, will be poured into your lap. For with the measure you use, it will be measured to you.

Luke 6:38

On the first day of every week, each one of you should set aside a sum of money in keeping with his income, saving it up, so that when I come no collections will have to be made.

1 Corinthians 16:2

Remember this: Whoever sows sparingly will also reap sparingly, and whoever sows generously will also reap generously.

Each man should give what he has decided in his heart to give, not reluctantly or under compulsion, for God loves a cheerful giver.

And God is able to make all grace abound to you, so that in all things at all times, having all that you need, you will abound in every good work.

2 Corinthians 9:6-8

Command those who are rich in this present world not to be arrogant nor to put their hope in wealth, which is so uncertain, but to put their hope in God, who richly provides us with everything for our enjoyment.

Command them to do good, to be rich in good deeds, and to be generous and willing to share.

In this way they will lay up treasure for themselves as a firm foundation for the coming age, so that they may take hold of the life that is truly life.

1 Timothy 6:17-19

If anyone has material possessions and sees his brother in need but has no pity on him, how can the love of God be in him?

Dear children, let us not love with words or tongue but with actions and in truth.

1 John 3:17,18

Dear friend, I pray that you may enjoy good health and that all may go well with you, even as your soul is getting along well.

3 John 1:2

A Resourceful Mother

But it is the spirit in a man, the breath of the Almighty, that gives him understanding.

Job 32:8

He may speak in their ears and terrify them with warnings.

Job 33:16

I will praise the LORD, who counsels me; even at night my heart instructs me.

Psalm 16:7

I will instruct you and teach you in the way you should go; I will counsel you and watch over you.

Psalm 32:8

Surely you desire truth in the inner parts; you teach me wisdom in the inmost place.

Psalm 51:6

The LORD will fulfill for me; your love, O LORD, endures forever — do not abandon the works of your hands.

Psalm 138:8

Let the wise listen and add to their learning, and let the discerning get guidance.

Proverbs 1:5

Wisdom is supreme; therefore get wisdom. Though it cost all you have, get understanding.

Esteem her, and she will exalt you; embrace her, and she will honor you.

Proverbs 4:7,8

I love those who love me, and those who seek me find me.

With me are riches and honor, enduring wealth and prosperity.

Bestowing wealth on those who love me and making their treasuries full.

Proverbs 8:17,18,21

The plans of the righteous are just, but the advice of the wicked is deceitful.

Proverbs 12:5

He who walks with the wise grows wise, but a companion of fools suffers harm.

Proverbs 13:20

Know also that wisdom is sweet to your soul; if you find it, there is a future hope for you, and your hope will not be cut off.

Proverbs 24:14

See, the former things have taken place, and new things I declare; before they spring into being I announce them to you.

Isaiah 42:9

Ask and it will be given to you; seek and you will find; knock and the door will be opened to you.

Matthew 7:7

Suppose one of you wants to build a tower. Will he not first sit down and estimate the cost to see if he has enough money to complete it?

Luke 14:28

If any of you lacks wisdom, he should ask God, who gives generously to all without finding fault, and it will be given to him.

James 1:5

A Godly Example as a Mother

He did what was right in the eyes of the LORD, just as his father David had done.

2 Chronicles 29:2

He who walks with the wise grows wise, but a companion of fools suffers harm.

Proverbs 13:20

And if anyone gives even a cup of cold water to one of these little ones because he is my disciple, I tell you the truth, he will certainly not lose his reward.

Matthew 10:42

Just as the Son of Man did not come to be served, but to serve, and to give his life as a ransom for many.

Matthew 20:28

Not so with you. Instead, whoever wants to become great among you must be your servant, and whoever wants to be first must be slave of all.

Mark 10:43,44

The expert in the law replied, "The one who had mercy on him." Jesus told him, "Go and do likewise."

Luke 10:37

I have set you an example that you should do as I have done for you.

I tell you the truth, no servant is greater than his master, nor is a messenger greater than the one who sent him.

A new command I give you: Love one another. As I have loved you, so you must love one another.

John 13:15,16,34

May the God who gives endurance and encouragement give you a spirit of unity among yourselves as you follow Christ Jesus, so that with one heart and mouth you may glorify the God and Father of our Lord Jesus Christ.

Accept one another, then, just as Christ accepted you, in order to bring praise to God.

Romans 15:5-7

Now it is required that those who have been given a trust must prove faithful.

1 Corinthians 4:2

Therefore, my dear brothers, stand firm. Let nothing move you. Always give yourselves fully to the work of the Lord, because you know that your labor in the Lord is not in vain.

1 Corinthians 15:58

Carry each other's burdens, and in this way you will fulfill the law of Christ.

Therefore, as we have opportunity, let us do good to all people, especially to those who belong to the family of believers.

Galatians 6:2,10

Be imitators of God, therefore, as dearly loved children and live a life of love, just as Christ loved us and gave himself up for us as a fragrant offering and sacrifice to God.

Ephesians 5:1,2

Slaves, obey your earthly masters with respect and fear, and with sincerity of heart, just as you would obey Christ.

Obey them not only to win their favor when their eye is on you, but like slaves of Christ, doing the will of God from your heart.

Serve wholeheartedly, as if you were serving the Lord, not men.

Ephesians 6:5-7

Your attitude should be the same as that of Christ Jesus:

Who, being in very nature God, did not consider equality with God something to be grasped, but made himself nothing, taking the very nature of a servant, being made in human likeness.

And being found in appearance as a man, he humbled himself and became obedient to death — even death on a cross!

Philippians 2:5-8

Bear with each other and forgive whatever grievances you may have against one another. Forgive as the Lord forgave you.

Slaves, obey your earthly masters in everything; and do it, not only when their eye is on you and to win their favor, but with sincerity of heart and reverence for the Lord.

Colossians 3:13,22

To this you were called, because Christ suffered for you, leaving you an example, that you should follow in his steps.

1 Peter 2:21

For everything in the world — the cravings of sinful man, the lust of his eyes and the boasting of what he has and does — comes not from the Father but from the world.

1 John 2:16

This is how we know what love is: Jesus Christ laid down his life for us. And we ought to lay down our lives for our brothers.

1 John 3:16

A Diligent Mother

But as for you, be strong and do not give up, for your work will be rewarded.

2 Chronicles 15:7

And who knows but that you have come to royal position for such a time as this?

Esther 4:14b

He who gathers crops in summer is a wise son, but he who sleeps during harvest is a disgraceful son.

Proverbs 10:5

Diligent hands will rule, but laziness ends in slave labor.

Proverbs 12:24

The sluggard craves and gets nothing, but the desires of the diligent are fully satisfied.

Proverbs 13:4

The plans of the diligent lead to profit as surely as haste leads to poverty.

Proverbs 21:5

Do you see a man skilled in his work? He will serve before kings; he will not serve before obscure men.

Proverbs 22:29

The Sovereign LORD is my strength; he makes my feet like the feet of a deer, he enables me to go on the heights. For the director of music. On my stringed instruments.

Habakkuk 3:19

Do you not say, "Four months more and then the harvest"? I tell you, open your eyes and look at the fields! They are ripe for harvest.

John 4:35

As long as it is day, we must do the work of him who sent me. Night is coming, when no one can work.

John 9:4

Therefore, as we have opportunity, let us do good to all people, especially to those who belong to the family of believers.

Galatians 6:10

Now to him who is able to do immeasurably more than all we ask or imagine, according to his power that is at work within us.

Ephesians 3:20

I can do everything through him who gives me strength.

Philippians 4:13

We want each of you to show this same diligence to the very end, in order to make your hope sure.

Hebrews 6:11

If any of you lacks wisdom, he should ask God, who gives generously to all without finding fault, and it will be given to him.

James 1:5

So then, dear friends, since you are looking forward to this, make every effort to be found spotless, blameless and at peace with him.

2 Peter 3:14

I know your deeds. See, I have placed before you an open door that no one can shut. I know that you have little strength, yet you have kept my word and have not denied my name.

Revelation 3:8

An Honest Mother

Now if you obey me fully and keep my covenant, then out of all nations you will be my treasured possession. Although the whole earth is mine.

Exodus 19:5

And if you walk in my ways and obey my statutes and commands as David your father did, I will give you a long life.

1 Kings 3:14

Then the LORD said to Satan, "Have you considered my servant Job? There is no one on earth like him; he is blameless and upright, a man who fears God and shuns evil. And he still maintains his integrity, though you incited me against him to ruin him without any reason."

Job 2:3

Blessed is the man who does not walk in the counsel of the wicked or stand in the way of sinners or sit in the seat of mockers.

But his delight is in the law of the LORD, and on his law he meditates day and night.

Psalm 1:1,2

All the ways of the LORD are loving and faithful for those who keep the demands of his covenant.

Psalm 25:10

The fear of the LORD is the beginning of wisdom; all who follow his precepts have good understanding. To him belongs eternal praise.

Psalm 111:10

Blessed are they who keep his statutes and seek him with all their heart.

You have laid down precepts that are to be fully obeyed.

Psalm 119:2,4

Vindicate me, O LORD, for I have led a blameless life; I have trusted in the LORD without wavering.

Psalm 26:1

In my integrity you uphold me and set me in your presence forever.

Psalm 41:12

And David shepherded them with integrity of heart; with skillful hands he led them.

Psalm 78:72

The integrity of the upright guides them, but the unfaithful are destroyed by their duplicity.

Proverbs 11:3

Better a poor man whose walk is blameless than a fool whose lips are perverse.

He who obeys instructions guards his life, but he who is contemptuous of his ways will die.

Proverbs 19:1,16

The righteous man leads a blameless life; blessed are his children after him.

Proverbs 20:7

If you are willing and obedient, you will eat the best from the land.

Isaiah 1:19

Do not repay anyone evil for evil. Be careful to do what is right in the eyes of everybody.

Romans 12:17

Finally, brothers, whatever is true, whatever is noble, whatever is right, whatever is pure, whatever is lovely, whatever is admirable — if anything is excellent or praiseworthy — think about such things.

Philippians 4:8

Live such good lives among the pagans that, though they accuse you of doing wrong, they may see your good deeds and glorify God on the day he visits us.

1 Peter 2:12

An Understanding Mother

Trust in the LORD with all your heart and lean not on your own understanding; in all your ways acknowledge him, and he will make your paths straight.

Proverbs 3:5,6

As for God, his way is perfect; the word of the LORD is flawless. He is a shield for all who take refuge in him.

Psalm 18:30

Teach me your way, O LORD; lead me in a straight path because of my oppressors.

Psalm 27:11

I am your servant; give me discernment that I may understand your statutes.

The unfolding of your words gives light; it gives understanding to the simple.

May my cry come before you, O LORD; give me understanding according to your word.

Psalm 119:125,130,169

Counsel and sound judgment are mine; I have understanding and power.

Proverbs 8:14

Understanding is a fountain of life to those who have it, but folly brings punishment to fools.

A wise man's heart guides his mouth, and his lips promote instruction.

Proverbs 16:22,23

By wisdom a house is built, and through understanding it is established; through knowledge its rooms are filled with rare and beautiful treasures.

Proverbs 24:3,4

"For my thoughts are not your thoughts, neither are your ways my ways," declares the LORD.

"As the heavens are higher than the earth, so are my ways higher than your ways and my thoughts than your thoughts."

Isaiah 55:8,9

Call to me and I will answer you and tell you great and unsearchable things you do not know.

Jeremiah 33:3

Then he opened their minds so they could understand the Scriptures.

Luke 24:45

Because through Christ Jesus the law of the Spirit of life set me free from the law of sin and death.

Romans 8:2

I keep asking that the God of our Lord Jesus Christ, the glorious Father, may give you the Spirit of wisdom and revelation, so that you may know him better.

I pray also that the eyes of your heart may be enlightened in order that you may know the hope to which he has called you, the riches of his glorious inheritance in the saints.

Ephesians 1:17,18

Therefore do not be foolish, but understand what the Lord's will is.

Ephesians 5:17

We know also that the Son of God has come and has given us understanding, so that we may know him who is true. And we are in him who is true — even in his Son Jesus Christ. He is the true God and eternal life.

1 John 5:20

A Creative Mother

Now go; I will help you speak and will teach you what to say.

Exodus 4:12

Be strong and very courageous. Be careful to obey all the law my servant Moses gave you; do not turn from it to the right or to the left, that you may be successful wherever you go.

Joshua 1:7

But it is the spirit in a man, the breath of the Almighty, that gives him understanding.

Job 32:8

He may speak in their ears and terrify them with warnings.

Job 33:16

I will praise the LORD, who counsels me; even at night my heart instructs me.

Psalm 16:7

I will instruct you and teach you in the way you should go; I will counsel you and watch over you.

Psalm 32:8

The LORD will fulfill for me; your love, O LORD, endures forever — do not abandon the works of your hands.

Psalm 138:8

Let the wise listen and add to their learning, and let the discerning get guidance.

Proverbs 1:5

Wisdom is supreme; therefore get wisdom. Though it cost all you have, get understanding.

Esteem her, and she will exalt you; embrace her, and she will honor you.

Proverbs 4:7,8

I love those who love me, and those who seek me find me.

With me are riches and honor, enduring wealth and prosperity.

Proverbs 8:17,18

Bestowing wealth on those who love me and making their treasuries full.

Proverbs 8:21

Know also that wisdom is sweet to your soul; if you find it, there is a future hope for you, and your hope will not be cut off.

Proverbs 24:14

See, the former things have taken place, and new things I declare; before they spring into being I announce them to you.

Isaiah 42:9

See, I am doing a new thing! Now it springs up; do you not perceive it? I am making a way in the desert and streams in the wasteland.

Isaiah 43:19

You have heard these things; look at them all. Will you not admit them? From now on I will tell you of new things, of hidden things unknown to you.

They are created now, and not long ago; you have not heard of them before today. So you cannot say, "Yes, I knew of them."

Isaiah 48:6,7

The Sovereign LORD has given me an instructed tongue, to know the word that sustains the weary. He wakens me morning by morning, wakens my ear to listen like one being taught.

Isaiah 50:4

Then the LORD replied: "Write down the revelation and make it plain on tablets so that a herald may run with it.

For the revelation awaits an appointed time; it speaks of the end and will not prove false. Though it linger, wait for it; it will certainly come and will not delay."

Habakkuk 2:2,3

Who despises the day of small things? Men will rejoice when they see the plumb line in the hand of Zerubbabel. These seven are the eyes of the LORD, which range throughout the earth.

Zechariah 4:10

Ask and it will be given to you; seek and you will find; knock and the door will be opened to you.

Matthew 7:7

Suppose one of you wants to build a tower. Will he not first sit down and estimate the cost to see if he has enough money to complete it?

Luke 14:28

Because you know that the Lord will reward everyone for whatever good he does, whether he is slave or free.

Ephesians 6:8

A Hospitable Mother

Share with God's people who are in need. Practice hospitality.

Romans 12:13

Rather he must be hospitable, one who loves what is good, who is self-controlled, upright, holy and disciplined.

Titus 1:8

Offer hospitality to one another without grumbling.

1 Peter 4:9

I am a friend to all who fear you, to all who follow your precepts.

Psalm 119:63

A friend loves at all times.

Proverbs 17:17a

A man of many companions may come to ruin, but there is a friend who sticks closer than a brother.

Proverbs 18:24

Do not make friends with a hot-tempered man, do not associate with one easily angered.

Proverbs 22:24

"Though the mountains be shaken and the hills be removed, yet my unfailing love for you will not be shaken nor my covenant of peace be removed," says the LORD, who has compassion on you.

Isaiah 54:10

For whoever does the will of my Father in heaven is my brother and sister and mother.

Matthew 12:50

So I say to you: Ask and it will be given to you; seek and you will find; knock and the door will be opened to you.

Luke 11:9

But when you are invited, take the lowest place, so that when your host comes, he will say to you, "Friend, move up to a better place." Then you will be honored in the presence of all your fellow guests.

Luke 14:10

I will not leave you as orphans; I will come to you.

John 14:18

My command is this: Love each other as I have loved you.

Greater love has no one than this, that one lay down his life for his friends.

You are my friends if you do what I command.

I no longer call you servants, because a servant does not know his master's business. Instead, I have called you friends, for everything that I learned from my Father I have made known to you.

You did not choose me, but I chose you to go and bear fruit — fruit that will last. Then the Father will give you whatever you ask in my name.

John 15:12-16

God, who has called you into fellowship with his Son Jesus Christ our Lord, is faithful.

1 Corinthians 1:9

Keep your lives free from the love of money and be content with what you have, because God has said, "Never will I leave you; never will I forsake you."

Hebrews 13:5

But if we walk in the light, as he is in the light, we have fellowship with one another, and the blood of Jesus, his Son, purifies us from all sin.

1 John 1:7

Here I am! I stand at the door and knock. If anyone hears my voice and opens the door, I will come in and eat with him, and he with me.

Revelation 3:20

A Courageous Mother

Be strong and courageous. Do not be afraid or terrified because of them, for the LORD your God goes with you; he will never leave you nor forsake you.

Deuteronomy 31:6

Be strong and courageous, for you will bring the Israelites into the land I promised them on oath, and I myself will be with you.

Deuteronomy 31:23b

Be strong and courageous, because you will lead these people to inherit the land I swore to their forefathers to give them.

Joshua 1:6

David also said to Solomon his son, "Be strong and courageous, and do the work. Do not be afraid or discouraged, for the LORD God, my God, is with you. He will not fail you or forsake you until all the work for the service of the temple of the LORD is finished."

1 Chronicles 28:20

But as for you, be strong and do not give up, for your work will be rewarded.

2 Chronicles 15:7

Be strong and take heart, all you who hope in the LORD.

Psalm 31:24

Counsel and sound judgment are mine; I have understanding and power.

Proverbs 8:14

Strengthen the feeble hands, steady the knees that give way.

Isaiah 35:3

So do not fear, for I am with you; do not be dismayed, for I am your God. I will strengthen you and help you; I will uphold you with my righteous right hand.

Isaiah 41:10

The Sovereign LORD is my strength; he makes my feet like the feet of a deer, he enables me to go on the heights. For the director of music. On my stringed instruments.

Habakkuk 3:19

But you will receive power when the Holy Spirit comes on you; and you will be my witnesses in Jerusalem, and in all Judea and Samaria, and to the ends of the earth.

Acts 1:8

But God chose the foolish things of the world to shame the wise; God chose the weak things of the world to shame the strong.

1 Corinthians 1:27

To one there is given through the Spirit the message of wisdom, to another the message of knowledge by means of the same Spirit.

1 Corinthians 12:8

And God is able to make all grace abound to you, so that in all things at all times, having all that you need, you will abound in every good work.

2 Corinthians 9:8

Now to him who is able to do immeasurably more than all we ask or imagine, according to his power that is at work within us.

Ephesians 3:20

I can do everything through him who gives me strength.

Philippians 4:13

So do not throw away your confidence; it will be richly rewarded.

You need to persevere so that when you have done the will of God, you will receive what he has promised.

Hebrews 10:35,36

If any of you lacks wisdom, he should ask God, who gives generously to all without finding fault, and it will be given to him.

James 1:5

A Joyful Mother

Let the heavens rejoice, let the earth be glad; let them say among the nations, "The LORD reigns!"

1 Chronicles 16:31

You have filled my heart with greater joy than when their grain and new wine abound.

Psalm 4:7

But let all who take refuge in you be glad; let them ever sing for joy. Spread your protection over them, that those who love your name may rejoice in you.

Psalm 5:11

Weeping may remain for a night, but rejoicing comes in the morning.

Psalm 30:5b

Delight yourself in the LORD and he will give you the desires of your heart.

Psalm 37:4

Blessed are those who have learned to acclaim you, who walk in the light of your presence, O LORD.

Psalm 89:15

Shout for joy to the LORD, all the earth.

Worship the LORD with gladness; come before him with joyful songs.

Know that the LORD is God. It is he who made us, and we are his; we are his people, the sheep of his pasture.

Enter his gates with thanksgiving and his courts with praise; give thanks to him and praise his name.

Psalm 100:1-4

Those who sow in tears will reap with songs of joy.

Psalm 126:5

A happy heart makes the face cheerful, but heartache crushes the spirit.

Proverbs 15:13

A cheerful heart is good medicine, but a crushed spirit dries up the bones.

Proverbs 17:22

You will go out in joy and be led forth in peace; the mountains and hills will burst into song before you, and all the trees of the field will clap their hands.

Isaiah 55:12

Though the fig tree does not bud and there are no grapes on the vines, though the olive crop fails and the fields produce no food, though there are no sheep in the pen and no cattle in the stalls, yet I will rejoice in the LORD, I will be joyful in God my Savior.

Habakkuk 3:17,18

However, do not rejoice that the spirits submit to you, but rejoice that your names are written in heaven.

Luke 10:20

May the God of hope fill you with all joy and peace as you trust in him, so that you may overflow with hope by the power of the Holy Spirit.

Romans 15:13

But the fruit of the Spirit is love, joy, peace, patience, kindness, goodness, faithfulness.

Galatians 5:22

Speak to one another with psalms, hymns and spiritual songs. Sing and make music in your heart to the Lord.

Ephesians 5:19

We write this to make our joy complete.

1 John 1:4

A Consistent Mother

I the LORD do not change.

Malachi 3:6a

I will establish his kingdom forever if he is unswerving in carrying out my commands and laws, as is being done at this time.

1 Chronicles 28:7

But you are a shield around me, O LORD; you bestow glory on me and lift up my head.

Psalm 3:3

The LORD is my light and my salvation — whom shall I fear? The LORD is the stronghold of my life — of whom shall I be afraid?

Though an army besiege me, my heart will not fear; though war break out against me, even then will I be confident.

For in the day of trouble he will keep me safe in his dwelling; he will hide me in the shelter of his tabernacle and set me high upon a rock.

Psalm 27:1,3,5

It is better to take refuge in the LORD than to trust in man.

Psalm 118:8

Trust in the LORD with all your heart and lean not on your own understanding; in all your ways acknowledge him, and he will make your paths straight.

Proverbs 3:5,6

For the LORD will be your confidence and will keep your foot from being snared.

Proverbs 3:26

In his heart a man plans his course, but the LORD determines his steps.

Proverbs 16:9

He gives strength to the weary and increases the power of the weak.

Isaiah 40:29

Because the Sovereign LORD helps me, I will not be disgraced.

Isaiah 50:7a

Whoever serves me must follow me; and where I am, my servant also will be. My Father will honor the one who serves me.

John 12:26

Love never fails. But where there are prophecies, they will cease; where there are tongues, they will be stilled; where there is knowledge, it will pass away.

1 Corinthians 13:8

If any of you lacks wisdom, he should ask God, who gives generously to all without finding fault, and it will be given to him.

James 1:5

A Good Listener as a Mother

Let the wise listen and add to their learning, and let the discerning get guidance — for understanding proverbs and parables, the sayings and riddles of the wise.

The fear of the LORD is the beginning of knowledge, but fools despise wisdom and discipline.

Listen, my son, to your father's instruction and do not forsake your mother's teaching.

Proverbs 1:5-8

The heart of the discerning acquires knowledge; the ears of the wise seek it out.

Proverbs 18:15

Therefore hear the word of the LORD, you scoffers who rule this people in Jerusalem.

Isaiah 28:14

The man said to me, "Son of man, look with your eyes and hear with your ears and pay attention to everything I am going to show you."

Ezekiel 40:4a

But everyone who hears these words of mine and does not put them into practice is like a foolish man who built his house on sand.

The rain came down, the streams rose, and the winds blew and beat against that house, and it fell with a great crash.

Matthew 7:26,27

But blessed are your eyes because they see, and your ears because they hear.

Matthew 13:16

Therefore consider carefully how you listen. Whoever has will be given more; whoever does not have, even what he thinks he has will be taken from him.

Luke 8:18

He who listens to you listens to me; he who rejects you rejects me; but he who rejects me rejects him who sent me.

Luke 10:16

He who belongs to God hears what God says. The reason you do not hear is that you do not belong to God.

John 8:47

"You are a king, then!" said Pilate. Jesus answered, "You are right in saying I am a king. In fact, for this reason I was born, and for this I came into the world, to testify to the truth. Everyone on the side of truth listens to me."

John 18:37

Do not merely listen to the word, and so deceive yourselves. Do what it says.

James 1:22

Anyone who listens to the word but does not do what it says is like a man who looks at his face in a mirror.

James 1:23

But the man who looks intently into the perfect law that gives freedom, and continues to do this, not forgetting what he has heard, but doing it — he will be blessed in what he does.

James 1:25

He who has an ear, let him hear what the Spirit says to the churches.

Revelation 2:29

A Compassionate Mother

Then you will call, and the LORD will answer; you will cry for help, and he will say: Here am I. ''If you do away with the yoke of oppression, with the pointing finger and malicious talk, and if you spend yourselves in behalf of the hungry and satisfy the needs of the oppressed, then your light will rise in the darkness, and your night will become like the noonday.

The LORD will guide you always; he will satisfy your needs in a sun-scorched land and will strengthen your frame. You will be like a well-watered garden, like a spring whose waters never fail.''

Isaiah 58:9-11

The LORD is my shepherd, I shall not be in want.

Psalm 23:1

All the ways of the LORD are loving and faithful for those who keep the demands of his covenant.

Psalm 25:10

The wicked borrow and do not repay, but the righteous give generously.

Psalm 37:21

Yet he was merciful; he forgave their iniquities and did not destroy them. Time after time he restrained his anger and did not stir up his full wrath.

Psalm 78:38

He who pursues righteousness and love finds life, prosperity and honor.

Proverbs 21:21

He who conceals his sins does not prosper, but whoever confesses and renounces them finds mercy.

Proverbs 28:13

Can a mother forget the baby at her breast and have no compassion on the child she has borne? Though she may forget, I will not forget you!

Isaiah 49:15

But after I uproot them, I will again have compassion and will bring each of them back to his own inheritance and his own country.

Jeremiah 12:15

When Jesus landed and saw a large crowd, he had compassion on them, because they were like sheep without a shepherd. So he began teaching them many things.

Mark 6:34

As he approached the town gate, a dead person was being carried out — the only son of his mother, and she was a widow. And a large crowd from the town was with her.

When the Lord saw her, his heart went out to her and he said, "Don't cry."

Luke 7:12,13

Love is patient, love is kind. It does not envy, it does not boast, it is not proud.

It is not rude, it is not self-seeking, it is not easily angered, it keeps no record of wrongs.

Love does not delight in evil but rejoices with the truth.

It always protects, always trusts, always hopes, always perseveres.

1 Corinthians 13:4-7

Finally, all of you, live in harmony with one another; be sympathetic, love as brothers, be compassionate and humble.

1 Peter 3:8

When Your Child...

When Your Child Becomes Unruly

But Samuel replied: "Does the LORD delight in burnt offerings and sacrifices as much as in obeying the voice of the LORD? To obey is better than sacrifice, and to heed is better than the fat of rams.

For rebellion is like the sin of divination, and arrogance like the evil of idolatry. Because you have rejected the word of the LORD, he has rejected you as king."

1 Samuel 15:22,23

A man's wisdom gives him patience; it is to his glory to overlook an offense.

Proverbs 19:11

It is to a man's honor to avoid strife, but every fool is quick to quarrel.

Proverbs 20:3

If a ruler's anger rises against you, do not leave your post; calmness can lay great errors to rest.

Ecclesiastes 10:4

"If you are willing and obedient, you will eat the best from the land; but if you resist and rebel, you will be devoured by the sword.'' For the mouth of the LORD has spoken.

Isaiah 1:19,20

Blessed are the peacemakers, for they will be called sons of God.

Matthew 5:9

If it is possible, as far as it depends on you, live at peace with everyone.

Romans 12:18

Love is patient, love is kind. It does not envy, it does not boast, it is not proud.

It is not rude, it is not self-seeking, it is not easily angered, it keeps no record of wrongs.

Love does not delight in evil but rejoices with the truth.

It always protects, always trusts, always hopes, always perseveres.

1 Corinthians 13:4-7

And we urge you, brothers, warn those who are idle.

1 Thessalonians 5:14a

And the Lord's servant must not quarrel; instead, he must be kind to everyone, able to teach, not resentful.

2 Timothy 2:24

To slander no one, to be peaceable and considerate, and to show true humility toward all men.

Titus 3:2

Make every effort to live in peace with all men and to be holy; without holiness no one will see the Lord.

Hebrews 12:14

Peacemakers who sow in peace raise a harvest of righteousness.

James 3:18

Young men, in the same way be submissive to those who are older. All of you, clothe yourselves with humility toward one another, because, "God opposes the proud but gives grace to the humble."

Humble yourselves, therefore, under God's mighty hand, that he may lift you up in due time.

1 Peter 5:5,6

When Your Child Becomes Sick

The LORD will keep you free from every disease. He will not inflict on you the horrible diseases you knew in Egypt, but he will inflict them on all who hate you.

Deuteronomy 7:15

Praise the LORD, O my soul, and forget not all his benefits — who forgives all your sins and heals all your diseases.

Psalm 103:2,3

My son, pay attention to what I say; listen closely to my words.

Do not let them out of your sight, keep them within your heart; for they are life to those who find them and health to a man's whole body.

Proverbs 4:20-22

Surely he took up our infirmities and carried our sorrows, yet we considered him stricken by God, smitten by him, and afflicted.

But he was pierced for our transgressions, he was crushed for our iniquities; the punishment that brought us peace was upon him, and by his wounds we are healed.

Isaiah 53:4,5

Heal me, O LORD, and I will be healed; save me and I will be saved, for you are the one I praise.

Jeremiah 17:14

"But I will restore you to health and heal your wounds," declares the LORD.

Jeremiah 30:17a

Jesus said to him, "I will go and heal him."

Matthew 8:7

Jesus Christ is the same yesterday and today and forever.

Hebrews 13:8

Is any one of you in trouble? He should pray. Is anyone happy? Let him sing songs of praise.

Is any one of you sick? He should call the elders of the church to pray over him and anoint him with oil in the name of the Lord.

And the prayer offered in faith will make the sick person well; the Lord will raise him up. If he has sinned, he will be forgiven.

Therefore confess your sins to each other and pray for each other so that you may be healed. The prayer of a righteous man is powerful and effective.

James 5:13-16

Dear friend, I pray that you may enjoy good health and that all may go well with you, even as your soul is getting along well.

3 John 1:2

When Your Child Becomes Rebellious Toward You

Train a child in the way he should go, and when he is old he will not turn from it.

Proverbs 22:6

Now go; I will help you speak and will teach you what to say.

Exodus 4:12

Teach me, and I will be quiet; show me where I have been wrong.

Job 6:24

Show me your ways, O LORD, teach me your paths.

Who, then, is the man that fears the LORD? He will instruct him in the way chosen for him.

Psalm 25:4,12

The LORD is my strength and my shield; my heart trusts in him, and I am helped. My heart leaps for joy and I will give thanks to him in song.

Psalm 28:7

Cast your cares on the LORD and he will sustain you; he will never let the righteous fall.

Psalm 55:22

Though I walk in the midst of trouble, you preserve my life; you stretch out your hand against the anger of my foes, with your right hand you save me.

Psalm 138:7

Teach me to do your will, for you are my God; may your good Spirit lead me on level ground.

Psalm 143:10

Do not answer a fool according to his folly, or you will be like him yourself.

Proverbs 26:4

"If you are willing and obedient, you will eat the best from the land; but if you resist and rebel, you will be devoured by the sword." For the mouth of the LORD has spoken.

Isaiah 1:19,20

Can a mother forget the baby at her breast and have no compassion on the child she has borne? Though she may forget, I will not forget you!
Isaiah 49:15

I will give you the keys of the kingdom of heaven; whatever you bind on earth will be bound in heaven, and whatever you loose on earth will be loosed in heaven.
Matthew 16:19

I have given you authority to trample on snakes and scorpions and to overcome all the power of the enemy; nothing will harm you.
Luke 10:19

So watch yourselves. "If your brother sins, rebuke him, and if he repents, forgive him."
Luke 17:3

Peter and the other apostles replied: "We must obey God rather than men!"
Acts 5:29

Slaves, obey your earthly masters with respect and fear, and with sincerity of heart, just as you would obey Christ.

Serve wholeheartedly, as if you were serving the Lord, not men.
Ephesians 6:5,7

Therefore, prepare your minds for action; be self-controlled; set your hope fully on the grace to be given you when Jesus Christ is revealed.

As obedient children, do not conform to the evil desires you had when you lived in ignorance.

1 Peter 1:13,14

Submit yourselves for the Lord's sake to every authority instituted among men: whether to the king, as the supreme authority, or to governors, who are sent by him to punish those who do wrong and to commend those who do right.

For it is God's will that by doing good you should silence the ignorant talk of foolish men.

1 Peter 2:13-15

When Your Child Becomes Rebellious Toward God

Train a child in the way he should go, and when he is old he will not turn from it.

Proverbs 22:6

Wait for the LORD; be strong and take heart and wait for the LORD.

Psalm 27:14

We wait in hope for the LORD; he is our help and our shield.

Psalm 33:20

Delight yourself in the LORD and he will give you the desires of your heart.

Commit your way to the LORD; trust in him and he will do this.

Psalm 37:4,5

Cast your cares on the LORD and he will sustain you; he will never let the righteous fall.

Psalm 55:22

For the LORD will not reject his people; he will never forsake his inheritance.

Psalm 94:14

I wait for the LORD, my soul waits, and in his word I put my hope.

Psalm 130:5

The LORD will fulfill for me; your love, O LORD, endures forever — do not abandon the works of your hands.

Psalm 138:8

Discipline your son, and he will give you peace; he will bring delight to your soul.

Proverbs 29:17

So do not fear, for I am with you; do not be dismayed, for I am your God. I will strengthen you and help you; I will uphold you with my righteous right hand.

Isaiah 41:10

All your sons will be taught by the LORD, and great will be your children's peace.

Isaiah 54:13

We live by faith, not by sight.

2 Corinthians 5:7

Let us hold unswervingly to the hope we profess, for he who promised is faithful.

Hebrews 10:23

Now faith is being sure of what we hope for and certain of what we do not see.

And without faith it is impossible to please God, because anyone who comes to him must believe that he exists and that he rewards those who earnestly seek him.

Hebrews 11:1,6

These have come so that your faith — of greater worth than gold, which perishes even though refined by fire — may be proved genuine and may result in praise, glory and honor when Jesus Christ is revealed.

1 Peter 1:7

But you are a chosen people, a royal priesthood, a holy nation, a people belonging to God, that you may declare the praises of him who called you out of darkness into his wonderful light.

1 Peter 2:9

Cast all your anxiety on him because he cares for you.

1 Peter 5:7

When Your Child Becomes Quarrelsome

I am still confident of this: I will see the goodness of the LORD in the land of the living.

Psalm 27:13

Commit your way to the LORD; trust in him and he will do this.

Psalm 37:5

Trust in the LORD with all your heart and lean not on your own understanding.

Proverbs 3:5

Discipline your son, and he will give you peace; he will bring delight to your soul.

Proverbs 29:17

Because the Sovereign LORD helps me, I will not be disgraced. Therefore have I set my face like flint, and I know I will not be put to shame.

Isaiah 50:7

I have given you authority to trample on snakes and scorpions and to overcome all the power of the enemy; nothing will harm you.

Luke 10:19

In the same way, any of you who does not give up everything he has cannot be my disciple.

Luke 14:33

Peace I leave with you; my peace I give you. I do not give to you as the world gives. Do not let your hearts be troubled and do not be afraid.
John 14:27

They replied, ''Believe in the Lord Jesus, and you will be saved — you and your household.''
Acts 16:31

Get rid of all bitterness, rage and anger, brawling and slander, along with every form of malice.

Be kind and compassionate to one another, forgiving each other, just as in Christ God forgave you.

Ephesians 4:31,32

Fathers, do not exasperate your children; instead, bring them up in the training and instruction of the Lord.

Ephesians 6:4

For God did not give us a spirit of timidity, but a spirit of power, of love and of self-discipline.
2 Timothy 1:7

When Your Child Pursues Unwholesome Relationships

I am a friend to all who fear you, to all who follow your precepts.

Psalm 119:63

Thus you will walk in the ways of good men and keep to the paths of the righteous.

Proverbs 2:20

In all your ways acknowledge him, and he will make your paths straight.

Proverbs 3:6

The righteousness of the blameless makes a straight way for them, but the wicked are brought down by their own wickedness.

Proverbs 11:5

He who walks with the wise grows wise, but a companion of fools suffers harm.

Proverbs 13:20

A friend loves at all times, and a brother is born for adversity.

Proverbs 17:17

A man of many companions may come to ruin, but there is a friend who sticks closer than a brother.

Proverbs 18:24

Do not make friends with a hot-tempered man, do not associate with one easily angered, or you may learn his ways and get yourself ensnared.

Proverbs 22:24,25

Wounds from a friend can be trusted, but an enemy multiplies kisses.

Perfume and incense bring joy to the heart, and the pleasantness of one's friend springs from his earnest counsel.

Do not forsake your friend and the friend of your father, and do not go to your brother's house when disaster strikes you — better a neighbor nearby than a brother far away.

Proverbs 27:6,9,10

"Though the mountains be shaken and the hills be removed, yet my unfailing love for you will not be shaken nor my covenant of peace be removed," says the LORD, who has compassion on you.

All your sons will be taught by the LORD, and great will be your children's peace.

Isaiah 54:10,13

My command is this: Love each other as I have loved you.

Greater love has no one than this, that he lay down his life for his friends.

You are my friends if you do what I command.

I no longer call you servants, because a servant does not know his master's business. Instead, I have called you friends, for everything that I learned from my Father I have made known to you.

You did not choose me, but I chose you and appointed you to go and bear fruit — fruit that will last. Then the Father will give you whatever you ask in my name.

John 15:12-16

But now I am writing you that you must not associate with anyone who calls himself a brother but is sexually immoral or greedy, an idolater or a slanderer, a drunkard or a swindler. With such a man do not even eat.

1 Corinthians 5:11

Do not be yoked together with unbelievers. For what do righteousness and wickedness have in common? Or what fellowship can light have with darkness?

2 Corinthians 6:14

Do not be hasty in the laying on of hands, and do not share in the sins of others. Keep yourself pure.

1 Timothy 5:22

When Your Child Lacks a Sense of Worth

So God created man in his own image, in the image of God he created him; male and female he created them.

Genesis 1:27

But you are a shield around me, O LORD; you bestow glory on me and lift up my head.

Psalm 3:3

I will not fear the tens of thousands drawn up against me on every side.

Psalm 3:6

The LORD is my light and my salvation — whom shall I fear? The LORD is the stronghold of my life — of whom shall I be afraid?

Though an army besiege me, my heart will not fear; though war break out against me, even then will I be confident.

For in the day of trouble he will keep me safe in his dwelling; he will hide me in the shelter of his tabernacle and set me high upon a rock.

Psalm 27:1,3,5

It is better to take refuge in the LORD than to trust in man.

Psalm 118:8

I praise you because I am fearfully and wonderfully made; your works are wonderful, I know that full well.

Psalm 139:14

For the LORD will be your confidence and will keep your foot from being snared.

Proverbs 3:26

He who fears the LORD has a secure fortress, and for his children it will be a refuge.

Proverbs 14:26

But now, this is what the LORD says — he who created you, O Jacob, he who formed you, O Israel: "Fear not, for I have redeemed you; I have summoned you by name; you are mine.

Everyone who is called by my name, whom I created for my glory, whom I formed and made.

The people I formed for myself that they may proclaim my praise.

Isaiah 43:1,7,21

This is what the LORD says — your Redeemer, who formed you in the womb: I am the LORD, who has made all things, who alone stretched out the heavens, who spread out the earth by myself.

Isaiah 44:24

Before I formed you in the womb I knew you, before you were born I set you apart; I appointed you as a prophet to the nations.

Jeremiah 1:5

And exchanged the glory of the immortal God for images made to look like mortal man and birds and animals and reptiles.

Romans 1:23

For who has known the mind of the Lord that he may instruct him? But we have the mind of Christ.

1 Corinthians 2:16

The god of this age has blinded the minds of unbelievers, so that they cannot see the light of the gospel of the glory of Christ, who is the image of God.

2 Corinthians 4:4

Being confident of this, that he who began a good work in you will carry it on to completion until the day of Christ Jesus.

Philippians 1:6

Do nothing out of selfish ambition or vain conceit, but in humility consider others better than yourselves.

Each of you should look not only to your own interests, but also to the interests of others.

Your attitude should be the same as that of Christ Jesus.

Philippians 2:3-5

He is the image of the invisible God, the firstborn over all creation.

Colossians 1:15

And have put on the new self, which is being renewed in knowledge in the image of its Creator.

Colossians 3:10

You, dear children, are from God and have overcome them, because the one who is in you is greater than the one who is in the world.

They are from the world and therefore speak from the viewpoint of the world, and the world listens to them.

We are from God, and whoever knows God listens to us; but whoever is not from God does not listen to us. This is how we recognize the Spirit of truth and the spirit of falsehood.

1 John 4:4-6

When Your Child Becomes Unforgiving Toward You

I will instruct you and teach you in the way you should go; I will counsel you and watch over you.

Psalm 32:8

Cast your cares on the LORD and he will sustain you; he will never let the righteous fall.

Psalm 55:22

Unless the LORD had given me help, I would soon have dwelt in the silence of death.

When I said, "My foot is slipping," your love, O LORD, supported me.

Psalm 94:17,18

Great peace have they who love your law, and nothing can make them stumble.

Psalm 119:165

For your name's sake, O LORD, preserve my life; in your righteousness, bring me out of trouble.

Psalm 143:11

Instruct a wise man and he will be wiser still; teach a righteous man and he will add to his learning.

Proverbs 9:9

Better is open rebuke than hidden love.

Proverbs 27:5

Because the Sovereign LORD helps me, I will not be disgraced.

Isaiah 50:7a

No temptation has seized you except what is common to man. And God is faithful; he will not let you be tempted beyond what you can bear. But when you are tempted, he will also provide a way out so that you can stand up under it.

1 Corinthians 10:13

I pray that out of his glorious riches he may strengthen you with power through his Spirit in your inner being.

Ephesians 3:16

Finally, be strong in the Lord and in his mighty power.

Ephesians 6:10

And over all these virtues put on love, which binds them all together in perfect unity.

And whatever you do, whether in word or deed, do it all in the name of the Lord Jesus, giving thanks to God the Father through him.

Colossians 3:14,17

If any of you lacks wisdom, he should ask God, who gives generously to all without finding fault, and it will be given to him.

James 1:5

Dear friends, do not be surprised at the painful trial you are suffering, as though something strange were happening to you.

But rejoice that you participate in the sufferings of Christ, so that you may be overjoyed when his glory is revealed.

1 Peter 4:12,13

When Your Child Begins To Withdraw from You

Commit to the LORD whatever you do, and your plans will succeed.

Proverbs 16:3

Everyone who is called by my name, whom I created for my glory, whom I formed and made.

The people I formed for myself that they may proclaim my praise.

Isaiah 43:7,21

He will turn the hearts of the fathers to their children, and the hearts of the children to their fathers; or else I will come and strike the land with a curse.

Malachi 4:6

Those who are wise will shine like the brightness of the heavens, and those who lead many to righteousness, like the stars for ever and ever.

Daniel 12:3

At least there is hope for a tree: If it is cut down, it will sprout again, and its new shoots will not fail.

Its roots may grow old in the ground and its stump die in the soil, yet at the scent of water it will bud and put forth shoots like a plant.

Job 14:7-9

Be strong and take heart, all you who hope in the LORD.

Psalm 31:24

Why are you downcast, O my soul? Why so disturbed within me? Put your hope in God, for I will yet praise him, my Savior and my God.

Psalm 43:5

You are the salt of the earth. But if the salt loses its saltiness, how can it be made salty again?

Matthew 5:13a

And when you stand praying, if you hold anything against anyone, forgive him, so that your Father in heaven may forgive you your sins.

Mark 11:25

Now faith is being sure of what we hope for and certain of what we do not see.

This is what the ancients were commended for.

By faith we understand that the universe was formed at God's command, so that what is seen was not made out of what was visible.

Hebrews 11:1-3

When Your Child Has Thoughts of Suicide

This day I call heaven and earth as witnesses against you that I have set before you life and death, blessings and curses. Now choose life, so that you and your children may live and that you may love the LORD your God, listen to his voice, and hold fast to him. For the LORD is your life, and he will give you many years in the land he swore to give to your fathers, Abraham, Isaac and Jacob.

Deuteronomy 30:19,20

One of you routs a thousand, because the LORD your God fights for you, just as he promised.

Joshua 23:10

He will guard the feet of his saints, but the wicked will be silenced in darkness. It is not by strength that one prevails.

1 Samuel 2:9

''The LORD who delivered me from the paw of the lion and the paw of the bear will deliver me from the hand of this Philistine.'' Saul said to David, ''Go, and the LORD be with you.''

1 Samuel 17:37

But you are a shield around me, O LORD; you bestow glory on me and lift up my head.

Psalm 3:3

I will not fear the tens of thousands drawn up against me on every side.

Psalm 3:6

Before the mountains were settled in place, before the hills, I was given birth.

Proverbs 8:25

Blessed is the man who does not walk in the counsel of the wicked or stand in the way of sinners or sit in the seat of mockers.

Though an army besiege me, my heart will not fear; though war break out against me, even then will I be confident.

For in the day of trouble he will keep me safe in his dwelling; he will hide me in the shelter of his tabernacle and set me high upon a rock.

Psalm 27:1,3,5

It is better to take refuge in the LORD than to trust in man.

Psalm 118:8

I have hidden your word in my heart that I might not sin against you.

Psalm 119:11

For the LORD will be your confidence and will keep your foot from being snared.

Proverbs 3:26

He who fears the LORD has a secure fortress, and for his children it will be a refuge.

Proverbs 14:26

But those who hope in the LORD will renew their strength. They will soar on wings like eagles; they will run and not grow weary, they will walk and not be faint.

Isaiah 40:31

But now, this is what the LORD says — he who created you, O Jacob, he who formed you, O Israel: "Fear not, for I have redeemed you; I have summoned you by name; you are mine.

Everyone who is called by my name, whom I created for my glory, whom I formed and made.

The people I formed for myself that they may proclaim my praise."

Isaiah 43:1,7,21

For God so loved the world that he gave his one and only Son, that whoever believes in him shall not perish but have eternal life.

John 3:16

The Spirit gives life; the flesh counts for nothing. The words I have spoken to you are spirit and they are life.

John 6:63

I am the gate; whoever enters through me will be saved. He will come in and go out, and find pasture.

The thief comes only to steal and kill and destroy; I have come that they may have life, and have it to the full.

John 10:9,10

For who has known the mind of the Lord that he may instruct him? But we have the mind of Christ.

1 Corinthians 2:16

The god of this age has blinded the minds of unbelievers, so that they cannot see the light of the gospel of the glory of Christ, who is the image of God.

2 Corinthians 4:4

Being confident of this, that he who began a good work in you will carry it on to completion until the day of Christ Jesus.

Philippians 1:6

You, dear children, are from God and have overcome them, because the one who is in you is greater than the one who is in the world.

They are from the world and therefore speak from the viewpoint of the world, and the world listens to them.

We are from God, and whoever knows God listens to us; but whoever is not from God does not listen to us. This is how we recognize the Spirit of truth and the spirit of falsehood.

1 John 4:4-6

When Your Child Must Bear the Burden of a Physical Handicap

In my distress I called to the LORD; I cried to my God for help. From his temple he heard my voice; my cry came before him, into his ears.

Psalm 18:6

Weeping may remain for a night, but rejoicing comes in the morning.

Psalm 30:5b

You are my hiding place; you will protect me from trouble and surround me with songs of deliverance. Selah.

Psalm 32:7

Teach us to number our days aright, that we may gain a heart of wisdom.

Psalm 90:12

Praise the LORD, O my soul, and forget not all his benefits — who forgives all your sins and heals all your diseases.

Psalm 103:2,3

Let your compassion come to me that I may live, for your law is my delight.

Psalm 119:77

Surely he took up our infirmities and carried our sorrows, yet we considered him stricken by God, smitten by him, and afflicted.

But he was pierced for our transgressions, he was crushed for our iniquities; the punishment that brought us peace was upon him, and by his wounds we are healed.

Isaiah 53:4,5

"But I will restore you to health and heal your wounds," declares the LORD.

Jeremiah 30:17a

Jesus said to him, "I will go and heal him."
Matthew 8:7

Finally, brothers, whatever is true, whatever is noble, whatever is right, whatever is pure, whatever is lovely, whatever is admirable — if anything is excellent or praiseworthy — think about such things.

I can do everything through him who gives me strength.

Philippians 4:8,13

Is any one of you in trouble? He should pray. Is anyone happy? Let him sing songs of praise.

Is any one of you sick? He should call the elders of the church to pray over him and anoint him with oil in the name of the Lord.

And the prayer offered in faith will make the sick person well; the Lord will raise him up. If he has sinned, he will be forgiven.

Therefore confess your sins to each other and pray for each other so that you may be healed. The prayer of a righteous man is powerful and effective.

James 5:13-16

These have come so that your faith — of greater worth than gold, which perishes even though refined by fire — may be proved genuine and may result in praise, glory and honor when Jesus Christ is revealed.

1 Peter 1:7

When Your Child Becomes Lazy and Disinterested in Life

Whatever you do, work at it with all your heart, as working for the Lord, not for men.

Colossians 3:23

Be wise in the way you act toward outsiders; make the most of every opportunity.

Colossians 4:5

The sluggard craves and gets nothing, but the desires of the diligent are fully satisfied.

Proverbs 13:4

Whatever your hand finds to do, do it with all your might, for in the grave, where you are going, there is neither working nor planning nor knowledge nor wisdom.

Ecclesiastes 9:10

If a man is lazy, the rafters sag; if his hands are idle, the house leaks.

Ecclesiastes 10:18

As for me, far be it from me that I should sin against the LORD by failing to pray for you. And I will teach you the way that is good and right.

1 Samuel 12:23

Now there were four men with leprosy at the entrance of the city gate. They said to each other, "Why stay here until we die?"

2 Kings 7:3

I will instruct you and teach you in the way you should go; I will counsel you and watch over you.

Psalm 32:8

Why are you downcast, O my soul? Why so disturbed within me? Put your hope in God, for I will yet praise him, my Savior and my God.

Psalm 43:5

Blessed is he whose help is the God of Jacob, whose hope is in the LORD his God.

Psalm 146:5

Hope deferred makes the heart sick, but a longing fulfilled is a tree of life.

Proverbs 13:12

When the king heard this, he was greatly distressed; he was determined to rescue Daniel and made every effort until sundown to save him.

Daniel 6:14

In the same way, let your light shine before men, that they may see your good deeds and praise your Father in heaven.

Matthew 5:16

May the God of hope fill you with all joy and peace as you trust in him, so that you may overflow with hope by the power of the Holy Spirit.

Romans 15:13

Put on the full armor of God so that you can take your stand against the devil's schemes.

Therefore put on the full armor of God, so that when the day of evil comes, you may be able to stand your ground, and after you have done everything, to stand.

And pray in the Spirit on all occasions with all kinds of prayers and requests. With this in mind, be alert and always keep on praying for all the saints.

Ephesians 6:11,13,18

And the peace of God, which transcends all understanding, will guard your hearts and your minds in Christ Jesus.

Philippians 4:7

When Your Child Becomes Disillusioned Toward Religion

Such is the destiny of all who forget God; so perishes the hope of the godless.

Job 8:13

Since you are my rock and my fortress, for the sake of your name lead and guide me.

Free me from the trap that is set for me, for you are my refuge.

Into your hands I commit my spirit; redeem me, O LORD, the God of truth.

Psalm 31:3-5

You are my hiding place; you will protect me from trouble and surround me with songs of deliverance. Selah.

Psalm 32:7

Commit your way to the LORD; trust in him and he will do this:

He will make your righteousness shine like the dawn, the justice of your cause like the noonday sun.

Be still before the LORD and wait patiently for him; do not fret when men succeed in their ways, when they carry out their wicked schemes.

Psalm 37:5-7

I wait for you, O LORD; you will answer, O Lord my God.

Psalm 38:15

I call on the LORD in my distress, and he answers me.

Save me, O LORD, from lying lips and from deceitful tongues.

Psalm 120:1,2

Though I walk in the midst of trouble, you preserve my life; you stretch out your hand against the anger of my foes, with your right hand you save me.

Psalm 138:7

Truthful lips endure forever, but a lying tongue lasts only a moment.

Proverbs 12:19

Commit to the LORD whatever you do, and your plans will succeed.

Proverbs 16:3

Do not say, ''I'll do to him as he has done to me; I'll pay that man back for what he did.''

Proverbs 24:29

When you pass through the waters, I will be with you; and when you pass through the rivers, they will not sweep over you. When you walk through the fire, you will not be burned; the flames will not set you ablaze.

Isaiah 43:2

The LORD will guide you always; he will satisfy your needs in a sun-scorched land and will strengthen your frame. You will be like a well-watered garden, like a spring whose waters never fail.

Isaiah 58:11

I the LORD search the heart and examine the mind, to reward a man according to his conduct, according to what his deeds deserve.

Jeremiah 17:10

The LORD is good, a refuge in times of trouble. He cares for those who trust in him.

Nahum 1:7

Woe to you, teachers of the law and Pharisees, you hypocrites! You are like whitewashed tombs, which look beautiful on the outside but on the inside are full of dead men's bones and everything unclean.

In the same way, on the outside you appear to people as righteous but on the inside you are full of hypocrisy and wickedness.

Matthew 23:27,28

And when you stand praying, if you hold anything against anyone, forgive him, so that your Father in heaven may forgive you your sins.

Mark 11:25

If anyone considers himself religious and yet does not keep a tight rein on his tongue, he deceives himself and his religion is worthless.

Religion that God our Father accepts as pure and faultless is this: to look after orphans and widows in their distress and to keep oneself from being polluted by the world.

James 1:26,27

Who is going to harm you if you are eager to do good?

1 Peter 3:13

When Your Child Lacks the Desire To Attend Church

Be strong and courageous. Do not be afraid or terrified because of them, for the LORD your God goes with you; he will never leave you nor forsake you.

Deuteronomy 31:6

But if serving the LORD seems undesirable to you, then choose for yourselves this day whom you will serve, whether the gods your forefathers served beyond the River, or the gods of the Amorites, in whose land you are living. But as for me and my household, we will serve the LORD.

Joshua 24:15

As for me, far be it from me that I should sin against the LORD by failing to pray for you. And I will teach you the way that is good and right.

1 Samuel 12:23

Splendor and majesty are before him; strength and joy in his dwelling place.

1 Chronicles 16:27

Through you we push back our enemies; through your name we trample our foes.

Psalm 44:5

An offended brother is more unyielding than a fortified city, and disputes are like the barred gates of a citadel.

Proverbs 18:19

The Spirit of the Sovereign LORD is on me, because the LORD has anointed me to preach good news to the poor. He has sent me to bind up the brokenhearted, to proclaim freedom for the captives and release from darkness for the prisoners.

Isaiah 61:1

Those who are wise will shine like the brightness of the heavens, and those who lead many to righteousness, like the stars for ever and ever.

Daniel 12:3

Ask and it will be given to you; seek and you will find; knock and the door will be opened to you.

For everyone who asks receives; he who seeks finds; and to him who knocks, the door will be opened.

Matthew 7:7,8

Then you will know the truth, and the truth will set you free.

So if the Son sets you free, you will be free indeed.

John 8:32,36

I tell you the truth, anyone who has faith in me will do what I have been doing. He will do even greater things than these, because I am going to the Father.

John 14:12

But you will receive power when the Holy Spirit comes on you; and you will be my witnesses in Jerusalem, and in all Judea and Samaria, and to the ends of the earth.

Acts 1:8

For it is light that makes everything visible. This is why it is said: "Wake up, O sleeper, rise from the dead, and Christ will shine on you."

Ephesians 5:14

I can do everything through him who gives me strength.

Philippians 4:13

Being strengthened with all power according to his glorious might so that you may have great endurance and patience, and joyfully giving thanks to the Father, who has qualified you to share in the inheritance of the saints in the kingdom of light.

Colossians 1:11,12

Do not neglect your gift, which was given you through a prophetic message when the body of elders laid their hands on you.

1 Timothy 4:14

For this reason I remind you to fan into flame the gift of God, which is in you through the laying on of my hands.

2 Timothy 1:6

Do your best to present yourself to God as one approved, a workman who does not need to be ashamed and who correctly handles the word of truth.

2 Timothy 2:15

When Your Child Is Heartbroken by Divorce

For the LORD your God is a merciful God; he will not abandon or destroy you or forget the covenant with your forefathers, which he confirmed to them by oath.

Deuteronomy 4:31

Be strong and courageous. Do not be afraid or terrified because of them, for the LORD your God goes with you; he will never leave you nor forsake you.

Deuteronomy 31:6

For the sake of his great name the LORD will not reject his people, because the LORD was pleased to make you his own.

1 Samuel 12:22

Those who know your name will trust in you,
for you, LORD, have never forsaken those who
seek you.

Psalm 9:10

Though my father and mother forsake me, the
LORD will receive me.

Teach me your way, O LORD; lead me in a
straight path because of my oppressors.

Psalm 27:10,11

Weeping may remain for a night, but rejoicing
comes in the morning.

Psalm 30:5b

I was young and now I am old, yet I have never
seen the righteous forsaken or their children
begging bread.

Psalm 37:25

Why are you downcast, O my soul? Why so
disturbed within me? Put your hope in God, for
I will yet praise him, my Savior and my God.

Psalm 43:5

''Because he loves me,'' says the LORD, ''I
will rescue him; I will protect him, for he
acknowledges my name.

He will call upon me, and I will answer him;
I will be with him in trouble, I will deliver him
and honor him.''

Psalm 91:14-15

For the LORD will not reject his people; he will never forsake his inheritance.

Psalm 94:14

The poor and needy search for water, but there is none; their tongues are parched with thirst. But I the LORD will answer them; I, the God of Israel, will not forsake them.

Isaiah 41:17

Can a mother forget the baby at her breast and have no compassion on the child she has borne? Though she may forget, I will not forget you!

See, I have engraved you on the palms of my hands; your walls are ever before me.

Isaiah 49:15,16

No longer will they call you Deserted, or name your land Desolate. But you will be called Hephzibah, and your land Beulah; for the LORD will take delight in you, and your land will be married.

Isaiah 62:4

The Spirit of the Lord is on me, because he has anointed me to preach good news to the poor. He has sent me to proclaim freedom for the prisoners and recovery of sight for the blind, to release the oppressed, to proclaim the year of the Lord's favor.

Luke 4:18,19

I will not leave you as orphans; I will come to you.

John 14:18

Persecuted, but not abandoned; struck down, but not destroyed.

2 Corinthians 4:9

Keep your lives free from the love of money and be content with what you have, because God has said, ''Never will I leave you; never will I forsake you.''

Hebrews 13:5

Cast all your anxiety on him because he cares for you.

1 Peter 5:7

When Your Child Experiences Personal Failure or Loss

He makes me lie down in green pastures, he leads me beside quiet waters, he restores my soul. He guides me in paths of righteousness for his name's sake.

Psalm 23:2,3

Show me your ways, O LORD, teach me your paths; guide me in your truth and teach me, for you are God my Savior, and my hope is in you all day long.

Psalm 25:4,5

May integrity and uprightness protect me, because my hope is in you.

Psalm 25:21

Wait for the LORD; be strong and take heart and wait for the LORD.

Psalm 27:14

Be still before the LORD and wait patiently for him; do not fret when men succeed in their ways, when they carry out their wicked schemes.

If the LORD delights in a man's way, he makes his steps firm; though he stumble, he will not fall, for the LORD upholds him with his hand.

Psalm 37:7,23,24

Blessed is the man who listens to me, watching daily at my doors, waiting at my doorway.

Proverbs 8:34

By wisdom a house is built, and through understanding it is established; for though a righteous man falls seven times, he rises again, but the wicked are brought down by calamity.

Proverbs 24:3,16

This is what the Sovereign LORD, the Holy One of Israel, says: "In repentance and rest is your salvation, in quietness and trust is your strength, but you would have none of it."

Isaiah 30:15

But those who hope in the LORD will renew their strength. They will soar on wings like eagles; they will run and not grow weary, they will walk and not be faint.

Isaiah 40:31

Then, because so many people were coming and going that they did not even have a chance to eat, he said to them, ''Come with me by yourselves to a quiet place and get some rest.''

Mark 6:31

Therefore, since we are surrounded by such a great cloud of witnesses, let us throw off everything that hinders and the sin that so easily entangles, and let us run with perseverance the race marked out for us.

Hebrews 12:1

If any of you lacks wisdom, he should ask God, who gives generously to all without finding fault, and it will be given to him.

James 1:5

Who through faith are shielded by God's power until the coming of the salvation that is ready to be revealed in the last time.

In this you greatly rejoice, though now for a little while you may have had to suffer grief in all kinds of trials.

These have come so that your faith — of greater worth than gold, which perishes even though refined by fire — may be proved genuine and may result in praise, glory and honor when Jesus Christ is revealed.

Though you have not seen him, you love him; and even though you do not see him now, you believe in him and are filled with an inexpressible and glorious joy.

1 Peter 1:5-8

Be self-controlled and alert. Your enemy the devil prowls around like a roaring lion looking for someone to devour.

Resist him, standing firm in the faith, because you know that your brothers throughout the world are undergoing the same kind of sufferings.

1 Peter 5:8,9

When Your Child Possesses
Exceptional Abilities

I will instruct you and teach you in the way you should go; I will counsel you and watch over you.

Psalm 32:8

The LORD will fulfill for me; your love, O LORD, endures forever — do not abandon the works of your hands.

Psalm 138:8

I praise you because I am fearfully and wonderfully made; your works are wonderful, I know that full well.

Psalm 139:14

Praise the LORD, O my soul, and forget not all his benefits — who forgives all your sins and heals all your diseases, who redeems your life from the pit and crowns you with love and compassion.

Psalm 103:2-4

My son, pay attention to what I say; listen closely to my words.

Proverbs 4:20

Counsel and sound judgment are mine; I have understanding and power.

Proverbs 8:14

Whether you turn to the right or to the left, your ears will hear a voice behind you, saying, "This is the way; walk in it."

Isaiah 30:21

Young men without any physical defect, handsome, showing aptitude for every kind of learning, well informed, quick to understand, and qualified to serve in the king's palace.

Daniel 1:4a

Heal the sick, raise the dead, cleanse those who have leprosy, drive out demons. Freely you have received, freely give.

Matthew 10:8

But the one who does not know and does things deserving punishment will be beaten with few blows. From everyone who has been given much, much will be demanded; and from the one who has been entrusted with much, much more will be asked.

Luke 12:48

So then, no more boasting about men! All things are yours, and you are of Christ, and Christ is of God.

1 Corinthians 3:21,23

If you belong to Christ, then you are Abraham's seed, and heirs according to the promise.

Galatians 3:29

All Scripture is God-breathed and is useful for teaching, rebuking, correcting and training in righteousness, so that the man of God may be thoroughly equipped for every good work.

2 Timothy 3:16,17

When Your Child Is Beyond Your Daily Influence

The LORD turn his face toward you and give you peace.

Numbers 6:26

For the LORD your God is a merciful God; he will not abandon or destroy you or forget the covenant with your forefathers, which he confirmed to them by oath.

Deuteronomy 4:31

Be strong and courageous. Do not be afraid or terrified because of them, for the LORD your God goes with you; he will never leave you nor forsake you.

The LORD himself goes before you and will be with you; he will never leave you nor forsake you. Do not be afraid; do not be discouraged.

Deuteronomy 31:6,8

Wait for the LORD; be strong and take heart and wait for the LORD.

Psalm 27:14

Delight yourself in the LORD and he will give you the desires of your heart.

I was young and now I am old, yet I have never seen the righteous forsaken or their children begging bread.

Psalm 37:4,25

Sons are a heritage from the LORD, children a reward from him.

Like arrows in the hands of a warrior are sons born in one's youth.

Blessed is the man whose quiver is full of them. They will not be put to shame.

Psalm 127:3-5a

In his heart a man plans his course, but the LORD determines his steps.

Proverbs 16:9

Train a child in the way he should go, and when he is old he will not turn from it.

Proverbs 22:6

The father of a righteous man has great joy; he who has a wise son delights in him.

Proverbs 23:24

Discipline your son, and he will give you peace; he will bring delight to your soul.

Proverbs 29:17

Can a mother forget the baby at her breast and have no compassion on the child she has borne? Though she may forget, I will not forget you!

See, I have engraved you on the palms of my hands; your walls are ever before me.

Isaiah 49:15,16

And teaching them to obey everything I have commanded you. And surely I am with you always, to the very end of the age.

Matthew 28:20

These have come so that your faith — of greater worth than gold, which perishes even though refined by fire — may be proved genuine and may result in praise, glory and honor when Jesus Christ is revealed.

1 Peter 1:7

Cast all your anxiety on him because he cares for you.

1 Peter 5:7

When Your Child Departs From His/Her Commitment to God

The eternal God is your refuge, and underneath are the everlasting arms. He will drive out your enemy before you, saying, "Destroy him!"

Deuteronomy 33:27

Be still, and know that I am God; I will be exalted among the nations, I will be exalted in the earth.

Psalm 46:10

And call upon me in the day of trouble; I will deliver you, and you will honor me.

Psalm 50:15

Cast your cares on the LORD and he will sustain you; he will never let the righteous fall.

Psalm 55:22

My flesh and my heart may fail, but God is the strength of my heart and my portion forever.

Psalm 73:26

When anxiety was great within me, your consolation brought joy to my soul.

Psalm 94:19

He heals the brokenhearted and binds up their wounds.

Psalm 147:3

So do not fear, for I am with you; do not be dismayed, for I am your God. I will strengthen you and help you; I will uphold you with my righteous right hand.

For I am the LORD, your God, who takes hold of your right hand and says to you, Do not fear; I will help you.

Isaiah 41:10,13

I have not come to call the righteous, but sinners to repentance.

Luke 5:32

For the Son of Man came to seek and to save what was lost.

Luke 19:10

By standing firm you will gain life.

Luke 21:19

The Lord is not slow in keeping his promise, as some understand slowness. He is patient with you, not wanting anyone to perish, but everyone to come to repentance.

2 Peter 3:9

When Your Child Neglects
Regular Contact With You

I will instruct you and teach you in the way you should go; I will counsel you and watch over you.

Psalm 32:8

Teach me knowledge and good judgment, for I believe in your commands.

Psalm 119:66

For the LORD will be your confidence and will keep your foot from being snared.

Proverbs 3:26

Can a mother forget the baby at her breast and have no compassion on the child she has borne? Though she may forget, I will not forget you!

See, I have engraved you on the palms of my hands; your walls are ever before me.

Isaiah 49:15,16

All your sons will be taught by the LORD, and great will be your children's peace.

Isaiah 54:13

No longer will they call you Deserted, or name your land Desolate.

Isaiah 62:4a

Call to me and I will answer you and tell you great and unsearchable things you do not know.
Jeremiah 33:3

If your brother sins against you, go and show him his fault, just between the two of you. If he listens to you, you have won your brother over.
Matthew 18:15

And teaching them to obey everything I have commanded you. And surely I am with you always, to the very end of the age.

Matthew 28:20

What, then, shall we say in response to this? If God is for us, who can be against us?

Romans 8:31

Be joyful in hope, patient in affliction, faithful in prayer.

Romans 12:12

May the God of hope fill you with all joy and peace as you trust in him, so that you may overflow with hope by the power of the Holy Spirit.
Romans 15:13

Love is patient, love is kind. It does not envy, it does not boast, it is not proud.

It is not rude, it is not self-seeking, it is not easily angered, it keeps no record of wrongs.

Love does not delight in evil but rejoices with the truth.

It always protects, always trusts, always hopes, always perseveres.

1 Corinthians 13:4-7

When Your Child's Mistakes Grieve You

For the LORD your God is a merciful God; he will not abandon or destroy you or forget the covenant with your forefathers, which he confirmed to them by oath.

Deuteronomy 4:31

Wait for the LORD; be strong and take heart and wait for the LORD.

Psalm 27:14

We wait in hope for the LORD; he is our help and our shield.

Psalm 33:20

Cast your cares on the LORD and he will sustain you; he will never let the righteous fall.

Psalm 55:22

For the LORD will not reject his people; he will never forsake his inheritance.

Psalm 94:14

I wait for the LORD, my soul waits, and in his word I put my hope.

Psalm 130:5

The LORD will fulfill for me; your love, O LORD, endures forever — do not abandon the works of your hands.

Psalm 138:8

So do not fear, for I am with you; do not be dismayed, for I am your God. I will strengthen you and help you; I will uphold you with my righteous right hand.

Isaiah 41:10

And we know that in all things God works for the good of those who love him, who have been called according to his purpose.

Romans 8:28

We live by faith, not by sight.

2 Corinthians 5:7

Let us hold unswervingly to the hope we profess, for he who promised is faithful.

Hebrews 10:23

Now faith is being sure of what we hope for and certain of what we do not see.

And without faith it is impossible to please God, because anyone who comes to him must believe that he exists and that he rewards those who earnestly seek him.

Hebrews 11:1,6

These have come so that your faith — of greater worth than gold, which perishes even though refined by fire — may be proved genuine and may result in praise, glory and honor when Jesus Christ is revealed.

1 Peter 1:7

But you are a chosen people, a royal priesthood, a holy nation, a people belonging to God, that you may declare the praises of him who called you out of darkness into his wonderful light.

1 Peter 2:9

Cast all your anxiety on him because he cares for you.

1 Peter 5:7

When Your Child Blames You for His/Her Problems

A righteous man may have many troubles, but the LORD delivers him from them all;

Psalm 34:19

O LORD, you have seen this; be not silent. Do not be far from me, O Lord.

Psalm 35:22

Cast your cares on the LORD and he will sustain you; he will never let the righteous fall.

Psalm 55:22

He alone is my rock and my salvation; he is my fortress, I will never be shaken.

Psalm 62:2

The LORD will fulfill for me; your love, O LORD, endures forever — do not abandon the works of your hands.

Psalm 138:8

Trust in the LORD with all your heart and lean not on your own understanding; in all your ways acknowledge him, and he will make your paths straight.

Proverbs 3:5,6

Whoever gives heed to instruction prospers, and blessed is he who trusts in the LORD.

Proverbs 16:20

Fear of man will prove to be a snare, but whoever trusts in the LORD is kept safe.

Proverbs 29:25

Surely God is my salvation; I will trust and not be afraid. The LORD, the LORD, is my strength and my song; he has become my salvation.

Isaiah 12:2

You will keep in perfect peace him whose mind is steadfast, because he trusts in you.

Trust in the LORD forever, for the LORD, the LORD, is the Rock eternal.

Isaiah 26:3,4

O LORD, be gracious to us; we long for you. Be our strength every morning, our salvation in time of distress.

Isaiah 33:2

So do not fear, for I am with you; do not be dismayed, for I am your God. I will strengthen you and help you; I will uphold you with my righteous right hand.

Isaiah 41:10

But as for me, I watch in hope for the LORD, I wait for God my Savior; my God will hear me.

Micah 7:7

What, then, shall we say in response to this? If God is for us, who can be against us?

Romans 8:31

''In your anger do not sin'': Do not let the sun go down while you are still angry.

Get rid of all bitterness, rage and anger, brawling and slander, along with every form of malice.

Ephesians 4:26,31

See to it that no one misses the grace of God and that no bitter root grows up to cause trouble and defile many.

Hebrews 12:15

Dear friends, do not be surprised at the painful trial you are suffering, as though something strange were happening to you.

But rejoice that you participate in the sufferings of Christ, so that you may be overjoyed when his glory is revealed.

1 Peter 4:12,13

When You Fear the Consequences of Your Child's Lifestyle

I am still confident of this: I will see the goodness of the LORD in the land of the living.

Psalm 27:13

Commit your way to the LORD; trust in him and he will do this.

Psalm 37:5

Blessed are they who keep his statutes and seek him with all their heart.

I have hidden your word in my heart that I might not sin against you.

Give me understanding, and I will keep your law and obey it with all my heart.

Your word is a lamp to my feet and a light for my path.

Psalm 119:2,11,34,105

Trust in the LORD with all your heart and lean not on your own understanding.

Proverbs 3:5

Discipline your son, and he will give you peace; he will bring delight to your soul.

Proverbs 29:17

Because the Sovereign LORD helps me, I will not be disgraced. Therefore have I set my face like flint, and I know I will not be put to shame.

Isaiah 50:7

You will seek me and find me when you seek me with all your heart.

Jeremiah 29:13

I have given you authority to trample on snakes and scorpions and to overcome all the power of the enemy; nothing will harm you.

Luke 10:19

In the same way, any of you who does not give up everything he has cannot be my disciple.

Luke 14:33

Peace I leave with you; my peace I give you. I do not give to you as the world gives. Do not let your hearts be troubled and do not be afraid.

John 14:27

They replied, ''Believe in the Lord Jesus, and you will be saved — you and your household.''

Acts 16:31

Get rid of all bitterness, rage and anger, brawling and slander, along with every form of malice.

Be kind and compassionate to one another, forgiving each other, just as in Christ God forgave you.

Ephesians 4:31,32

Fathers, do not exasperate your children; instead, bring them up in the training and instruction of the Lord.

Ephesians 6:4

But whatever was to my profit I now consider loss for the sake of Christ.

Philippians 3:7

For God did not give us a spirit of timidity, but a spirit of power, of love and of self-discipline.

2 Timothy 1:7

There is no fear in love. But perfect love drives out fear, because fear has to do with punishment. The one who fears is not made perfect in love.

1 John 4:18

When Your Husband...

When Your Husband Is Not Committed to Christ

The eternal God is your refuge, and underneath are the everlasting arms. He will drive out your enemy before you, saying, "Destroy him!"

Deuteronomy 33:27

But if serving the LORD seems undesirable to you, then choose for yourselves this day whom you will serve.

Joshua 24:15a

Be still, and know that I am God; I will be exalted among the nations, I will be exalted in the earth.

Psalm 46:10

And call upon me in the day of trouble; I will deliver you, and you will honor me.

Psalm 50:15

Cast your cares on the LORD and he will sustain you; he will never let the righteous fall.

Psalm 55:22

My flesh and my heart may fail, but God is the strength of my heart and my portion forever.

Psalm 73:26

When anxiety was great within me, your consolation brought joy to my soul.

Psalm 94:19

He heals the brokenhearted and binds up their wounds.

Psalm 147:3

So do not fear, for I am with you; do not be dismayed, for I am your God. I will strengthen you and help you; I will uphold you with my righteous right hand.

All who rage against you will surely be ashamed and disgraced; those who oppose you will be as nothing and perish.

Though you search for your enemies, you will not find them. Those who wage war against you will be as nothing at all.

For I am the LORD, your God, who takes hold of your right hand and says to you, Do not fear; I will help you.

Isaiah 41:10-13

The Sovereign LORD has given me an instructed tongue, to know the word that sustains the weary. He wakens me morning by morning, wakens my ear to listen like one being taught.

Isaiah 50:4

I tell you the truth, if anyone says to this mountain, ''Go, throw yourself into the sea,'' and does not doubt in his heart but believes that what he says will happen, it will be done for him.

Mark 11:23

For nothing is impossible with God.

Luke 1:37

I have not come to call the righteous, but sinners to repentance.

Luke 5:32

For the Son of Man came to seek and to save what was lost.

Luke 19:10

By standing firm you will gain life.

Luke 21:19

I am not saying this because I am in need, for I have learned to be content whatever the circumstances.

I know what it is to be in need, and I know what it is to have plenty. I have learned the secret of being content in any and every situation, whether well fed or hungry, whether living in plenty or in want.

I can do everything through him who gives me strength.

Philippians 4:11-13

Endure hardship with us like a good soldier of Christ Jesus.

2 Timothy 2:3

The Lord is not slow in keeping his promise, as some understand slowness. He is patient with you, not wanting anyone to perish, but everyone to come to repentance.

2 Peter 3:9

When Your Husband Does Not Assume His Role as a Spiritual Leader

Now go; I will help you speak and will teach you what to say.

Exodus 4:12

Teach me, and I will be quiet; show me where I have been wrong.

Job 6:24

Show me your ways, O LORD, teach me your paths.
Who, then, is the man that fears the LORD? He will instruct him in the way chosen for him.

Psalm 25:4,12

Teach me your way, O LORD; lead me in a straight path because of my oppressors.

Psalm 27:11

Teach me to do your will, for you are my God; may your good Spirit lead me on level ground.

Psalm 143:10

Keep my commands and you will live; guard my teachings as the apple of your eye.

Proverbs 7:2

"If you are willing and obedient, you will eat the best from the land; but if you resist and rebel, you will be devoured by the sword." For the mouth of the LORD has spoken.

Isaiah 1:19,20

Peter and the other apostles replied: "We must obey God rather than men!"

Acts 5:29

Slaves, obey your earthly masters with respect and fear, and with sincerity of heart, just as you would obey Christ.
Serve wholeheartedly, as if you were serving the Lord, not men.

Ephesians 6:5,7

Therefore, prepare your minds for action; be self-controlled; set your hope fully on the grace to be given you when Jesus Christ is revealed.
As obedient children, do not conform to the evil desires you had when you lived in ignorance.

1 Peter 1:13,14

Submit yourselves for the Lord's sake to every authority instituted among men: whether to the king, as the supreme authority, or to governors, who are sent by him to punish those who do wrong and to commend those who do right.

For it is God's will that by doing good you should silence the ignorant talk of foolish men.

1 Peter 2:13-15

Wives, in the same way be submissive to your husbands so that, if any of them do not believe the word, they may be won over without words by the behavior of their wives.

1 Peter 3:1

When Your Husband Seems Overly Strict With the Children

The LORD is my light and my salvation — whom shall I fear? The LORD is the stronghold of my life — of whom shall I be afraid?

Though an army besiege me, my heart will not fear; though war break out against me, even then will I be confident.

Wait for the LORD; be strong and take heart and wait for the LORD.

Psalm 27:1,3,14

Since you are my rock and my fortress, for the sake of your name lead and guide me.

Psalm 31:3

You are my hiding place; you will protect me from trouble and surround me with songs of deliverance. Selah.

I will instruct you and teach you in the way you should go; I will counsel you and watch over you.

Psalm 32:7,8

Train a child in the way he should go, and when he is old he will not turn from it.

Proverbs 22:6

Finally, brothers, whatever is true, whatever is noble, whatever is right, whatever is pure, whatever is lovely, whatever is admirable — if anything is excellent or praiseworthy — think about such things.

I know what it is to be in need, and I know what it is to have plenty. I have learned the secret of being content in any and every situation, whether well fed or hungry, whether living in plenty or in want.

I can do everything through him who gives me strength.

Philippians 4:8,12,13

For we know him who said, "It is mine to avenge; I will repay," and again, "The Lord will judge his people."

Hebrews 10:30

Bear with each other and forgive whatever grievances you may have against one another. Forgive as the Lord forgave you.

And over all these virtues put on love, which binds them all together in perfect unity.

Fathers, do not embitter your children, or they will become discouraged.

Colossians 3:13,14,21

If any of you lacks wisdom, he should ask God, who gives generously to all without finding fault, and it will be given to him.

James 1:5

But if you harbor bitter envy and selfish ambition in your hearts, do not boast about it or deny the truth.

For where you have envy and selfish ambition, there you find disorder and every evil practice.

But the wisdom that comes from heaven is first of all pure; then peace-loving, considerate, submissive, full of mercy and good fruit, impartial and sincere.

Peacemakers who sow in peace raise a harvest of righteousness.

James 3:14,16-18

Therefore confess your sins to each other and pray for each other so that you may be healed. The prayer of a righteous man is powerful and effective.

James 5:16

When Your Husband Seems Uncaring Toward Your Children

The LORD your God, who is going before you, will fight for you, as he did for you in Egypt, before your very eyes.

Deuteronomy 1:30

For the eyes of the LORD range throughout the earth to strengthen those whose hearts are fully committed to him.

2 Chronicles 16:9a

But you are a shield around me, O LORD; you bestow glory on me and lift up my head.

Psalm 3:3

The LORD is close to the brokenhearted and saves those who are crushed in spirit.

Psalm 34:18

By day the LORD directs his love, at night his song is with me — a prayer to the God of my life.

Psalm 42:8

The LORD will fulfill for me; your love, O LORD, endures forever — do not abandon the works of your hands.

Psalm 138:8

But I tell you: Love your enemies and pray for those who persecute you.

Matthew 5:44

And now these three remain: faith, hope and love. But the greatest of these is love.

1 Corinthians 13:13

And live a life of love, just as Christ loved us and gave himself up for us as a fragrant offering and sacrifice to God.

Ephesians 5:2

Bear with each other and forgive whatever grievances you may have against one another. Forgive as the Lord forgave you.

Colossians 3:13

When Your Husband Must Be Away From Home

I am a friend to all who fear you, to all who follow your precepts.

Psalm 119:63

A friend loves at all times, and a brother is born for adversity.

Proverbs 17:17

A man of many companions may come to ruin, but there is a friend who sticks closer than a brother.

Proverbs 18:24

Do not make friends with a hot-tempered man, do not associate with one easily angered.

Proverbs 22:24

Wounds from a friend can be trusted, but an enemy multiplies kisses.

Perfumé and incense bring joy to the heart, and the pleasantness of one's friend springs from his earnest counsel.

Do not forsake your friend and the friend of your father, and do not go to your brother's house when disaster strikes you — better a neighbor nearby than a brother far away.

Proverbs 27:6,9,10

Two are better than one, because they have a good return for their work:

If one falls down, his friend can help him up. But pity the man who falls and has no one to help him up!

Ecclesiastes 4:9,10

''Though the mountains be shaken and the hills be removed, yet my unfailing love for you will not be shaken nor my covenant of peace be removed,'' says the LORD, who has compassion on you.

Isaiah 54:10

For whoever does the will of my Father in heaven is my brother and sister and mother.

Matthew 12:50

But when you are invited, take the lowest place, so that when your host comes, he will say to you, "Friend, move up to a better place." Then you will be honored in the presence of all your fellow guests.

Luke 14:10

I will not leave you as orphans; I will come to you.

John 14:18

My command is this: Love each other as I have loved you.

Greater love has no one than this, that he lay down his life for his friends.

You are my friends if you do what I command.

I no longer call you servants, because a servant does not know his master's business. Instead, I have called you friends, for everything that I learned from my Father I have made known to you.

You did not choose me, but I chose you and appointed you to go and bear fruit — fruit that will last. Then the Father will give you whatever you ask in my name.

John 15:12-16

If it is encouraging, let him encourage; if it is contributing to the needs of others, let him give generously; if it is leadership, let him govern diligently; if it is showing mercy, let him do it cheerfully.

Romans 12:8

If anyone does not provide for his relatives, and especially for his immediate family, he has denied the faith and is worse than an unbeliever.

1 Timothy 5:8

When Your Husband Becomes Distant or Untalkative

I wait for you, O LORD; you will answer, O Lord my God.

Psalm 38:15

Why are you downcast, O my soul? Why so disturbed within me? Put your hope in God, for I will yet praise him, my Savior and my God.

Psalm 43:5

But as for me, I will always have hope; I will praise you more and more.

Psalm 71:14

I am a friend to all who fear you, to all who follow your precepts.

Psalm 119:63

Blessed is he whose help is the God of Jacob, whose hope is in the LORD his God.

Psalm 146:5

Hope deferred makes the heart sick, but a longing fulfilled is a tree of life.

Proverbs 13:12

Do not let your heart envy sinners, but always be zealous for the fear of the LORD.

There is surely a future hope for you, and your hope will not be cut off.

Proverbs 23:17,18

Blessed are the merciful, for they will be shown mercy.

But I tell you, Do not resist an evil person. If someone strikes you on the right cheek, turn to him the other also.

But I tell you: Love your enemies and pray for those who persecute you.

Matthew 5:7,39,44

Forgive us our debts, as we also have forgiven our debtors.

For if you forgive men when they sin against you, your heavenly Father will also forgive you.

But if you do not forgive men their sins, your Father will not forgive your sins.

Matthew 6:12,14,15

Then Peter came to Jesus and asked, "Lord, how many times shall I forgive my brother when he sins against me? Up to seven times?" Jesus answered, "I tell you, not seven times, but seventy-seven times."

Matthew 18:21,22

May the God of hope fill you with all joy and peace as you trust in him, so that you may overflow with hope by the power of the Holy Spirit.

Romans 15:13

And God is able to make all grace abound to you, so that in all things at all times, having all that you need, you will abound in every good work.

2 Corinthians 9:8

That is why, for Christ's sake, I delight in weaknesses, in insults, in hardships, in persecutions, in difficulties. For when I am weak, then I am strong.

2 Corinthians 12:10

I pray that out of his glorious riches he may strengthen you with power through his Spirit in your inner being.

Ephesians 3:16

Put on the full armor of God so that you can take your stand against the devil's schemes.

Therefore put on the full armor of God, so that when the day of evil comes, you may be able to stand your ground, and after you have done everything, to stand.

And pray in the Spirit on all occasions with all kinds of prayers and requests. With this in mind, be alert and always keep on praying for all the saints.

Ephesians 6:11,13,18

When Your Husband Becomes Abusive Toward You or the Children

Who can discern his errors? Forgive my hidden faults.

Psalm 19:12

Remember not the sins of my youth and my rebellious ways; according to your love remember me, for you are good, O LORD.

For the sake of your name, O LORD, forgive my iniquity, though it is great.

Look upon my affliction and my distress and take away all my sins.

Psalm 25:7,11,18

Then I acknowledged my sin to you and did not cover up my iniquity. I said, "I will confess my transgressions to the LORD" — and you forgave the guilt of my sin. Selah.

Psalm 32:5

Create in me a pure heart, O God, and renew a steadfast spirit within me.

Psalm 51:10

Cast your cares on the LORD and he will sustain you; he will never let the righteous fall.

Psalm 55:22

Help us, O God our Savior, for the glory of your name; deliver us and forgive our sins for your name's sake.

Psalm 79:9

As far as the east is from the west, so far has he removed our transgressions from us.

Psalm 103:12

Great peace have they who love your law, and nothing can make them stumble.

Psalm 119:165

Sons are a heritage from the LORD, children a reward from him.

Psalm 127:3

But with you there is forgiveness; therefore you are feared.

Psalm 130:4

He heals the brokenhearted and binds up their wounds.

Psalm 147:3

So do not fear, for I am with you; do not be dismayed, for I am your God. I will strengthen you and help you; I will uphold you with my righteous right hand.

Isaiah 41:10

Because the Sovereign LORD helps me, I will not be disgraced. Therefore have I set my face like flint, and I know I will not be put to shame.

Isaiah 50:7

Seek the LORD while he may be found; call on him while he is near.

Let the wicked forsake his way and the evil man his thoughts. Let him turn to the LORD, and he will have mercy on him, and to our God, for he will freely pardon.

Isaiah 55:6,7

Forgive us our debts, as we also have forgiven our debtors.

Matthew 6:12

I have given you authority to trample on snakes and scorpions and to overcome all the power of the enemy; nothing will harm you.

Luke 10:19

It would be better for him to be thrown into the sea with a millstone tied around his neck than for him to cause one of these little ones to sin.

Luke 17:2

And will not God bring about justice for his chosen ones, who cry out to him day and night? Will he keep putting them off?

I tell you, he will see that they get justice, and quickly.

Luke 18:7,8a

Praise be to the God and Father of our Lord Jesus Christ, the Father of compassion and the God of all comfort, who comforts us in all our troubles,

so that we can comfort those in any trouble with the comfort we ourselves have received from God.
2 Corinthians 1:3,4

Do not be anxious about anything, but in everything, by prayer and petition, with thanksgiving, present your requests to God.
Philippians 4:6

For I will forgive their wickedness and will remember their sins no more.
Hebrews 8:12

But if we walk in the light, as he is in the light, we have fellowship with one another, and the blood of Jesus, his Son, purifies us from all sin.

If we confess our sins, he is faithful and just and will forgive us our sins and purify us from all unrighteousness.
1 John 1:7,9

My dear children, I write this to you so that you will not sin. But if anybody does sin, we have one who speaks to the Father in our defense — Jesus Christ, the Righteous One.

He is the atoning sacrifice for our sins, and not only for ours but also for the sins of the whole world.
1 John 2:1,2

When Your Husband Seems Jealous of Your Attention Toward the Children

Surely you desire truth in the inner parts; you teach me wisdom in the inmost place.

Create in me a pure heart, O God, and renew a steadfast spirit within me.

Psalm 51:6,10

In God, whose word I praise, in God I trust; I will not be afraid. What can mortal man do to me?

Psalm 56:4

Teach me your way, O LORD, and I will walk in your truth; give me an undivided heart, that I may fear your name.

Psalm 86:11

Trust in the LORD with all your heart and lean not on your own understanding; in all your ways acknowledge him, and he will make your paths straight.

For the LORD will be your confidence.

Proverbs 3:5,6,26a

Fear of man will prove to be a snare, but whoever trusts in the LORD is kept safe.

Proverbs 29:25

Place me like a seal over your heart, like a seal on your arm; for love is as strong as death, its jealousy unyielding as the grave. It burns like blazing fire, like a mighty flame.

Song of Solomon 8:6

Surely God is my salvation; I will trust and not be afraid. The LORD, the LORD, is my strength and my song; he has become my salvation.

Isaiah 12:2

Love is patient, love is kind. It does not envy, it does not boast, it is not proud.

It is not rude, it is not self-seeking, it is not easily angered, it keeps no record of wrongs.

1 Corinthians 13:4,5

The weapons we fight with are not the weapons of the world. On the contrary, they have divine power to demolish strongholds.

2 Corinthians 10:4

Finally, be strong in the Lord and in his mighty power.

Ephesians 6:10

If any of you lacks wisdom, he should ask God, who gives generously to all without finding fault, and it will be given to him.

James 1:5

Dear friends, do not be surprised at the painful trial you are suffering, as though something strange were happening to you.

1 Peter 4:12

Your Work

When You Must Balance Family and Career

He must manage his own family well and see that his children obey him with proper respect.

(If anyone does not know how to manage his own family, how can he take care of God's church?)

1 Timothy 3:4,5

If anyone does not provide for his relatives, and especially for his immediate family, he has denied the faith and is worse than an unbeliever.

1 Timothy 5:8

Only be careful, and watch yourselves closely so that you do not forget the things your eyes have seen or let them slip from your heart as long as you live. Teach them to your children and to their children after them.

Deuteronomy 4:9

I will establish his kingdom forever if he is unswerving in carrying out my commands and laws, as is being done at this time.

1 Chronicles 28:7

He decreed statutes for Jacob and established the law in Israel, which he commanded our forefathers to teach their children, so the next generation would know them, even the children yet to be born, and they in turn would tell their children.

Then they would put their trust in God and would not forget his deeds but would keep his commands.

Psalm 78:5-7

Teach us to number our days aright, that we may gain a heart of wisdom.

Psalm 90:12

Blessed are all who fear the LORD, who walk in his ways.

You will eat the fruit of your labor; blessings and prosperity will be yours.

Your wife will be like a fruitful vine within your house; your sons will be like olive shoots around your table.

Thus is the man blessed who fears the LORD.

Psalm 128:1-4

The sluggard craves and gets nothing, but the desires of the diligent are fully satisfied.

Proverbs 13:4

In his heart a man plans his course, but the LORD determines his steps.

Proverbs 16:9

The righteous man leads a blameless life; blessed are his children after him.

Proverbs 20:7

Train a child in the way he should go, and when he is old he will not turn from it.

Proverbs 22:6

By wisdom a house is built, and through understanding it is established.

Proverbs 24:3

Discipline your son, and he will give you peace; he will bring delight to your soul.

Proverbs 29:17

A wife of noble character who can find? She is worth far more than rubies.

Her husband has full confidence in her and lacks nothing of value.

She brings him good, not harm, all the days of her life.

She selects wool and flax and works with eager hands.

She is like the merchant ships, bringing her food from afar.

She gets up while it is still dark; she provides food for her family and portions for her servant girls.

She considers a field and buys it; out of her earnings she plants a vineyard.

She sets about her work vigorously; her arms are strong for her tasks.

She sees that her trading is profitable, and her lamp does not go out at night.

In her hand she holds the distaff and grasps the spindle with her fingers.

She opens her arms to the poor and extends her hands to the needy. When it snows, she has no fear for her household; for all of them are clothed in scarlet.

She makes coverings for her bed; she is clothed in fine linen and purple.

Her husband is respected at the city gate, where he takes his seat among the elders of the land.

She makes linen garments and sells them, and supplies the merchants with sashes.

She is clothed with strength and dignity; she can laugh at the days to come.

She speaks with wisdom, and faithful instruction is on her tongue. She watches over the affairs of her household and does not eat the bread of idleness.

Her children arise and call her blessed; her husband also, and he praises her:

"Many women do noble things, but you surpass them all."

Charm is deceptive, and beauty is fleeting; but a woman who fears the LORD is to be praised.

Proverbs 31:10-30

He will be the sure foundation for your times, a rich store of salvation and wisdom and knowledge; the fear of the LORD is the key to this treasure.

Isaiah 33:6

All your sons will be taught by the LORD, and great will be your children's peace.

In righteousness you will be established: Tyranny will be far from you; you will have nothing to fear. Terror will be far removed; it will not come near you.

Isaiah 54:13,14

But seek first his kingdom and his righteousness, and all these things will be given to you as well.

Matthew 6:33

Be very careful, then, how you live — not as unwise but as wise, making the most of every opportunity, because the days are evil.

Ephesians 5:15,16

Fathers, do not exasperate your children; instead, bring them up in the training and instruction of the Lord.

Ephesians 6:4

Be wise in the way you act toward outsiders; make the most of every opportunity.

Colossians 4:5

When Your Daily Duties Become a Drudgery

I will instruct you and teach you in the way you should go; I will counsel you and watch over you.

Psalm 32:8

I wait for you, O LORD; you will answer, O Lord my God.

Psalm 38:15

Why are you downcast, O my soul? Why so disturbed within me? Put your hope in God, for I will yet praise him, my Savior and my God.

Psalm 43:5

But as for me, I will always have hope; I will praise you more and more.

Psalm 71:14

Blessed is he whose help is the God of Jacob, whose hope is in the LORD his God.

Psalm 146:5

Hope deferred makes the heart sick, but a longing fulfilled is a tree of life.

Proverbs 13:12

Do not let your heart envy sinners, but always be zealous for the fear of the LORD.
There is surely a future hope for you, and your hope will not be cut off.

Proverbs 23:17,18

"The glory of this present house will be greater than the glory of the former house," says the LORD Almighty. "And in this place I will grant peace," declares the LORD Almighty.

Haggai 2:9

May the God of hope fill you with all joy and peace as you trust in him, so that you may overflow with hope by the power of the Holy Spirit.

Romans 15:13

Therefore we do not lose heart. Though outwardly we are wasting away, yet inwardly we are being renewed day by day.

2 Corinthians 4:16

And God is able to make all grace abound to you, so that in all things at all times, having all that you need, you will abound in every good work.

2 Corinthians 9:8

That is why, for Christ's sake, I delight in weaknesses, in insults, in hardships, in persecutions, in difficulties. For when I am weak, then I am strong.

2 Corinthians 12:10

Let us not become weary in doing good, for at the proper time we will reap a harvest if we do not give up.

Galatians 6:9

I pray that out of his glorious riches he may strengthen you with power through his Spirit in your inner being.

Ephesians 3:16

Put on the full armor of God so that you can take your stand against the devil's schemes.

Therefore put on the full armor of God, so that when the day of evil comes, you may be able to stand your ground, and after you have done everything, to stand.

And pray in the Spirit on all occasions with all kinds of prayers and requests. With this in mind, be alert and always keep on praying for all the saints.

Ephesians 6:11,13,18

And the peace of God, which transcends all understanding, will guard your hearts and your minds in Christ Jesus.

Philippians 4:7

Therefore, prepare your minds for action; be self-controlled; set your hope fully on the grace to be given you when Jesus Christ is revealed.

"But the word of the Lord stands forever." And this is the word that was preached to you.

1 Peter 1:13,25

When No One Seems To Appreciate Your Efforts

A righteous man may have many troubles, but the LORD delivers him from them all.

Psalm 34:19

O LORD, you have seen this; be not silent. Do not be far from me, O Lord.

Psalm 35:22

Cast your cares on the LORD and he will sustain you; he will never let the righteous fall.
Psalm 55:22

He alone is my rock and my salvation; he is my fortress, I will never be shaken.
Psalm 62:2

The LORD will fulfill for me; your love, O LORD, endures forever — do not abandon the works of your hands.
Psalm 138:8

Trust in the LORD with all your heart and lean not on your own understanding; in all your ways acknowledge him, and he will make your paths straight.
Proverbs 3:5,6

Whoever gives heed to instruction prospers, and blessed is he who trusts in the LORD.
Proverbs 16:20

Whoever trusts in the LORD is kept safe.
Proverbs 29:25b

Whatever your hand finds to do, do it with all your might, for in the grave, where you are going, there is neither working nor planning nor knowledge nor wisdom.
Ecclesiastes 9:10

The LORD, the LORD, is my strength and my song; he has become my salvation.

Isaiah 12:2b

Trust in the LORD forever, for the LORD, the LORD, is the Rock eternal.

Isaiah 26:4

O LORD, be gracious to us; we long for you. Be our strength every morning, our salvation in time of distress.

Isaiah 33:2

So do not fear, for I am with you; do not be dismayed, for I am your God. I will strengthen you and help you; I will uphold you with my righteous right hand.

Isaiah 41:10

But as for me, I watch in hope for the LORD, I wait for God my Savior; my God will hear me.

Micah 7:7

So that your giving may be in secret. Then your Father, who sees what is done in secret, will reward you.

Matthew 6:4

What, then, shall we say in response to this? If God is for us, who can be against us?

Romans 8:31

"In your anger do not sin": Do not let the sun go down while you are still angry.

Get rid of all bitterness, rage and anger, brawling and slander, along with every form of malice.

Ephesians 4:26,31

See to it that no one misses the grace of God and that no bitter root grows up to cause trouble and defile many.

Hebrews 12:15

Dear friends, do not be surprised at the painful trial you are suffering, as though something strange were happening to you.

But rejoice that you participate in the sufferings of Christ, so that you may be overjoyed when his glory is revealed.

1 Peter 4:12,13

When You Are Your Family's Sole Support

The LORD is good, a refuge in times of trouble. He cares for those who trust in him.

Nahum 1:7

Since you are my rock and my fortress, for the sake of your name lead and guide me.

Psalm 31:3

I will instruct you and teach you in the way you should go; I will counsel you and watch over you.

Psalm 32:8

You guide me with your counsel, and afterward you will take me into glory.

Psalm 73:24

For the LORD gives wisdom, and from his mouth come knowledge and understanding.

Proverbs 2:6

Trust in the LORD with all your heart and lean not on your own understanding.

Proverbs 3:5

Lazy hands make a man poor, but diligent hands bring wealth.

Proverbs 10:4

Diligent hands will rule, but laziness ends in slave labor.

Proverbs 12:24

The sluggard craves and gets nothing, but the desires of the diligent are fully satisfied.

Proverbs 13:4

Plans fail for lack of counsel, but with many advisers they succeed.

Proverbs 15:22

Do not love sleep or you will grow poor; stay awake and you will have food to spare.

Proverbs 20:13

Do you see a man skilled in his work? He will serve before kings; he will not serve before obscure men.

Proverbs 22:29

By wisdom a house is built, and through understanding it is established.

Proverbs 24:3

A wife of noble character who can find? She is worth far more than rubies.

She is clothed with strength and dignity; she can laugh at the days to come.

She speaks with wisdom, and faithful instruction is on her tongue.

She watches over the affairs of her household and does not eat the bread of idleness.

Her children arise and call her blessed; her husband also, and he praises her:

"Many women do noble things, but you surpass them all."

Charm is deceptive, and beauty is fleeting; but a woman who fears the LORD is to be praised.

Give her the reward she has earned, and let her works bring her praise at the city gate.

Proverbs 31:10,25-31

Sow your seed in the morning, and at evening let not your hands be idle, for you do not know which will succeed, whether this or that, or whether both will do equally well.

Ecclesiastes 11:6

So do not fear, for I am with you; do not be dismayed, for I am your God. I will strengthen you and help you; I will uphold you with my righteous right hand.

Isaiah 41:10

This is what the LORD says — your Redeemer, the Holy One of Israel: "I am the LORD your God, who teaches you what is best for you, who directs you in the way you should go."

Isaiah 48:17

But seek first his kingdom and his righteousness, and all these things will be given to you as well.

Matthew 6:33

Never be lacking in zeal, but keep your spiritual fervor, serving the Lord.

Romans 12:11

And my God will meet all your needs according to his glorious riches in Christ Jesus.

Philippians 4:19

When You Feel Guilty About Working Outside the Home

The name of the LORD is a strong tower; the righteous run to it and are safe.

Proverbs 18:10

A wife of noble character who can find? She is worth far more than rubies.

She is clothed with strength and dignity; she can laugh at the days to come.

She speaks with wisdom, and faithful instruction is on her tongue.

She watches over the affairs of her household and does not eat the bread of idleness.

Her children arise and call her blessed; her husband also, and he praises her:

"Many women do noble things, but you surpass them all."

Proverbs 31:10,25-29

Whatever your hand finds to do, do it with all your might.

Ecclesiastes 9:10a

Now it is required that those who have been given a trust must prove faithful.

1 Corinthians 4:2

For this reason, since the day we heard about you, we have not stopped praying for you and asking God to fill you with the knowledge of his will through all spiritual wisdom and understanding.

And we pray this in order that you may live a life worthy of the Lord and may please him in every way: bearing fruit in every good work, growing in the knowledge of God, being strengthened with all power according to his glorious might so that you may have great endurance and patience, and joyfully giving thanks to the Father, who has qualified you to share in the inheritance of the saints in the kingdom of light.

Colossians 1:9-12

When Your Are Fearful for Your Child's Safety

The LORD is my light and my salvation — whom shall I fear? The LORD is the stronghold of my life — of whom shall I be afraid?

Though an army besiege me, my heart will not fear; though war break out against me, even then will I be confident.

Psalm 27:1,3

He who dwells in the shelter of the Most High will rest in the shadow of the Almighty.

He will cover you with his feathers, and under his wings you will find refuge; his faithfulness will be your shield and rampart.

You will not fear the terror of night, nor the arrow that flies by day, nor the pestilence that stalks in the darkness, nor the plague that destroys at midday.

A thousand may fall at your side, ten thousand at your right hand, but it will not come near you.

Psalm 91:1,4-7

Then no harm will befall you, no disaster will come near your tent.

For he will command his angels concerning you to guard you in all your ways.

Psalm 91:10,11

Great peace have they who love your law, and nothing can make them stumble.

Psalm 119:165

Have no fear of sudden disaster or of the ruin that overtakes the wicked, for the LORD will be your confidence and will keep your foot from being snared.

Proverbs 3:25,26

A time to be born and a time to die, a time to plant and a time to uproot.

Ecclesiastes 3:2

You will keep in perfect peace him whose mind is steadfast, because he trusts in you.

Isaiah 26:3

So do not fear, for I am with you; do not be dismayed, for I am your God. I will strengthen you and help you; I will uphold you with my righteous right hand.

Isaiah 41:10

In righteousness you will be established: Tyranny will be far from you; you will have nothing to fear. Terror will be far removed; it will not come near you.

Isaiah 54:14

Peace I leave with you; my peace I give you. I do not give to you as the world gives. Do not let your hearts be troubled and do not be afraid.

John 14:27

For you did not receive a spirit that makes you a slave again to fear, but you received the Spirit of sonship. And by him we cry, ''Abba, Father.''
Romans 8:15

Do not be anxious about anything, but in everything, by prayer and petition, with thanksgiving, present your requests to God.

And the peace of God, which transcends all understanding, will guard your hearts and your minds in Christ Jesus.

Finally, brothers, whatever is true, whatever is noble, whatever is right, whatever is pure, whatever is lovely, whatever is admirable — if anything is excellent or praiseworthy — think about such things.
Philippians 4:6-8

For God did not give us a spirit of timidity, but a spirit of power, of love and of self-discipline.
2 Timothy 1:7

There is no fear in love. But perfect love drives out fear, because fear has to do with punishment. The one who fears is not made perfect in love.
1 John 4:18

Your Daily Schedule

When You Feel Disorganized

Show me your ways, O LORD, teach me your paths.

Psalm 25:4

I will instruct you and teach you in the way you should go; I will counsel you and watch over you.

Psalm 32:8

Cast your cares on the LORD and he will sustain you; he will never let the righteous fall.

Psalm 55:22

Trust in the LORD with all your heart and lean not on your own understanding; in all your ways acknowledge him, and he will make your paths straight.

Proverbs 3:5,6

In his heart a man plans his course, but the LORD determines his steps.

Proverbs 16:9

Whether you turn to the right or to the left, your ears will hear a voice behind you, saying, "This is the way; walk in it."

Isaiah 30:21

He gives strength to the weary and increases the power of the weak.

Isaiah 40:29

When you pass through the waters, I will be with you; and when you pass through the rivers, they will not sweep over you. When you walk through the fire, you will not be burned; the flames will not set you ablaze.

Isaiah 43:2

Because the Sovereign LORD helps me, I will not be disgraced.

Isaiah 50:7a

For God is not a God of disorder but of peace. As in all the congregations of the saints.

1 Corinthians 14:33

Do not be anxious about anything, but in everything, by prayer and petition, with thanksgiving, present your requests to God.

And the peace of God, which transcends all understanding, will guard your hearts and your minds in Christ Jesus.

Philippians 4:6,7

If any of you lacks wisdom, he should ask God, who gives generously to all without finding fault, and it will be given to him.

James 1:5

When You Feel Overwhelmed by Your Responsibilities

The name of the LORD is a strong tower; the righteous run to it and are safe.

Proverbs 18:10

Whatever your hand finds to do, do it with all your might.

Ecclesiastes 9:10a

Now all has been heard; here is the conclusion of the matter: Fear God and keep his commandments, for this is the whole of man.

Ecclesiastes 12:13

Now it is required that those who have been given a trust must prove faithful.

1 Corinthians 4:2

And we, who with unveiled faces all reflect the Lord's glory, are being transformed into his likeness with ever-increasing glory, which comes from the Lord, who is the Spirit.

2 Corinthians 3:18

For though we live in the world, we do not wage war as the world does.

The weapons we fight with are not the weapons of the world. On the contrary, they have divine power to demolish strongholds.

We demolish arguments and every pretension that sets itself up against the knowledge of God, and we take captive every thought to make it obedient to Christ.

2 Corinthians 10:3-5

Then we will no longer be infants, tossed back and forth by the waves, and blown here and there by every wind of teaching and by the cunning and craftiness of men in their deceitful scheming.

Instead, speaking the truth in love, we will in all things grow up into him who is the Head, that is, Christ.

Ephesians 4:14,15

Being confident of this, that he who began a good work in you will carry it on to completion until the day of Christ Jesus.

And this is my prayer: that your love may abound more and more in knowledge and depth of insight, so that you may be able to discern what is best and may be pure and blameless until the day of Christ.

Philippians 1:6,9,10

For this reason, since the day we heard about you, we have not stopped praying for you and asking God to fill you with the knowledge of his will through all spiritual wisdom and understanding.

And we pray this in order that you may live a life worthy of the Lord and may please him in every way: bearing fruit in every good work, growing in the knowledge of God, being strengthened with all power according to his glorious might so that you may have great endurance and patience, and joyfully giving thanks to the Father, who has qualified you to share in the inheritance of the saints in the kingdom of light.

Colossians 1:9-12

Let the word of Christ dwell in you richly as you teach and admonish one another with all wisdom, and as you sing psalms, hymns and spiritual songs with gratitude in your hearts to God.

Colossians 3:16

When You Become Bored

Be strong and take heart, all you who hope in the LORD.

Psalm 31:24

I will instruct you and teach you in the way you should go; I will counsel you and watch over you.

Psalm 32:8

I wait for you, O LORD; you will answer, O Lord my God.

Psalm 38:15

Why are you downcast, O my soul? Why so disturbed within me? Put your hope in God, for I will yet praise him, my Savior and my God.

Psalm 43:5

But as for me, I will always have hope; I will praise you more and more.

Psalm 71:14

Blessed is he whose help is the God of Jacob, whose hope is in the LORD his God.

Psalm 146:5

Hope deferred makes the heart sick, but a longing fulfilled is a tree of life.

Proverbs 13:12

Do not let your heart envy sinners, but always be zealous for the fear of the LORD.

There is surely a future hope for you, and your hope will not be cut off.

Proverbs 23:17,18

Against all hope, Abraham in hope believed and so became the father of many nations, just as it had been said to him, ''So shall your offspring be.''

Romans 4:18

May the God of hope fill you with all joy and peace as you trust in him, so that you may overflow with hope by the power of the Holy Spirit.

Romans 15:13

And God is able to make all grace abound to you, so that in all things at all times, having all that you need, you will abound in every good work.

2 Corinthians 9:8

That is why, for Christ's sake, I delight in weaknesses, in insults, in hardships, in persecutions, in difficulties. For when I am weak, then I am strong.

2 Corinthians 12:10

I pray that out of his glorious riches he may strengthen you with power through his Spirit in your inner being.

Ephesians 3:16

Put on the full armor of God so that you can take your stand against the devil's schemes.

Therefore put on the full armor of God, so that when the day of evil comes, you may be able to stand your ground, and after you have done everything, to stand.

And pray in the Spirit on all occasions with all kinds of prayers and requests. With this in mind, be alert and always keep on praying for all the saints.

Ephesians 6:11,13,18

And the peace of God, which transcends all understanding, will guard your hearts and your minds in Christ Jesus.

Philippians 4:7

Therefore, prepare your minds for action; be self-controlled; set your hope fully on the grace to be given you when Jesus Christ is revealed.

But the word of the Lord stands forever. And this is the word that was preached to you.

1 Peter 1:13,25

When You Continually Procrastinate Necessary Tasks

But you are a shield around me, O LORD; you bestow glory on me and lift up my head.

Psalm 3:3

I will instruct you and teach you in the way you should go; I will counsel you and watch over you.

Psalm 32:8

It is better to take refuge in the LORD than to trust in man.

Psalm 118:8

I have hidden your word in my heart that I might not sin against you.

Psalm 119:11

Trust in the LORD with all your heart and lean not on your own understanding; in all your ways acknowledge him, and he will make your paths straight.

Proverbs 3:5,6

For the LORD will be your confidence and will keep your foot from being snared.

Proverbs 3:26

In his heart a man plans his course, but the LORD determines his steps.

Proverbs 16:9

He gives strength to the weary and increases the power of the weak.

Isaiah 40:29

Because the Sovereign LORD helps me, I will not be disgraced.

Isaiah 50:7a

I the LORD do not change.

Malachi 3:6a

Do you not say, ''Four months more and then the harvest''? I tell you, open your eyes and look at the fields! They are ripe for harvest.

John 4:35

And do this, understanding the present time. The hour has come for you to wake up from your slumber, because our salvation is nearer now than when we first believed.

Romans 13:11

Do you not know that the saints will judge the world? And if you are to judge the world, are you not competent to judge trivial cases?

1 Corinthians 6:2

Making the most of every opportunity, because the days are evil.

Ephesians 5:16

Be wise in the way you act toward outsiders; make the most of every opportunity.

Colossians 4:5

If any of you lacks wisdom, he should ask God, who gives generously to all without finding fault, and it will be given to him.

James 1:5

When You Feel Robbed of Your Private Time

I have set the LORD always before me. Because he is at my right hand, I will not be shaken.
Psalm 16:8

Vindicate me, O LORD, for I have led a blameless life; I have trusted in the LORD without wavering.

For your love is ever before me, and I walk continually in your truth.

Psalm 26:1,3

If the LORD delights in a man's way, he makes his steps firm.

Psalm 37:23

Your statutes are my delight; they are my counselors.

Psalm 119:24

The wicked man flees though no one pursues, but the righteous are as bold as a lion.

Proverbs 28:1

Therefore, I urge you, brothers, in view of God's mercy, to offer your bodies as living sacrifices, holy and pleasing to God — this is your spiritual act of worship.

Do not conform any longer to the pattern of this world, but be transformed by the renewing of your mind. Then you will be able to test and approve what God's will is — his good, pleasing and perfect will.

Be devoted to one another in brotherly love. Honor one another above yourselves.

Never be lacking in zeal, but keep your spiritual fervor, serving the Lord.

Be joyful in hope, patient in affliction, faithful in prayer.

Share with God's people who are in need. Practice hospitality.

Romans 12:1,2,10-13

Be on your guard; stand firm in the faith; be men of courage; be strong.

1 Corinthians 16:13

We demolish arguments and every pretension that sets itself up against the knowledge of God, and we take captive every thought to make it obedient to Christ.

2 Corinthians 10:5

Therefore each of you must put off falsehood and speak truthfully to his neighbor, for we are all members of one body.

Ephesians 4:25

Finally, be strong in the Lord and in his mighty power.

Ephesians 6:10

Do not be anxious about anything, but in everything, by prayer and petition, with thanksgiving, present your requests to God.

And the peace of God, which transcends all understanding, will guard your hearts and your minds in Christ Jesus.

I can do everything through him who gives me strength.

Philippians 4:6,7,13

You then, my son, be strong in the grace that is in Christ Jesus.

2 Timothy 2:1

See to it that no one misses the grace of God and that no bitter root grows up to cause trouble and defile many.

Hebrews 12:15

When Family Devotions Seem Difficult

Only be careful, and watch yourselves closely so that you do not forget the things your eyes have seen or let them slip from your heart as long as you live. Teach them to your children and to their children after them.

Deuteronomy 4:9

These commandments that I give you today are to be upon your hearts.

Impress them on your children. Talk about them when you sit at home and when you walk along the road, when you lie down and when you get up.

Deuteronomy 6:6,7

Fix these words of mine in your hearts and minds; tie them as symbols on your hands and bind them on your foreheads.

Teach them to your children, talking about them when you sit at home and when you walk along the road, when you lie down and when you get up.

Deuteronomy 11:18,19

So the next generation would know them, even the children yet to be born, and they in turn would tell their children.

Then they would put their trust in God and would not forget his deeds but would keep his commands.

Psalm 78:6,7

Blessed are all who fear the LORD, who walk in his ways.

You will eat the fruit of your labor; blessings and prosperity will be yours.

Your wife will be like a fruitful vine within your house; your sons will be like olive shoots around your table.

Thus is the man blessed who fears the LORD.
Psalm 128:1-4

Train a child in the way he should go, and when he is old he will not turn from it.
Proverbs 22:6

By wisdom a house is built, and through understanding it is established.
Proverbs 24:3

Discipline your son, and he will give you peace; he will bring delight to your soul.
Proverbs 29:17

A wife of noble character who can find? She is worth far more than rubies.

She is clothed with strength and dignity; she can laugh at the days to come.

She speaks with wisdom, and faithful instruction is on her tongue. She watches over the affairs of her household and does not eat the bread of idleness.

Her children arise and call her blessed; her husband also, and he praises her:

"Many women do noble things, but you surpass them all."

Charm is deceptive, and beauty is fleeting; but a woman who fears the LORD is to be praised.

Give her the reward she has earned, and let her works bring her praise at the city gate.
Proverbs 31:10,25-31

All your sons will be taught by the LORD, and great will be your children's peace.

In righteousness you will be established: Tyranny will be far from you; you will have nothing to fear. Terror will be far removed; it will not come near you.

Isaiah 54:13,14

Tell it to your children, and let your children tell it to their children, and their children to the next generation.

Joel 1:3

But seek first his kingdom and his righteousness, and all these things will be given to you as well.

Matthew 6:33

Your Finances

When It Seems Impossible To Pay Your Bills

But as for you, be strong and do not give up, for your work will be rewarded.

2 Chronicles 15:7

The LORD is good, a refuge in times of trouble. He cares for those who trust in him.

Nahum 1:7

Since you are my rock and my fortress, for the sake of your name lead and guide me.

Psalm 31:3

I will instruct you and teach you in the way you should go; I will counsel you and watch over you.

Psalm 32:8

You guide me with your counsel, and afterward you will take me into glory.

Psalm 73:24

Though I walk in the midst of trouble, you preserve my life; you stretch out your hand against the anger of my foes, with your right hand you save me.

Psalm 138:7

For the LORD gives wisdom, and from his mouth come knowledge and understanding.

Proverbs 2:6

Trust in the LORD with all your heart and lean not on your own understanding.

Proverbs 3:5

Lazy hands make a man poor, but diligent hands bring wealth.

Proverbs 10:4

Diligent hands will rule, but laziness ends in slave labor.

Proverbs 12:24

The sluggard craves and gets nothing, but the desires of the diligent are fully satisfied.

Proverbs 13:4

Plans fail for lack of counsel, but with many advisers they succeed.

Proverbs 15:22

He who is kind to the poor lends to the LORD, and he will reward him for what he has done.

Proverbs 19:17

Do not love sleep or you will grow poor; stay awake and you will have food to spare.

Proverbs 20:13

Do you see a man skilled in his work? He will serve before kings; he will not serve before obscure men.

Proverbs 22:29

By wisdom a house is built, and through understanding it is established.

Proverbs 24:3

He who works his land will have abundant food, but the one who chases fantasies will have his fill of poverty.

Proverbs 28:19

Sow your seed in the morning, and at evening let not your hands be idle, for you do not know which will succeed, whether this or that, or whether both will do equally well.

Ecclesiastes 11:6

So do not fear, for I am with you; do not be dismayed, for I am your God. I will strengthen you and help you; I will uphold you with my righteous right hand.

Isaiah 41:10

But seek first his kingdom and his righteousness, and all these things will be given to you as well.

Matthew 6:33

Never be lacking in zeal, but keep your spiritual fervor, serving the Lord.

Romans 12:11

When You Face the Loss of Your Job

The LORD is good, a refuge in times of trouble. He cares for those who trust in him.

Nahum 1:7

Since you are my rock and my fortress, for the sake of your name lead and guide me.

Psalm 31:3

I will instruct you and teach you in the way you should go; I will counsel you and watch over you.

Psalm 32:8

You guide me with your counsel, and afterward you will take me into glory.

Psalm 73:24

Good will come to him who is generous and lends freely, who conducts his affairs with justice.

Psalm 112:5

Though I walk in the midst of trouble, you preserve my life; you stretch out your hand against the anger of my foes, with your right hand you save me.

Psalm 138:7

For the LORD gives wisdom, and from his mouth come knowledge and understanding.

Proverbs 2:6

Trust in the LORD with all your heart and lean not on your own understanding.

Proverbs 3:5

Lazy hands make a man poor, but diligent hands bring wealth.

Proverbs 10:4

Diligent hands will rule, but laziness ends in slave labor.

Proverbs 12:24

The sluggard craves and gets nothing, but the desires of the diligent are fully satisfied.

Proverbs 13:4

Do not love sleep or you will grow poor; stay awake and you will have food to spare.

Proverbs 20:13

Do you see a man skilled in his work? He will serve before kings; he will not serve before obscure men.

Proverbs 22:29

By wisdom a house is built, and through understanding it is established.

Proverbs 24:3

Sow your seed in the morning, and at evening let not your hands be idle, for you do not know which will succeed, whether this or that, or whether both will do equally well.

Ecclesiastes 11:6

So do not fear, for I am with you; do not be dismayed, for I am your God. I will strengthen you and help you; I will uphold you with my righteous right hand.

Isaiah 41:10

But seek first his kingdom and his righteousness, and all these things will be given to you as well.

Matthew 6:33

Never be lacking in zeal, but keep your spiritual fervor, serving the Lord.

Romans 12:11

When Your Husband's Pay Seems Inadequate

All these blessings will come upon you and accompany you if you obey the LORD your God:

You will be blessed in the city and blessed in the country.

The fruit of your womb will be blessed, and the crops of your land and the young of your livestock — the calves of your herds and the lambs of your flocks.

Your basket and your kneading trough will be blessed.

You will be blessed when you come in and blessed when you go out.

The LORD will grant that the enemies who rise up against you will be defeated before you. They will come at you from one direction but flee from you in seven.

The LORD will send a blessing on your barns and on everything you put your hand to. The LORD your God will bless you in the land he is giving you.

Deuteronomy 28:2-8

The LORD is good, a refuge in times of trouble. He cares for those who trust in him.

Nahum 1:7

The LORD is my shepherd, I shall not be in want.

Psalm 23:1

I was young and now I am old, yet I have never seen the righteous forsaken or their children begging bread.

Psalm 37:25

Lazy hands make a man poor, but diligent hands bring wealth.

Proverbs 10:4

Diligent hands will rule, but laziness ends in slave labor.

Proverbs 12:24

Do you see a man skilled in his work? He will serve before kings; he will not serve before obscure men.

Proverbs 22:29

Be sure you know the condition of your flocks, give careful attention to your herds.

Proverbs 27:23

Whatever your hand finds to do, do it with all your might.

Ecclesiastes 9:10a

The Sovereign LORD has given me an instructed tongue, to know the word that sustains the weary. He wakens me morning by morning, wakens my ear to listen like one being taught.

Isaiah 50:4

Therefore, my dear brothers, stand firm. Let nothing move you. Always give yourselves fully to the work of the Lord, because you know that your labor in the Lord is not in vain.

1 Corinthians 15:58

And my God will meet all your needs according to his glorious riches in Christ Jesus.

Philippians 4:19

Dear friend, I pray that you may enjoy good health and that all may go well with you, even as your soul is getting along well.

3 John 1:2

When Tithing Seems Too Difficult

Make vows to the LORD your God and fulfill them; let all the neighboring lands bring gifts to the One to be feared.

Psalm 76:11

Honor the LORD with your wealth, with the firstfruits of all your crops; then your barns will be filled to overflowing, and your vats will brim over with new wine.

Proverbs 3:9,10

He who is kind to the poor lends to the LORD, and he will reward him for what he has done.

Proverbs 19:17

He who gives to the poor will lack nothing, but he who closes his eyes to them receives many curses.

Proverbs 28:27

Cast your bread upon the waters, for after many days you will find it again.

Ecclesiastes 11:1

"Bring the whole tithe into the storehouse, that there may be food in my house. Test me in this," says the LORD Almighty, "and see if I will not throw open the floodgates of heaven and pour out so much blessing that you will not have room enough for it.

I will prevent pests from devouring your crops, and the vines in your fields will not cast their fruit," says the LORD Almighty.

Malachi 3:10,11

Give, and it will be given to you. A good measure, pressed down, shaken together and running over, will be poured into your lap. For with the measure you use, it will be measured to you.

Luke 6:38

On the first day of every week, each one of you should set aside a sum of money in keeping with his income, saving it up, so that when I come no collections will have to be made.

1 Corinthians 16:2

Remember this: Whoever sows sparingly will also reap sparingly, and whoever sows generously will also reap generously.

Each man should give what he has decided in his heart to give, not reluctantly or under compulsion, for God loves a cheerful giver.

And God is able to make all grace abound to you, so that in all things at all times, having all that you need, you will abound in every good work.

2 Corinthians 9:6-8

And my God will meet all your needs according to his glorious riches in Christ Jesus.

Philippians 4:19

If anyone has material possessions and sees his brother in need but has no pity on him, how can the love of God be in him?

Dear children, let us not love with words or tongue but with actions and in truth.

1 John 3:17,18

When Your Children Need To Learn the Blessing of Work

But as for you, be strong and do not give up, for your work will be rewarded.

2 Chronicles 15:7

And who knows but that you have come to royal position for such a time as this?

Esther 4:14b

He who gathers crops in summer is a wise son, but he who sleeps during harvest is a disgraceful son.

Proverbs 10:5

Diligent hands will rule, but laziness ends in slave labor.

Proverbs 12:24

The sluggard craves and gets nothing, but the desires of the diligent are fully satisfied.

Proverbs 13:4

The plans of the diligent lead to profit as surely as haste leads to poverty.

Proverbs 21:5

Do you see a man skilled in his work? He will serve before kings; he will not serve before obscure men.

Proverbs 22:29

The Sovereign LORD is my strength; he makes my feet like the feet of a deer, he enables me to go on the heights. For the director of music. On my stringed instruments.

Habakkuk 3:19

Do you not say, ''Four months more and then the harvest''? I tell you, open your eyes and look at the fields! They are ripe for harvest.

John 4:35

As long as it is day, we must do the work of him who sent me. Night is coming, when no one can work.

John 9:4

Therefore, as we have opportunity, let us do good to all people, especially to those who belong to the family of believers.

Galatians 6:10

Now to him who is able to do immeasurably more than all we ask or imagine, according to his power that is at work within us.

Ephesians 3:20

I can do everything through him who gives me strength.

Philippians 4:13

Be wise in the way you act toward outsiders; make the most of every opportunity.

Colossians 4:5

If any of you lacks wisdom, he should ask God, who gives generously to all without finding fault, and it will be given to him.

James 1:5

So then, dear friends, since you are looking forward to this, make every effort to be found spotless, blameless and at peace with him.

2 Peter 3:14

I know your deeds. See, I have placed before you an open door that no one can shut. I know that you have little strength, yet you have kept my word and have not denied my name.

Revelation 3:8

Your Role in the Church

When You Are Asked To Teach or Assume Special Assignments

And you, my son Solomon, acknowledge the God of your father, and serve him with wholehearted devotion and with a willing mind, for the LORD searches every heart and understands every motive behind the thoughts. If you seek him, he will be found by you; but if you forsake him, he will reject you forever.

1 Chronicles 28:9

I have set the LORD always before me. Because he is at my right hand, I will not be shaken.

Therefore my heart is glad and my tongue rejoices; my body also will rest secure.

Psalm 16:8,9

For your love is ever before me, and I walk continually in your truth.

Psalm 26:3

If the LORD delights in a man's way, he makes his steps firm.

Psalm 37:23

Shout for joy to the LORD, all the earth.

Worship the LORD with gladness; come before him with joyful songs.

Enter his gates with thanksgiving and his courts with praise; give thanks to him and praise his name.

Psalm 100:1,2,4

Your statutes are my delight; they are my counselors.

Psalm 119:24

The wicked man flees though no one pursues, but the righteous are as bold as a lion.

Proverbs 28:1

Therefore, I urge you, brothers, in view of God's mercy, to offer your bodies as living sacrifices, holy and pleasing to God — this is your spiritual act of worship.

Do not conform any longer to the pattern of this world, but be transformed by the renewing of your mind. Then you will be able to test and approve what God's will is — his good, pleasing and perfect will.

Be devoted to one another in brotherly love. Honor one another above yourselves.

Never be lacking in zeal, but keep your spiritual fervor, serving the Lord.

Be joyful in hope, patient in affliction, faithful in prayer.

Share with God's people who are in need. Practice hospitality.

Romans 12:1,2,10-13

Be on your guard; stand firm in the faith; be men of courage; be strong.

1 Corinthians 16:13

We demolish arguments and every pretension that sets itself up against the knowledge of God, and we take captive every thought to make it obedient to Christ.

2 Corinthians 10:5

Finally, be strong in the Lord and in his mighty power.

Ephesians 6:10

Do not be anxious about anything, but in everything, by prayer and petition, with thanksgiving, present your requests to God.

And the peace of God, which transcends all understanding, will guard your hearts and your minds in Christ Jesus.

I can do everything through him who gives me strength.

Philippians 4:6,7,13

When You Feel Unqualified for Leadership

But as for you, be strong and do not give up, for your work will be rewarded.

2 Chronicles 15:7

Be strong and take heart, all you who hope in the LORD.

Psalm 31:24

Counsel and sound judgment are mine; I have understanding and power.

Proverbs 8:14

Now you dwellers in Jerusalem and men of Judah, judge between me and my vineyard.

Isaiah 35:3

So do not fear, for I am with you; do not be dismayed, for I am your God. I will strengthen you and help you; I will uphold you with my righteous right hand.

Isaiah 41:10

The Sovereign LORD is my strength; he makes my feet like the feet of a deer, he enables me to go on the heights. For the director of music. On my stringed instruments.

Habakkuk 3:19

But you will receive power when the Holy Spirit comes on you; and you will be my witnesses in Jerusalem, and in all Judea and Samaria, and to the ends of the earth.

Acts 1:8

But God chose the foolish things of the world to shame the wise; God chose the weak things of the world to shame the strong.

1 Corinthians 1:27

To one there is given through the Spirit the message of wisdom, to another the message of knowledge by means of the same Spirit.

1 Corinthians 12:8

And God is able to make all grace abound to you, so that in all things at all times, having all that you need, you will abound in every good work.

2 Corinthians 9:8

But he said to me, "My grace is sufficient for you, for my power is made perfect in weakness." Therefore I will boast all the more gladly about my weaknesses, so that Christ's power may rest on me.

2 Corinthians 12:9

Now to him who is able to do immeasurably more than all we ask or imagine, according to his power that is at work within us.

Ephesians 3:20

I can do everything through him who gives me strength.

Philippians 4:13

So do not throw away your confidence; it will be richly rewarded.

You need to persevere so that when you have done the will of God, you will receive what he has promised.

Hebrews 10:35,36

By faith Abraham, even though he was past age — and Sarah herself was barren — was enabled to become a father because he considered him faithful who had made the promise.

Hebrews 11:11

If any of you lacks wisdom, he should ask God, who gives generously to all without finding fault, and it will be given to him.

James 1:5

When You Hear Slander

Keep me as the apple of your eye; hide me in the shadow of your wings.

Psalm 17:8

For in the day of trouble he will keep me safe in his dwelling; he will hide me in the shelter of his tabernacle and set me high upon a rock.

Then my head will be exalted above the enemies who surround me; at his tabernacle will I sacrifice with shouts of joy; I will sing and make music to the LORD.

Psalm 27:5,6

You are my hiding place; you will protect me from trouble and surround me with songs of deliverance. Selah.

Psalm 32:7

Hide me from the conspiracy of the wicked, from that noisy crowd of evildoers.

Psalm 64:2

Do not hide your face from me when I am in distress. Turn your ear to me; when I call, answer me quickly.

Psalm 102:2

I have hidden your word in my heart that I might not sin against you.

Your word is a lamp to my feet and a light for my path.

You are my refuge and my shield; I have put my hope in your word.

Psalm 119:11,105,114

Set a guard over my mouth, O LORD; keep watch over the door of my lips.

Psalm 141:3

Answer me quickly, O LORD; my spirit fails. Do not hide your face from me or I will be like those who go down to the pit.

Rescue me from my enemies, O LORD, for I hide myself in you.

Teach me to do your will, for you are my God; may your good Spirit lead me on level ground.

Psalm 143:7,9,10

He who guards his mouth and his tongue keeps himself from calamity.

Proverbs 21:23

A word aptly spoken is like apples of gold in settings of silver.

Proverbs 25:11

A time to tear and a time to mend, a time to be silent and a time to speak.

Ecclesiastes 3:7

For by your words you will be acquitted, and by your words you will be condemned.

Matthew 12:37

Do not let any unwholesome talk come out of your mouths, but only what is helpful for building others up according to their needs, that it may benefit those who listen.

Ephesians 4:29

Let your conversation be always full of grace, seasoned with salt, so that you may know how to answer everyone.

Colossians 4:6

My dear brothers, take note of this: Everyone should be quick to listen, slow to speak and slow to become angry.

James 1:19

When Someone Has Offended You

Do not seek revenge or bear a grudge against one of your people, but love your neighbor as yourself. I am the LORD.

Leviticus 19:18

O LORD my God, I take refuge in you; save and deliver me from all who pursue me.

Psalm 7:1

Those who know your name will trust in you, for you, LORD, have never forsaken those who seek you.

Psalm 9:10

To you, O LORD, I lift up my soul; in you I trust, O my God. Do not let me be put to shame, nor let my enemies triumph over me.

Psalm 25:1,2

Trust in the LORD and do good; dwell in the land and enjoy safe pasture.

Delight yourself in the LORD and he will give you the desires of your heart.

Commit your way to the LORD; trust in him and he will do this:

He will make your righteousness shine like the dawn, the justice of your cause like the noonday sun.

Refrain from anger and turn from wrath; do not fret — it leads only to evil.

Psalm 37:3-6,8

"Because he loves me," says the LORD, "I will rescue him; I will protect him, for he acknowledges my name.

He will call upon me, and I will answer him; I will be with him in trouble, I will deliver him and honor him."

Psalm 91:14,15

For the LORD will not reject his people; he will never forsake his inheritance.

Psalm 94:14

Do not say, "I'll pay you back for this wrong!" Wait for the LORD, and he will deliver you.

Proverbs 20:22

For if you forgive men when they sin against you, your heavenly Father will also forgive you.

Matthew 6:14

If he sins against you seven times in a day, and seven times comes back to you and says, "I repent," forgive him.

Luke 17:4

Do not repay anyone evil for evil. Be careful to do what is right in the eyes of everybody.

Romans 12:17

Love is patient, love is kind. It does not envy, it does not boast, it is not proud.

1 Corinthians 13:4

And the Lord's servant must not quarrel; instead, he must be kind to everyone, able to teach, not resentful.

2 Timothy 2:24

But the Lord stood at my side and gave me strength, so that through me the message might be fully proclaimed and all the Gentiles might hear it. And I was delivered from the lion's mouth.

The Lord will rescue me from every evil attack and will bring me safely to his heavenly kingdom. To him be glory for ever and ever. Amen.

2 Timothy 4:17,18

When Church Conflicts Disillusion You

Since you are my rock and my fortress, for the sake of your name lead and guide me.

Free me from the trap that is set for me, for you are my refuge.

Into your hands I commit my spirit; redeem me, O LORD, the God of truth.

Psalm 31:3-5

You are my hiding place; you will protect me from trouble and surround me with songs of deliverance. Selah.

Psalm 32:7

Commit your way to the LORD; trust in him and he will do this:

He will make your righteousness shine like the dawn, the justice of your cause like the noonday sun.

Be still before the LORD and wait patiently for him; do not fret when men succeed in their ways, when they carry out their wicked schemes.

Psalm 37:5-7

I wait for you, O LORD; you will answer, O Lord my God.

Psalm 38:15

I call on the LORD in my distress, and he answers me.

Save me, O LORD, from lying lips and from deceitful tongues.

Psalm 120:1,2

Though I walk in the midst of trouble, you preserve my life; you stretch out your hand against the anger of my foes, with your right hand you save me.

Psalm 138:7

Truthful lips endure forever, but a lying tongue lasts only a moment.

Proverbs 12:19

Commit to the LORD whatever you do, and your plans will succeed.

Proverbs 16:3

Do not say, "I'll do to him as he has done to me; I'll pay that man back for what he did."

Proverbs 24:29

When you pass through the waters, I will be with you; and when you pass through the rivers, they will not sweep over you. When you walk through the fire, you will not be burned; the flames will not set you ablaze.

Isaiah 43:2

The LORD will guide you always; he will satisfy your needs in a sun-scorched land and will strengthen your frame. You will be like a well-watered garden, like a spring whose waters never fail.

Isaiah 58:11

I the LORD search the heart and examine the mind, to reward a man according to his conduct, according to what his deeds deserve.

Jeremiah 17:10

The LORD is good, a refuge in times of trouble. He cares for those who trust in him,

Nahum 1:7

And when you stand praying, if you hold anything against anyone, forgive him, so that your Father in heaven may forgive you your sins.

Mark 11:25

Who is going to harm you if you are eager to do good?

1 Peter 3:13

Cast all your anxiety on him because he cares for you.

1 Peter 5:7

When a Church Leader Fails

As the eyes of slaves look to the hand of their master, as the eyes of a maid look to the hand of her mistress, so our eyes look to the LORD our God, till he shows us his mercy.

Psalm 123:2

He who walks with the wise grows wise, but a companion of fools suffers harm.

Proverbs 13:20

And if anyone gives even a cup of cold water to one of these little ones because he is my disciple, I tell you the truth, he will certainly not lose his reward.

Matthew 10:42

Just as the Son of Man did not come to be served, but to serve, and to give his life as a ransom for many.

Matthew 20:28

Not so with you. Instead, whoever wants to become great among you must be your servant, and whoever wants to be first must be slave of all.

Mark 10:43,44

The expert in the law replied, "The one who had mercy on him." Jesus told him, "Go and do likewise."

Luke 10:37

The son said to him, "Father, I have sinned against heaven and against you. I am no longer worthy to be called your son."

But the father said to his servants, "Quick! Bring the best robe and put it on him. Put a ring on his finger and sandals on his feet.

Bring the fattened calf and kill it. Let's have a feast and celebrate.

For this son of mine was dead and is alive again; he was lost and is found." So they began to celebrate.

Luke 15:21-24

I tell you the truth, no servant is greater than his master, nor is a messenger greater than the one who sent him.

A new command I give you: Love one another. As I have loved you, so you must love one another.

John 13:16,34

May the God who gives endurance and encouragement give you a spirit of unity among yourselves as you follow Christ Jesus, so that with one heart and mouth you may glorify the God and Father of our Lord Jesus Christ.

Accept one another, then, just as Christ accepted you, in order to bring praise to God.

Romans 15:5-7

Now it is required that those who have been given a trust must prove faithful.

1 Corinthians 4:2

Therefore, my dear brothers, stand firm. Let nothing move you. Always give yourselves fully to the work of the Lord, because you know that your labor in the Lord is not in vain.

1 Corinthians 15:58

Brothers, if someone is caught in a sin, you who are spiritual should restore him gently. But watch yourself, or you also may be tempted.

Carry each other's burdens, and in this way you will fulfill the law of Christ.

Therefore, as we have opportunity, let us do good to all people, especially to those who belong to the family of believers.

Galatians 6:1,2,10

Be imitators of God, therefore, as dearly loved children and live a life of love, just as Christ loved us and gave himself up for us as a fragrant offering and sacrifice to God.

Ephesians 5:1,2

Bear with each other and forgive whatever grievances you may have against one another. Forgive as the Lord forgave you.

Slaves, obey your earthly masters in everything; and do it, not only when their eye is on you and to win their favor, but with sincerity of heart and reverence for the Lord.

Colossians 3:13,22

Let us fix our eyes on Jesus, the author and perfecter of our faith, who for the joy set before him endured the cross, scorning its shame, and sat down at the right hand of the throne of God.

Consider him who endured such opposition from sinful men, so that you will not grow weary and lose heart.

Hebrews 12:2,3

To this you were called, because Christ suffered for you, leaving you an example, that you should follow in his steps.

1 Peter 2:21

If we confess our sins, he is faithful and just and will forgive us our sins and purify us from all unrighteousness.

1 John 1:9

For everything in the world — the cravings of sinful man, the lust of his eyes and the boasting of what he has and does — comes not from the Father but from the world.

1 John 2:16

This is how we know what love is: Jesus Christ laid down his life for us. And we ought to lay down our lives for our brothers.

1 John 3:16

Those whom I love I rebuke and discipline. So be earnest, and repent.

Revelation 3:19

Your Personal Needs

When You Need Strength

For the joy of the LORD is your strength.

Nehemiah 8:10b

The LORD is my rock, my fortress and my deliverer; my God is my rock, in whom I take refuge. He is my shield and the horn of my salvation, my stronghold.

Psalm 18:2

The LORD is my light and my salvation — whom shall I fear? The LORD is the stronghold of my life — of whom shall I be afraid?

Wait for the LORD; be strong and take heart and wait for the LORD.

Psalm 27:1,14

Be strong and take heart, all you who hope in the LORD.

Psalm 31:24

Be my rock of refuge, to which I can always go; give the command to save me, for you are my rock and my fortress.

Psalm 71:3

My soul is weary with sorrow; strengthen me according to your word.

Psalm 119:28

When I called, you answered me; you made me bold and stouthearted.

Psalm 138:3

Counsel and sound judgment are mine; I have understanding and power.

Proverbs 8:14

The way of the LORD is a refuge for the righteous, but it is the ruin of those who do evil.

Proverbs 10:29

He who fears the LORD has a secure fortress, and for his children it will be a refuge.

Proverbs 14:26

A wise man has great power, and a man of knowledge increases strength.

Proverbs 24:5

Surely God is my salvation; I will trust and not be afraid. The LORD, the LORD, is my strength and my song; he has become my salvation.

Isaiah 12:2

This is what the Sovereign LORD, the Holy One of Israel, says: "In repentance and rest is your salvation, in quietness and trust is your strength, but you would have none of it."

Isaiah 30:15

He gives strength to the weary and increases the power of the weak.

But those who hope in the LORD will renew their strength. They will soar on wings like eagles; they will run and not grow weary, they will walk and not be faint.

Isaiah 40:29,31

So do not fear, for I am with you; do not be dismayed, for I am your God. I will strengthen you and help you; I will uphold you with my righteous right hand.

Isaiah 41:10

"Do not be afraid, O man highly esteemed," he said. "Peace! Be strong now; be strong." When he spoke to me, I was strengthened and said, "Speak, my lord, since you have given me strength."

Daniel 10:19

The Sovereign LORD is my strength; he makes my feet like the feet of a deer, he enables me to go on the heights. For the director of music. On my stringed instruments.

Habakkuk 3:19

That is why, for Christ's sake, I delight in weaknesses, in insults, in hardships, in persecutions, in difficulties. For when I am weak, then I am strong.

2 Corinthians 12:10

I pray that out of his glorious riches he may strengthen you with power through his Spirit in your inner being, so that Christ may dwell in your hearts through faith. And I pray that you, being rooted and established in love.

Ephesians 3:16,17

I can do everything through him who gives me strength.

Philippians 4:13

And we pray this in order that you may live a life worthy of the Lord and may please him in every way: bearing fruit in every good work, growing in the knowledge of God, being strengthened with all power according to his glorious might so that you may have great endurance and patience, and joyfully giving thanks to the Father, who has qualified you to share in the inheritance of the saints in the kingdom of light.

Colossians 1:10-12

When You Need To Feel Loved

Delight yourself in the LORD and he will give you the desires of your heart.

Commit your way to the LORD; trust in him and he will do this:

He will make your righteousness shine like the dawn, the justice of your cause like the noonday sun.

Psalm 37:4-6

I love those who love me, and those who seek me find me.

Proverbs 8:17

I will betroth you to me forever; I will betroth you in righteousness and justice, in love and compassion.

Hosea 2:19

For God so loved the world that he gave his one and only Son, that whoever believes in him shall not perish but have eternal life.

John 3:16

Whoever has my commands and obeys them, he is the one who loves me. He who loves me will be loved by my Father, and I too will love him and show myself to him.

John 14:21

As the Father has loved me, so have I loved you. Now remain in my love.

If you obey my commands, you will remain in my love, just as I have obeyed my Father's commands and remain in his love.

I have told you this so that my joy may be in you and that your joy may be complete.

My command is this: Love each other as I have loved you.

Greater love has no one than this, that he lay down his life for his friends.

This is my command: Love each other.

John 15:9-13,17

No, the Father himself loves you because you have loved me and have believed that I came from God.

John 16:27

For I am convinced that neither death nor life, neither angels nor demons, neither the present nor the future, nor any powers, neither height nor depth, nor anything else in all creation, will be able to separate us from the love of God that is in Christ Jesus our Lord.

Romans 8:38,39

Finally, brothers, whatever is true, whatever is noble, whatever is right, whatever is pure, whatever is lovely, whatever is admirable — if anything is excellent or praiseworthy — think about such things.

Philippians 4:8

And to know this love that surpasses knowledge — that you may be filled to the measure of all the fullness of God.

Ephesians 3:19

Dear friends, let us love one another, for love comes from God. Everyone who loves has been born of God and knows God.

Whoever does not love does not know God, because God is love.

This is how God showed his love among us: He sent his one and only Son into the world that we might live through him.

This is love: not that we loved God, but that he loved us and sent his Son as an atoning sacrifice for our sins.

Dear friends, since God so loved us, we also ought to love one another.

No one has ever seen God; but if we love one another, God lives in us and his love is made complete in us.

And so we know and rely on the love God has for us. God is love. Whoever lives in love lives in God, and God in him.

We love because he first loved us.

1 John 4:7-12,16,19

When You Need To Forgive

The ordinances of the LORD are sure and altogether righteous.

They are more precious than gold, than much pure gold; they are sweeter than honey, than honey from the comb.

By them is your servant warned; in keeping them there is great reward.

Psalm 19:9b-11

Do not gloat when your enemy falls; when he stumbles, do not let your heart rejoice,

Do not say, "I'll do to him as he has done to me; I'll pay that man back for what he did."

Proverbs 24:17,29

If your enemy is hungry, give him food to eat; if he is thirsty, give him water to drink.

Proverbs 25:21

Blessed are the merciful, for they will be shown mercy.

Matthew 5:7

But I tell you, Do not resist an evil person. If someone strikes you on the right cheek, turn to him the other also.

Matthew 5:39

But I tell you: Love your enemies and pray for those who persecute you.

Matthew 5:44

Forgive us our debts, as we also have forgiven our debtors.

For if you forgive men when they sin against you, your heavenly Father will also forgive you.

But if you do not forgive men their sins, your Father will not forgive your sins.

Matthew 6:12,14,15

Then Peter came to Jesus and asked, "Lord, how many times shall I forgive my brother when he sins against me? Up to seven times?"

Jesus answered, "I tell you, not seven times, but seventy-seven times."

Matthew 18:21,22

And when you stand praying, if you hold anything against anyone, forgive him, so that your Father in heaven may forgive you your sins.

Mark 11:25

So watch yourselves. "If your brother sins, rebuke him, and if he repents, forgive him.

If he sins against you seven times in a day, and seven times comes back to you and says, "I repent," forgive him.

Luke 17:3,4

Bless those who persecute you; bless and do not curse.

Do not be overcome by evil, but overcome evil with good.

Romans 12:14,21

Be kind and compassionate to one another, forgiving each other, just as in Christ God forgave you.

Ephesians 4:32

Bear with each other and forgive whatever grievances you may have against one another. Forgive as the Lord forgave you.

Colossians 3:13

Do not repay evil with evil or insult with insult, but with blessing, because to this you were called so that you may inherit a blessing.

1 Peter 3:9

When You Need Personal Comfort

The LORD replied, "My Presence will go with you, and I will give you rest."

Exodus 33:14

Look to the LORD and his strength; seek his face always.

1 Chronicles 16:11

Nevertheless, the righteous will hold to their ways, and those with clean hands will grow stronger.

Job 17:9

Even though I walk through the valley of the shadow of death, I will fear no evil, for you are with me; your rod and your staff, they comfort me.

Psalm 23:4

Be strong and take heart, all you who hope in the LORD.

Psalm 31:24

He who dwells in the shelter of the Most High will rest in the shadow of the Almighty.

I will say of the LORD, ''He is my refuge and my fortress, my God, in whom I trust.''

Surely he will save you from the fowler's snare and from the deadly pestilence.

He will cover you with his feathers, and under his wings you will find refuge; his faithfulness will be your shield and rampart.

Psalm 91:1-4

My comfort in my suffering is this: Your promise preserves my life.

You are my refuge and my shield; I have put my hope in your word.

Psalm 119:50,114

Though I walk in the midst of trouble, you preserve my life; you stretch out your hand against the anger of my foes, with your right hand you save me.

Psalm 138:7

Trust in the LORD with all your heart and lean not on your own understanding.

Proverbs 3:5

So do not fear, for I am with you; do not be dismayed, for I am your God. I will strengthen you and help you; I will uphold you with my righteous right hand.

For I am the LORD, your God, who takes hold of your right hand and says to you, Do not fear; I will help you.

Isaiah 41:10,13

When you pass through the waters, I will be with you; and when you pass through the rivers, they will not sweep over you. When you walk through the fire, you will not be burned; the flames will not set you ablaze.

Isaiah 43:2

For the LORD comforts his people and will have compassion on his afflicted ones.

Isaiah 49:13b

Blessed are those who mourn, for they will be comforted.

Matthew 5:4

I will not leave you as orphans; I will come to you.

John 14:18

If you remain in me and my words remain in you, ask whatever you wish, and it will be given you.

John 15:7

No, in all these things we are more than conquerors through him who loved us.

For I am convinced that neither death nor life, neither angels nor demons, neither the present nor the future, nor any powers, neither height nor depth, nor anything else in all creation, will be able to separate us from the love of God that is in Christ Jesus our Lord.

Romans 8:37-39

Therefore, my dear brothers, stand firm. Let nothing move you. Always give yourselves fully to the work of the Lord, because you know that your labor in the Lord is not in vain.

1 Corinthians 15:58

Be on your guard; stand firm in the faith; be men of courage; be strong.

1 Corinthians 16:13

Praise be to the God and Father of our Lord Jesus Christ, the Father of compassion and the God of all comfort, who comforts us in all our troubles, so that we can comfort those in any trouble with the comfort we ourselves have received from God.

2 Corinthians 1:3,4

Being confident of this, that he who began a good work in you will carry it on to completion until the day of Christ Jesus.

Philippians 1:6

Therefore, my brothers, you whom I love and long for, my joy and crown, that is how you should stand firm in the Lord, dear friends!

Philippians 4:1

May our Lord Jesus Christ himself and God our Father, who loved us and by his grace gave us eternal encouragement and good hope, encourage your hearts and strengthen you in every good deed and word.

2 Thessalonians 2:16,17

Let us then approach the throne of grace with confidence, so that we may receive mercy and find grace to help us in our time of need.

Hebrews 4:16

Let us fix our eyes on Jesus, the author and perfecter of our faith, who for the joy set before him endured the cross, scorning its shame, and sat down at the right hand of the throne of God.

Hebrews 12:2

Cast all your anxiety on him because he cares for you.

1 Peter 5:7

He will wipe every tear from their eyes. There will be no more death or mourning or crying or pain, for the old order of things has passed away.

Revelation 21:4

When You Need Inner Peace

I will lie down and sleep in peace, for you alone, O LORD, make me dwell in safety.

Psalm 4:8

But the meek will inherit the land and enjoy great peace.

Consider the blameless, observe the upright; there is a future for the man of peace.

Psalm 37:11,37

I will listen to what God the LORD will say; he promises peace to his people, his saints — but let them not return to folly.

Psalm 85:8

Great peace have they who love your law, and nothing can make them stumble.

Psalm 119:165

You will keep in perfect peace him whose mind is steadfast, because he trusts in you.

LORD, you establish peace for us; all that we have accomplished you have done for us.

Isaiah 26:3,12

You will go out in joy and be led forth in peace; the mountains and hills will burst into song before you, and all the trees of the field will clap their hands.

Isaiah 55:12

Those who walk uprightly enter into peace; they find rest as they lie in death.

Isaiah 57:2

Peace I leave with you; my peace I give you. I do not give to you as the world gives. Do not let your hearts be troubled and do not be afraid.

John 14:27

I have told you these things, so that in me you may have peace. In this world you will have trouble. But take heart! I have overcome the world.

John 16:33

Therefore, since we have been justified through faith, we have peace with God through our Lord Jesus Christ.

Romans 5:1

The mind of sinful man is death, but the mind controlled by the Spirit is life and peace.

Romans 8:6

Because anyone who serves Christ in this way is pleasing to God and approved by men.

Let us therefore make every effort to do what leads to peace and to mutual edification.

Romans 14:18,19

May the God of hope fill you with all joy and peace as you trust in him, so that you may overflow with hope by the power of the Holy Spirit.

Romans 15:13

Finally, brothers, good-by. Aim for perfection, listen to my appeal, be of one mind, live in peace. And the God of love and peace will be with you.

2 Corinthians 13:11

Grace and peace to you from God our Father and the Lord Jesus Christ.

Galatians 1:3

But the fruit of the Spirit is love, joy, peace, patience, kindness, goodness, faithfulness.

Galatians 5:22

For he himself is our peace, who has made the two one and has destroyed the barrier, the dividing wall of hostility.

Ephesians 2:14

Do not be anxious about anything, but in everything, by prayer and petition, with thanksgiving, present your requests to God.

And the peace of God, which transcends all understanding, will guard your hearts and your minds in Christ Jesus.

Whatever you have learned or received or heard from me, or seen in me — put it into practice. And the God of peace will be with you.

Philippians 4:6,7,9

Let the peace of Christ rule in your hearts, since as members of one body you were called to peace. And be thankful.

Colossians 3:15

Through Jesus, therefore, let us continually offer to God a sacrifice of praise — the fruit of lips that confess his name.

Hebrews 13:15

Peacemakers who sow in peace raise a harvest of righteousness.

James 3:18

When You Need a Physical Healing

Praise the LORD, O my soul, and forget not all his benefits — who forgives all your sins and heals all your diseases.

Psalm 103:2,3

Surely he took up our infirmities and carried our sorrows, yet we considered him stricken by God, smitten by him, and afflicted.
But he was pierced for our transgressions, he was crushed for our iniquities; the punishment that brought us peace was upon him, and by his wounds we are healed.

Isaiah 53:4,5

"But I will restore you to health and heal your wounds," declares the LORD.

Jeremiah 30:17a

Jesus said to him, "I will go and heal him."
Matthew 8:7

Then the woman, seeing that she could not go unnoticed, came trembling and fell at his feet. In the presence of all the people, she told why she had touched him and how she had been instantly healed.

Luke 8:47

And a woman was there who had been crippled by a spirit for eighteen years. She was bent over and could not straighten up at all.

When Jesus saw her, he called her forward and said to her, "Woman, you are set free from your infirmity."

Then he put his hands on her, and immediately she straightened up and praised God.

Luke 13:11-13

Is any one of you in trouble? He should pray. Is anyone happy? Let him sing songs of praise.

Is any one of you sick? He should call the elders of the church to pray over him and anoint him with oil in the name of the Lord.

And the prayer offered in faith will make the sick person well; the Lord will raise him up. If he has sinned, he will be forgiven.

Therefore confess your sins to each other and pray for each other so that you may be healed. The prayer of a righteous man is powerful and effective.

James 5:13-16

When You Need Discernment

But it is the spirit in a man, the breath of the Almighty, that gives him understanding.

Job 32:8

I will praise the LORD, who counsels me; even at night my heart instructs me.

Psalm 16:7

As for God, his way is perfect; the word of the LORD is flawless. He is a shield for all who take refuge in him.

Psalm 18:30

Teach me your way, O LORD; lead me in a straight path because of my oppressors.

Psalm 27:11

Send forth your light and your truth, let them guide me; let them bring me to your holy mountain, to the place where you dwell.

Psalm 43:3

The LORD will fulfill for me; your love, O LORD, endures forever — do not abandon the works of your hands.

Psalm 138:8

Trust in the LORD with all your heart and lean not on your own understanding; in all your ways acknowledge him, and he will make your paths straight.

Proverbs 3:5,6

Counsel and sound judgment are mine; I have understanding and power.

Proverbs 8:14

Understanding is a fountain of life to those who have it, but folly brings punishment to fools.

A wise man's heart guides his mouth, and his lips promote instruction.

Proverbs 16:22,23

By wisdom a house is built, and through understanding it is established; through knowledge its rooms are filled with rare and beautiful treasures.

Proverbs 24:3,4

"For my thoughts are not your thoughts, neither are your ways my ways," declares the LORD.

"As the heavens are higher than the earth, so are my ways higher than your ways and my thoughts than your thoughts."

Isaiah 55:8,9

Call to me and I will answer you and tell you great and unsearchable things you do not know.

Jeremiah 33:3

Then he opened their minds so they could understand the Scriptures.

Luke 24:45

When You Need Wisdom

I will praise the LORD, who counsels me; even at night my heart instructs me.

Psalm 16:7

Teach me your way, O LORD; lead me in a straight path because of my oppressors.

Psalm 27:11

Send forth your light and your truth, let them guide me; let them bring me to your holy mountain, to the place where you dwell.

Psalm 43:3

Teach us to number our days aright, that we may gain a heart of wisdom.

Psalm 90:12

I am your servant; give me discernment that I may understand your statutes.
The unfolding of your words gives light; it gives understanding to the simple.

Psalm 119:125,130

For the LORD gives wisdom, and from his mouth come knowledge and understanding.

He holds victory in store for the upright, he is a shield to those whose walk is blameless.

Proverbs 2:6,7

Trust in the LORD with all your heart and lean not on your own understanding; in all your ways acknowledge him, and he will make your paths straight.

Proverbs 3:5,6

Whoever loves discipline loves knowledge, but he who hates correction is stupid.

Proverbs 12:1

To the man who pleases him, God gives wisdom, knowledge and happiness, but to the sinner he gives the task of gathering and storing up wealth to hand it over to the one who pleases God. This too is meaningless, a chasing after the wind.

Ecclesiastes 2:26

Whether you turn to the right or to the left, your ears will hear a voice behind you, saying, ''This is the way; walk in it.''

Isaiah 30:21

For I will give you words and wisdom that none of your adversaries will be able to resist or contradict.

Luke 21:15

To one there is given through the Spirit the message of wisdom, to another the message of knowledge by means of the same Spirit.

1 Corinthians 12:8

I have not stopped giving thanks for you, remembering you in my prayers.

I keep asking that the God of our Lord Jesus Christ, the glorious Father, may give you the Spirit of wisdom and revelation, so that you may know him better.

I pray also that the eyes of your heart may be enlightened in order that you may know the hope to which he has called you, the riches of his glorious inheritance in the saints.

Ephesians 1:16-18

For this reason, since the day we heard about you, we have not stopped praying for you and asking God to fill you with the knowledge of his will through all spiritual wisdom and understanding.

And we pray this in order that you may live a life worthy of the Lord and may please him in every way: bearing fruit in every good work, growing in the knowledge of God.

Colossians 1:9,10

If any of you lacks wisdom, he should ask God, who gives generously to all without finding fault, and it will be given to him.

James 1:5

When You Feel Inadequate

For the LORD your God is a merciful God; he will not abandon or destroy you or forget the covenant with your forefathers, which he confirmed to them by oath.

Deuteronomy 4:31

But you are a shield around me, O LORD; you bestow glory on me and lift up my head.

Psalm 3:3

In the morning, O LORD, you hear my voice; in the morning I lay my requests before you and wait in expectation.

Psalm 5:3

Though an army besiege me, my heart will not fear; though war break out against me, even then will I be confident.

For in the day of trouble he will keep me safe in his dwelling; he will hide me in the shelter of his tabernacle and set me high upon a rock.

Psalm 27:3,5

It is better to take refuge in the LORD than to trust in man.

Psalm 118:8

He gives strength to the weary and increases the power of the weak.

But those who hope in the LORD will renew their strength. They will soar on wings like eagles; they will run and not grow weary, they will walk and not be faint.

Isaiah 40:29,31

So do not fear, for I am with you; do not be dismayed, for I am your God. I will strengthen you and help you; I will uphold you with my righteous right hand.

Isaiah 41:10

When you pass through the waters, I will be with you; and when you pass through the rivers, they will not sweep over you. When you walk through the fire, you will not be burned; the flames will not set you ablaze.

Isaiah 43:2

I will not leave you as orphans; I will come to you.

John 14:18

In this you greatly rejoice, though now for a little while you may have had to suffer grief in all kinds of trials.

These have come so that your faith — of greater worth than gold, which perishes even though refined by fire — may be proved genuine and may result in praise, glory and honor when Jesus Christ is revealed.

Though you have not seen him, you love him; and even though you do not see him now, you believe in him and are filled with an inexpressible and glorious joy, for you are receiving the goal of your faith, the salvation of your souls.

1 Peter 1:6-9

When You Feel Physically Unattractive

It is God who arms me with strength and makes my way perfect.

Psalm 18:32

For the LORD takes delight in his people; he crowns the humble with salvation.

Psalm 149:4

A happy heart makes the face cheerful, but heartache crushes the spirit.

Proverbs 15:13

Charm is deceptive, and beauty is fleeting; but a woman who fears the LORD is to be praised.

Proverbs 31:30

But those who hope in the LORD will renew their strength. They will soar on wings like eagles; they will run and not grow weary, they will walk and not be faint.

Isaiah 40:31

"No weapon forged against you will prevail, and you will refute every tongue that accuses you. This is the heritage of the servants of the LORD, and this is their vindication from me," declares the LORD.

Isaiah 54:17

Stop judging by mere appearances, and make a right judgment.

John 7:24

You are looking only on the surface of things. If anyone is confident that he belongs to Christ, he should consider again that we belong to Christ just as much as he.

2 Corinthians 10:7

Being confident of this, that he who began a good work in you will carry it on to completion until the day of Christ Jesus.

Philippians 1:6

Your attitude should be the same as that of Christ Jesus.

Philippians 2:5

And have put on the new self, which is being renewed in knowledge in the image of its Creator.

Colossians 3:10

May the God of peace, who through the blood of the eternal covenant brought back from the dead our Lord Jesus, that great Shepherd of the sheep, equip you with everything good for doing his will, and may he work in us what is pleasing to him, through Jesus Christ, to whom be glory for ever and ever. Amen.

Hebrews 13:20,21

Your beauty should not come from outward adornment, such as braided hair and the wearing of gold jewelry and fine clothes.

Instead, it should be that of your inner self, the unfading beauty of a gentle and quiet spirit, which is of great worth in God's sight.

1 Peter 3:3,4

When You Face Sexual Temptation

But you are a shield around me, O LORD; you bestow glory on me and lift up my head.

Psalm 3:3

The LORD is my light and my salvation — whom shall I fear? The LORD is the stronghold of my life — of whom shall I be afraid?

Though an army besiege me, my heart will not fear; though war break out against me, even then will I be confident.

For in the day of trouble he will keep me safe in his dwelling; he will hide me in the shelter of his tabernacle and set me high upon a rock.

Psalm 27:1,3,5

Be pleased, O LORD, to save me; O LORD, come quickly to help me.

May all who seek to take my life be put to shame and confusion; may all who desire my ruin be turned back in disgrace.

Psalm 40:13,14

It is better to take refuge in the LORD than to trust in man.

Psalm 118:8

I have hidden your word in my heart that I might not sin against you.

Psalm 119:11

For the LORD will be your confidence and will keep your foot from being snared.

Proverbs 3:26

Let your eyes look straight ahead, fix your gaze directly before you.

Do not swerve to the right or the left; keep your foot from evil.

Proverbs 4:25,27

The way of the LORD is a refuge for the righteous, but it is the ruin of those who do evil.

Proverbs 10:29

He who fears the LORD has a secure fortress, and for his children it will be a refuge.

Proverbs 14:26

He who conceals his sins does not prosper, but whoever confesses and renounces them finds mercy.

Proverbs 28:13

He gives strength to the weary and increases the power of the weak.

Isaiah 40:29

So do not fear, for I am with you; do not be dismayed, for I am your God. I will strengthen you and help you; I will uphold you with my righteous right hand.

Isaiah 41:10

And lead us not into temptation, but deliver us from the evil one.

Matthew 6:13

Watch and pray so that you will not fall into temptation. The spirit is willing, but the body is weak.

Matthew 26:41

For sin shall not be your master, because you are not under law, but under grace.

Romans 6:14

No temptation has seized you except what is common to man. And God is faithful; he will not let you be tempted beyond what you can bear. But when you are tempted, he will also provide a way out so that you can stand up under it.

1 Corinthians 10:13

Even though my illness was a trial to you, you did not treat me with contempt or scorn. Instead, you welcomed me as if I were an angel of God, as if I were Christ Jesus himself.

Galatians 4:14

When tempted, no one should say, ''God is tempting me.'' For God cannot be tempted by evil, nor does he tempt anyone; but each one is tempted when, by his own evil desire, he is dragged away and enticed.

James 1:13,14

Be self-controlled and alert. Your enemy the devil prowls around like a roaring lion looking for someone to devour.

Resist him, standing firm in the faith, because you know that your brothers throughout the world are undergoing the same kind of sufferings.

1 Peter 5:8,9

If this is so, then the Lord knows how to rescue godly men from trials and to hold the unrighteous for the day of judgment, while continuing their punishment.

2 Peter 2:9

Since you have kept my command to endure patiently, I will also keep you from the hour of trial that is going to come upon the whole world to test those who live on the earth.

Revelation 3:10

When You Feel Angry or Resentful

I will praise the LORD, who counsels me; even at night my heart instructs me.

I have set the LORD always before me. Because he is at my right hand, I will not be shaken.

Therefore my heart is glad and my tongue rejoices; my body also will rest secure.

Psalm 16:7-9

Refrain from anger and turn from wrath; do not fret — it leads only to evil.

Psalm 37:8

Surely you desire truth in the inner parts; you teach me wisdom in the inmost place.

Create in me a pure heart, O God, and renew a steadfast spirit within me.

Psalm 51:6,10

In God, whose word I praise, in God I trust; I will not be afraid. What can mortal man do to me?

Psalm 56:4

Teach me your way, O LORD, and I will walk in your truth; give me an undivided heart, that I may fear your name.

Psalm 86:11

Trust in the LORD with all your heart and lean not on your own understanding; in all your ways acknowledge him, and he will make your paths straight.

For the LORD will be your confidence.

Proverbs 3:5,6,26a

A quick-tempered man does foolish things, and a crafty man is hated.

Proverbs 14:17

Better a patient man than a warrior, a man who controls his temper than one who takes a city.

Proverbs 16:32

Fear of man will prove to be a snare, but whoever trusts in the LORD is kept safe.

Proverbs 29:25

Do not be quickly provoked in your spirit, for anger resides in the lap of fools.

Ecclesiastes 7:9

Surely God is my salvation; I will trust and not be afraid. The LORD, the LORD, is my strength and my song; he has become my salvation.

Isaiah 12:2

Blessed are the peacemakers, for they will be called sons of God.

Matthew 5:9

Love is patient, love is kind. It does not envy, it does not boast, it is not proud.

It is not rude, it is not self-seeking, it is not easily angered, it keeps no record of wrongs.

1 Corinthians 13:4,5

The weapons we fight with are not the weapons of the world. On the contrary, they have divine power to demolish strongholds.

2 Corinthians 10:4

But the fruit of the Spirit is love, joy, peace, patience, kindness, goodness, faithfulness, gentleness and self-control. Against such things there is no law.

Galatians 5:22,23

He who descended is the very one who ascended higher than all the heavens, in order to fill the whole universe.

Ephesians 4:10

Finally, be strong in the Lord and in his mighty power.

Ephesians 6:10

Finally, brothers, whatever is true, whatever is noble, whatever is right, whatever is pure, whatever is lovely, whatever is admirable — if anything is excellent or praiseworthy — think about such things.

Philippians 4:8

Dear friends, do not be surprised at the painful trial you are suffering, as though something strange were happening to you.

1 Peter 4:12

When You Feel Lonely and Unappreciated

Be strong and courageous. Do not be afraid or terrified because of them, for the LORD your God goes with you; he will never leave you nor forsake you.

Deuteronomy 31:6

For the sake of his great name the LORD will not reject his people, because the LORD was pleased to make you his own.

1 Samuel 12:22

Those who know your name will trust in you, for you, LORD, have never forsaken those who seek you.

Psalm 9:10

As for God, his way is perfect; the word of the LORD is flawless. He is a shield for all who take refuge in him.

Psalm 18:30

May the LORD answer you when you are in distress; may the name of the God of Jacob protect you.

May he send you help from the sanctuary and grant you support from Zion.

Psalm 20:1,2

Even though I walk through the valley of the shadow of death, I will fear no evil, for you are with me; your rod and your staff, they comfort me.

Psalm 23:4

A righteous man may have many troubles, but the LORD delivers him from them all.

Psalm 34:19

Why are you downcast, O my soul? Why so disturbed within me? Put your hope in God, for I will yet praise him, my Savior and my God.

Psalm 43:5

Find rest, O my soul, in God alone; my hope comes from him.

Psalm 62:5

"Because he loves me," says the LORD, "I will rescue him; I will protect him, for he acknowledges my name.

He will call upon me, and I will answer him; I will be with him in trouble, I will deliver him and honor him."

Psalm 91:14,15

I wait for the LORD, my soul waits, and in his word I put my hope.

Psalm 130:5

The eyes of all look to you, and you give them their food at the proper time.

You open your hand and satisfy the desires of every living thing.

Psalm 145:15,16

Trust in the LORD with all your heart and lean not on your own understanding; in all your ways acknowledge him, and he will make your paths straight.

Proverbs 3:5,6

Above all else, guard your heart, for it is the wellspring of life.

Proverbs 4:23

So do not fear, for I am with you; do not be dismayed, for I am your God. I will strengthen you and help you; I will uphold you with my righteous right hand.

Isaiah 41:10

You have been a refuge for the poor, a refuge for the needy in his distress, a shelter from the storm and a shade from the heat. For the breath of the ruthless is like a storm driving against a wall.

Isaiah 25:4

Can a mother forget the baby at her breast and have no compassion on the child she has borne? Though she may forget, I will not forget you!

See, I have engraved you on the palms of my hands; your walls are ever before me.

Isaiah 49:15,16

And teaching them to obey everything I have commanded you. And surely I am with you always, to the very end of the age.

Matthew 28:20

I have given you authority to trample on snakes and scorpions and to overcome all the power of the enemy; nothing will harm you.

Luke 10:19

What, then, shall we say in response to this? If God is for us, who can be against us?

Romans 8:31

So we say with confidence, ''The Lord is my helper; I will not be afraid. What can man do to me?''

Hebrews 13:6

Cast all your anxiety on him because he cares for you.

1 Peter 5:7

They overcame him by the blood of the Lamb and by the word of their testimony; they did not love their lives so much as to shrink from death.

Revelation 12:11

When You Need Ability

I can do everything through him who gives me strength.

Philippians 4:13

You show that you are a letter from Christ, the result of our ministry, written not with ink but with the Spirit of the living God, not on tablets of stone but on tablets of human hearts.

Such confidence as this is ours through Christ before God.

2 Corinthians 3:3,4

I always thank God for you because of his grace given you in Christ Jesus.

For in him you have been enriched in every way — in all your speaking and in all your knowledge — because our testimony about Christ was confirmed in you.

Therefore you do not lack any spiritual gift as you eagerly wait for our Lord Jesus Christ to be revealed.

1 Corinthians 1:4-7

Each one should use whatever gift he has received to serve others, faithfully administering God's grace in its various forms.

If anyone speaks, he should do it as one speaking the very words of God. If anyone serves, he should do it with the strength God provides, so that in all things God may be praised through Jesus Christ. To him be the glory and the power for ever and ever. Amen.

1 Peter 4:10,11

And I have filled him with the Spirit of God, with skill, ability and knowledge in all kinds of crafts.

Exodus 31:3

Moreover, I have appointed Oholiab son of Ahisamach, of the tribe of Dan, to help him. Also I have given skill to all the craftsmen to make everything I have commanded you.

Exodus 31:6

Grace and peace be yours in abundance through the knowledge of God and of Jesus our Lord.

His divine power has given us everything we need for life and godliness through our knowledge of him who called us by his own glory and goodness.

2 Peter 1:2,3

Praise be to the LORD my Rock, who trains my hands for war, my fingers for battle.

Psalm 144:1

Remain in me, and I will remain in you. No branch can bear fruit by itself; it must remain in the vine. Neither can you bear fruit unless you remain in me.

I am the vine; you are the branches. If a man remains in me and I in him, he will bear much fruit; apart from me you can do nothing.

John 15:4,5

If you remain in me and my words remain in you, ask whatever you wish, and it will be given you.

John 15:7

With your help I can advance against a troop; with my God I can scale a wall.

Psalm 18:29

No, in all these things we are more than conquerors through him who loved us.

Romans 8:37

And my God will meet all your needs according to his glorious riches in Christ Jesus.

Philippians 4:19

When You Need a Friend

You are my hiding place; you will protect me from trouble and surround me with songs of deliverance. Selah.

Psalm 32:7

He will call upon me, and I will answer him; I will be with him in trouble, I will deliver him and honor him.

Psalm 91:15

A man of many companions may come to ruin, but there is a friend who sticks closer than a brother.

Proverbs 18:24

A friend loves at all times, and a brother is born for adversity.

Proverbs 17:17

He who walks with the wise grows wise, but a companion of fools suffers harm.

Proverbs 13:20

Do nothing out of selfish ambition or vain conceit, but in humility consider others better than yourselves.

Each of you should look not only to your own interests, but also to the interests of others.

Philippians 2:3,4

For the LORD God is a sun and shield; the LORD bestows favor and honor; no good thing does he withhold from those whose walk is blameless.

Psalm 84:11

Delight yourself in the LORD and he will give you the desires of your heart.

Psalm 37:4

Where can I go from your Spirit? Where can I flee from your presence?

Psalm 139:7

Even there your hand will guide me, your right hand will hold me fast.

Psalm 139:10

When You Need Encouragement

When I called, you answered me; you made me bold and stouthearted.

Psalm 138:3

Though I walk in the midst of trouble, you preserve my life; you stretch out your hand against the anger of my foes, with your right hand you save me.
The LORD will fulfill for me; your love, O LORD, endures forever — do not abandon the works of your hands.

Psalm 138:7,8

But you, O LORD, have mercy on me; raise me up, that I may repay them.

Psalm 41:10

When you pass through the waters, I will be with you; and when you pass through the rivers, they will not sweep over you. When you walk through the fire, you will not be burned; the flames will not set you ablaze.

Isaiah 43:2

The LORD will surely comfort Zion and will look with compassion on all her ruins; he will make her deserts like Eden, her wastelands like the garden of the LORD. Joy and gladness will be found in her, thanksgiving and the sound of singing.

Isaiah 51:3

I, even I, am he who comforts you. Who are you that you fear mortal men, the sons of men, who are but grass.

Isaiah 51:12

The LORD will fulfill for me; your love, O LORD, endures forever — do not abandon the works of your hands.

Psalm 138:8

"For I know the plans I have for you," declares the LORD, "plans to prosper you and not to harm you, plans to give you hope and a future."

Jeremiah 29:11

May our Lord Jesus Christ himself and God our Father, who loved us and by his grace gave us eternal encouragement and good hope, encourage your hearts and strengthen you in every good deed and word.

2 Thessalonians 2:16,17

God is not unjust; he will not forget your work and the love you have shown him as you have helped his people and continue to help them.

We want each of you to show this same diligence to the very end, in order to make your hope sure.

We do not want you to become lazy, but to imitate those who through faith and patience inherit what has been promised.

Hebrews 6:10-12

But from everlasting to everlasting the LORD's love is with those who fear him, and his righteousness with their children's children.

Psalm 103:17

Be strong and courageous. Do not be afraid or terrified because of them, for the LORD your God goes with you; he will never leave you nor forsake you.

Deuteronomy 31:6

Yet I am always with you; you hold me by my right hand.

Psalm 73:23

Have I not commanded you? Be strong and courageous. Do not be terrified; do not be discouraged, for the LORD your God will be with you wherever you go.

Joshua 1:9

So he said to me, "This is the word of the LORD to Zerubbabel: 'Not by might nor by power, but by my Spirit,' says the LORD Almighty."

Zechariah 4:6

Trust in the LORD and do good; dwell in the land and enjoy safe pasture.

Delight yourself in the LORD and he will give you the desires of your heart.

Commit your way to the LORD; trust in him and he will do this.

Psalm 37:3-5

Praise our God, O peoples, let the sound of his praise be heard; he has preserved our lives and kept our feet from slipping.

Psalm 66:8,9

But thanks be to God, who always leads us in triumphal procession in Christ and through us spreads everywhere the fragrance of the knowledge of him.

2 Corinthians 2:14

I will praise God's name in song and glorify him with thanksgiving.

Psalm 69:30

The poor will see and be glad — you who seek God, may your hearts live!

Psalm 69:32

Being confident of this, that he who began a good work in you will carry it on to completion until the day of Christ Jesus.

Philippians 1:6

The path of the righteous is like the first gleam of dawn, shining ever brighter till the full light of day.

Proverbs 4:18

When You Need Faith

But what does it say? "The word is near you; it is in your mouth and in your heart," that is, the word of faith we are proclaiming.

Romans 10:8

Consequently, faith comes from hearing the message, and the message is heard through the word of Christ.

Romans 10:17

As for God, his way is perfect; the word of the LORD is flawless. He is a shield for all who take refuge in him.

2 Samuel 22:31

The LORD is a refuge for the oppressed, a stronghold in times of trouble.

Those who know your name will trust in you, for you, LORD, have never forsaken those who seek you.

Psalm 9:9,10

It is better to take refuge in the LORD than to trust in man.

It is better to take refuge in the LORD than to trust in princes.

Psalm 118:8,9

Those who trust in the LORD are like Mount Zion, which cannot be shaken but endures forever.

Psalm 125:1

My help comes from the LORD, the Maker of heaven and earth.

He will not let your foot slip — he who watches over you will not slumber; indeed, he who watches over Israel will neither slumber nor sleep.

Psalm 121:2-4

But let all who take refuge in you be glad; let them ever sing for joy. Spread your protection over them, that those who love your name may rejoice in you.

Psalm 5:11

May the God of hope fill you with all joy and peace as you trust in him, so that you may overflow with hope by the power of the Holy Spirit.

Romans 15:13

And we also thank God continually because, when you received the word of God, which you heard from us, you accepted it not as the word of men, but as it actually is, the word of God, which is at work in you who believe.

1 Thessalonians 2:13

But those sacrifices are an annual reminder of sins.

Hebrews 10:3

But my righteous one will live by faith. And if he shrinks back, I will not be pleased with him.

But we are not of those who shrink back and are destroyed, but of those who believe and are saved.

Hebrews 10:38,39

For everyone born of God overcomes the world. This is the victory that has overcome the world, even our faith.

1 John 5:4

The LORD himself goes before you and will be with you; he will never leave you nor forsake you. Do not be afraid; do not be discouraged.

Deuteronomy 31:8

Early in the morning they left for the Desert of Tekoa. As they set out, Jehoshaphat stood and said, "Listen to me, Judah and people of Jerusalem! Have faith in the LORD your God and you will be upheld; have faith in his prophets and you will be successful."

2 Chronicles 20:20

"Be strong and courageous. Do not be afraid or discouraged because of the king of Assyria and the vast army with him, for there is a greater power with us than with him.

With him is only the arm of flesh, but with us is the LORD our God to help us and to fight our battles." And the people gained confidence from what Hezekiah the king of Judah said.

2 Chronicles 32:7,8

Be not afraid, O land; be glad and rejoice. Surely the LORD has done great things.

Joel 2:21

See, he is puffed up; his desires are not upright — but the righteous will live by his faith.

Habakkuk 2:4

David also said to Solomon his son, "Be strong and courageous, and do the work. Do not be afraid or discouraged, for the LORD God, my God, is with you. He will not fail you or forsake you until all the work for the service of the temple of the LORD is finished."

1 Chronicles 28:20

The LORD is my shepherd, I shall not be in want.

Psalm 23:1

When You Need Joy

You have made known to me the path of life; you will fill me with joy in your presence, with eternal pleasures at your right hand.

Psalm 16:11

Splendor and majesty are before him; strength and joy in his dwelling place.

1 Chronicles 16:27

And on that day they offered great sacrifices, rejoicing because God had given them great joy. The women and children also rejoiced. The sound of rejoicing in Jerusalem could be heard far away.

Nehemiah 12:43

You have filled my heart with greater joy than when their grain and new wine abound.

Psalm 4:7

I will be glad and rejoice in you; I will sing praise to your name, O Most High.

Psalm 9:2

The precepts of the LORD are right, giving joy to the heart. The commands of the LORD are radiant, giving light to the eyes.

Psalm 19:8

The LORD is my strength and my shield; my heart trusts in him, and I am helped. My heart leaps for joy and I will give thanks to him in song.

Psalm 28:7

Then my soul will rejoice in the LORD and delight in his salvation.

Psalm 35:9

Will you not revive us again, that your people may rejoice in you?

Psalm 85:6

Blessed are those who have learned to acclaim you, who walk in the light of your presence, O LORD.

They rejoice in your name all day long; they exult in your righteousness.

Psalm 89:15,16

Shout for joy to the LORD, all the earth.

Worship the LORD with gladness; come before him with joyful songs.

Psalm 100:1,2

When the LORD brought back the captives to Zion, we were like men who dreamed.

Our mouths were filled with laughter, our tongues with songs of joy. Then it was said among the nations, "The LORD has done great things for them."

Psalm 126:1,2

When your words came, I ate them; they were my joy and my heart's delight, for I bear your name, O LORD God Almighty.

Jeremiah 15:16

However, do not rejoice that the spirits submit to you, but rejoice that your names are written in heaven.

Luke 10:20

I have told you this so that my joy may be in you and that your joy may be complete.

John 15:11

You have made known to me the paths of life; you will fill me with joy in your presence.

Acts 2:28

And the disciples were filled with joy and with the Holy Spirit.

Acts 13:52

For the kingdom of God is not a matter of eating and drinking, but of righteousness, peace and joy in the Holy Spirit.

Romans 14:17

For you were once darkness, but now you are light in the Lord. Live as children of light.

Ephesians 5:8

Whatever you have learned or received or heard from me, or seen in me — put it into practice. And the God of peace will be with you.

Philippians 4:9

Though you have not seen him, you love him; and even though you do not see him now, you believe in him and are filled with an inexpressible and glorious joy.

1 Peter 1:8

When You Need Love

And hope does not disappoint us, because God has poured out his love into our hearts by the Holy Spirit, whom he has given us.

Romans 5:5

And this is my prayer: that your love may abound more and more in knowledge and depth of insight, so that you may be able to discern what is best and may be pure and blameless until the day of Christ, filled with the fruit of righteousness that comes through Jesus Christ — to the glory and praise of God.

Philippians 1:9-11

May the Lord make your love increase and overflow for each other and for everyone else, just as ours does for you.

May he strengthen your hearts so that you will be blameless and holy in the presence of our God and Father when our Lord Jesus comes with all his holy ones.

1 Thessalonians 3:12,13

Now about brotherly love we do not need to write to you, for you yourselves have been taught by God to love each other.

And in fact, you do love all the brothers throughout Macedonia. Yet we urge you, brothers, to do so more and more.

1 Thessalonians 4:9,10

May the Lord direct your hearts into God's love and Christ's perseverance.

2 Thessalonians 3:5

This is love: not that we loved God, but that he loved us and sent his Son as an atoning sacrifice for our sins.

Dear friends, since God so loved us, we also ought to love one another.

No one has ever seen God; but if we love one another, God lives in us and his love is made complete in us.

1 John 4:10-12

And so we know and rely on the love God has for us. God is love. Whoever lives in love lives in God, and God in him.

In this way, love is made complete among us so that we will have confidence on the day of judgment, because in this world we are like him.

There is no fear in love. But perfect love drives out fear, because fear has to do with punishment. The one who fears is not made perfect in love.

1 John 4:16-18

They want to be teachers of the law, but they do not know what they are talking about or what they so confidently affirm.

1 Timothy 1:7

Hatred stirs up dissension, but love covers over all wrongs.

Proverbs 10:12

Place me like a seal over your heart, like a seal on your arm; for love is as strong as death, its jealousy unyielding as the grave. It burns like blazing fire, like a mighty flame.

Many waters cannot quench love; rivers cannot wash it away. If one were to give all the wealth of his house for love, it would be utterly scorned.

Song of Solomon 8:6,7

He who covers over an offense promotes love, but whoever repeats the matter separates close friends.

Proverbs 17:9

A friend loves at all times, and a brother is born for adversity.

Proverbs 17:17

Honor your father and mother, and love your neighbor as yourself.

Matthew 19:19

Love the LORD your God with all your heart and with all your soul and with all your strength.

Deuteronomy 6:5

And now, O Israel, what does the LORD your God ask of you but to fear the LORD your God, to walk in all his ways, to love him, to serve the LORD your God with all your heart and with all your soul.

Deuteronomy 10:12

But be very careful to keep the commandment and the law that Moses the servant of the LORD gave you: to love the LORD your God, to walk in all his ways, to obey his commands, to hold fast to him and to serve him with all your heart and all your soul.

Joshua 22:5

I love the LORD, for he heard my voice; he heard my cry for mercy.

Psalm 116:1

Jesus replied, ''I will ask you one question. Answer me, and I will tell you by what authority I am doing these things.

John's baptism — was it from heaven, or from men? Tell me!

They discussed it among themselves and said, ''If we say, 'From heaven,' he will ask, 'Then why didn't you believe him?'

But if we say, 'From men' . . . .'' (They feared the people, for everyone held that John really was a prophet.)

So they answered Jesus, ''We don't know.'' Jesus said, ''Neither will I tell you by what authority I am doing these things.''

Mark 11:29-33

A new command I give you: Love one another. As I have loved you, so you must love one another.

By this all men will know that you are my disciples, if you love one another.

John 13:34,35

Now about food sacrificed to idols: We know that we all possess knowledge. Knowledge puffs up, but love builds up.

1 Corinthians 8:1

The goal of this command is love, which comes from a pure heart and a good conscience and a sincere faith.

1 Timothy 1:5

Above all, love each other deeply, because love covers over a multitude of sins.

1 Peter 4:8

Whoever loves his brother lives in the light, and there is nothing in him to make him stumble.

1 John 2:10

When You Need Motivation

Slaves, obey your earthly masters in everything; and do it, not only when their eye is on you and to win their favor, but with sincerity of heart and reverence for the Lord.

Whatever you do, work at it with all your heart, as working for the Lord, not for men.

Colossians 3:22,23

Stay in that house, eating and drinking whatever they give you, for the worker deserves his wages. Do not move around from house to house.

Luke 10:7

For this reason I remind you to fan into flame the gift of God, which is in you through the laying on of my hands.

For God did not give us a spirit of timidity, but a spirit of power, of love and of self-discipline.

2 Timothy 1:6,7

But the men of Israel encouraged one another and again took up their positions where they had stationed themselves the first day.

Judges 20:22

Lazy hands make a man poor, but diligent hands bring wealth.

Proverbs 10:4

Diligent hands will rule, but laziness ends in slave labor.

Proverbs 12:24

Do you see a man skilled in his work? He will serve before kings; he will not serve before obscure men.

Proverbs 22:29

I walk in the way of righteousness, along the paths of justice, bestowing wealth on those who love me and making their treasuries full.

Proverbs 8:20,21

Never be lacking in zeal, but keep your spiritual fervor, serving the Lord.

Romans 12:11

Laziness brings on deep sleep, and the shiftless man goes hungry.

Proverbs 19:15

He who gathers crops in summer is a wise son, but he who sleeps during harvest is a disgraceful son.

Proverbs 10:5

He who works his land will have abundant food, but he who chases fantasies lacks judgment.

Proverbs 12:11

Dishonest money dwindles away, but he who gathers money little by little makes it grow.

Proverbs 13:11

Do not love sleep or you will grow poor; stay awake and you will have food to spare.

Proverbs 20:13

Make it your ambition to lead a quiet life, to mind your own business and to work with your hands, just as we told you, so that your daily life may win the respect of outsiders and so that you will not be dependent on anybody.

1 Thessalonians 4:11,12

For even when we were with you, we gave you this rule: "If a man will not work, he shall not eat."

2 Thessalonians 3:10

We do not want you to become lazy, but to imitate those who through faith and patience inherit what has been promised.

Hebrews 6:12

If a man is lazy, the rafters sag; if his hands are idle, the house leaks.

Ecclesiastes 10:18

No, in all these things we are more than conquerors through him who loved us.

Romans 8:37

When You Need Patience

Be still before the LORD and wait patiently for him; do not fret when men succeed in their ways, when they carry out their wicked schemes.

Refrain from anger and turn from wrath; do not fret — it leads only to evil.

For evil men will be cut off, but those who hope in the LORD will inherit the land.

Psalm 37:7-9

The end of a matter is better than its beginning, and patience is better than pride.

Do not be quickly provoked in your spirit, for anger resides in the lap of fools.

Ecclesiastes 7:8,9

By standing firm you will gain life.

Luke 21:19

Not only so, but we also rejoice in our sufferings, because we know that suffering produces perseverance.

Romans 5:3

Let us not become weary in doing good, for at the proper time we will reap a harvest if we do not give up.

Galatians 6:9

As a prisoner for the Lord, then, I urge you to live a life worthy of the calling you have received.

Ephesians 4:1

Be completely humble and gentle; be patient, bearing with one another in love.

Ephesians 4:2

And we pray this in order that you may live a life worthy of the Lord and may please him in every way: bearing fruit in every good work, growing in the knowledge of God,

being strengthened with all power according to his glorious might so that you may have great endurance and patience, and joyfully

giving thanks to the Father, who has qualified you to share in the inheritance of the saints in the kingdom of light.

Colossians 1:10-12

And we urge you, brothers, warn those who are idle, encourage the timid, help the weak, be patient with everyone.

1 Thessalonians 5:14

May the Lord direct your hearts into God's love and Christ's perseverance.

2 Thessalonians 3:5

But you, man of God, flee from all this, and pursue righteousness, godliness, faith, love, endurance and gentleness.

1 Timothy 6:11

We do not want you to become lazy, but to imitate those who through faith and patience inherit what has been promised.

Hebrews 6:12

And so after waiting patiently, Abraham received what was promised.

Hebrews 6:15

You need to persevere so that when you have done the will of God, you will receive what he has promised.

Hebrews 10:36

Therefore, since we are surrounded by such a great cloud of witnesses, let us throw off everything that hinders and the sin that so easily entangles, and let us run with perseverance the race marked out for us.

Hebrews 12:1

Because you know that the testing of your faith develops perseverance.

Perseverance must finish its work so that you may be mature and complete, not lacking anything.

James 1:3,4

My dear brothers, take note of this: Everyone should be quick to listen, slow to speak and slow to become angry.

James 1:19

Be patient, then, brothers, until the Lord's coming. See how the farmer waits for the land to yield its valuable crop and how patient he is for the autumn and spring rains.

You too, be patient and stand firm, because the Lord's coming is near.

James 5:7,8

For this very reason, make every effort to add to your faith goodness; and to goodness, knowledge; and to knowledge, self-control; and to self-control, perseverance; and to perseverance, godliness.

2 Peter 1:5,6

This calls for patient endurance on the part of the saints who obey God's commandments and remain faithful to Jesus.

Revelation 14:12

The Lord is not slow in keeping his promise, as some understand slowness. He is patient with you, not wanting anyone to perish, but everyone to come to repentance.

2 Peter 3:9

When You Need Protection

He who dwells in the shelter of the Most High will rest in the shadow of the Almighty.

I will say of the LORD, "He is my refuge and my fortress, my God, in whom I trust."

Surely he will save you from the fowler's snare and from the deadly pestilence.

He will cover you with his feathers, and under his wings you will find refuge; his faithfulness will be your shield and rampart.

You will not fear the terror of night, nor the arrow that flies by day, nor the pestilence that stalks in the darkness, nor the plague that destroys at midday.

A thousand may fall at your side, ten thousand at your right hand, but it will not come near you.

You will only observe with your eyes and see the punishment of the wicked.

If you make the Most High your dwelling — even the LORD, who is my refuge — then no harm will befall you, no disaster will come near your tent.

For he will command his angels concerning you to guard you in all your ways; they will lift you up in their hands, so that you will not strike your foot against a stone.

You will tread upon the lion and the cobra; you will trample the great lion and the serpent.

"Because he loves me," says the LORD, "I will rescue him; I will protect him, for he acknowledges my name.

He will call upon me, and I will answer him; I will be with him in trouble, I will deliver him and honor him.

With long life will I satisfy him and show him my salvation."

Psalm 91:1-16

Therefore let everyone who is godly pray to you while you may be found; surely when the mighty waters rise, they will not reach him.

You are my hiding place; you will protect me from trouble and surround me with songs of deliverance. Selah.

Psalm 32:6,7

"And I myself will be a wall of fire around it," declares the LORD, "and I will be its glory within."

Zechariah 2:5

God is our refuge and strength, an ever-present help in trouble.

Therefore we will not fear, though the earth give way and the mountains fall into the heart of the sea.

Psalm 46:1,2

God is within her, she will not fall; God will help her at break of day.

Psalm 46:5

When I am afraid, I will trust in you.

In God, whose word I praise, in God I trust; I will not be afraid. What can mortal man do to me?

Psalm 56:3,4

Give us aid against the enemy, for the help of man is worthless.

With God we will gain the victory, and he will trample down our enemies.

Psalm 60:11,12

Hear my cry, O God; listen to my prayer.

From the ends of the earth I call to you, I call as my heart grows faint; lead me to the rock that is higher than I.

For you have been my refuge, a strong tower against the foe.

I long to dwell in your tent forever and take refuge in the shelter of your wings. Selah.

Psalm 61:1-4

He who fears the LORD has a secure fortress,
and for his children it will be a refuge.

The fear of the LORD is a fountain of life,
turning a man from the snares of death.

Proverbs 14:26,27

As for God, his way is perfect; the word of
the LORD is flawless. He is a shield for all who
take refuge in him.

2 Samuel 22:31

That is why I am suffering as I am. Yet I am
not ashamed, because I know whom I have
believed, and am convinced that he is able to guard
what I have entrusted to him for that day.

2 Timothy 1:12

To him who is able to keep you from falling
and to present you before his glorious presence
without fault and with great joy.

Jude 1:24

When You Need Self-Control

Rather, clothe yourselves with the Lord Jesus
Christ, and do not think about how to gratify the
desires of the sinful nature.

Romans 13:14

For we know that our old self was crucified
with him so that the body of sin might be done away
with, that we should no longer be slaves to sin.

Romans 6:6

And put a knife to your throat if you are given to gluttony.

Proverbs 23:2

Better a patient man than a warrior, a man who controls his temper than one who takes a city.

Proverbs 16:32

Everything is permissible for me — but not everything is beneficial. Everything is permissible for me — but I will not be mastered by anything.

1 Corinthians 6:12

I have been crucified with Christ and I no longer live, but Christ lives in me. The life I live in the body, I live by faith in the Son of God, who loved me and gave himself for me.

Galatians 2:20

So I say, live by the Spirit, and you will not gratify the desires of the sinful nature.

Galatians 5:16

Those who belong to Christ Jesus have crucified the sinful nature with its passions and desires.

Galatians 5:24

No one serving as a soldier gets involved in civilian affairs — he wants to please his commanding officer.

2 Timothy 2:4

Dear friends, I urge you, as aliens and strangers in the world, to abstain from sinful desires, which war against your soul.

1 Peter 2:11

Therefore, since Christ suffered in his body, arm yourselves also with the same attitude, because he who has suffered in his body is done with sin.

As a result, he does not live the rest of his earthly life for evil human desires, but rather for the will of God.

1 Peter 4:1,2

If you find honey, eat just enough — too much of it, and you will vomit.

Proverbs 25:16

Everyone who competes in the games goes into strict training. They do it to get a crown that will not last; but we do it to get a crown that will last forever.

Therefore I do not run like a man running aimlessly; I do not fight like a man beating the air.

No, I beat my body and make it my slave so that after I have preached to others, I myself will not be disqualified for the prize.

1 Corinthians 9:25-27

Let your gentleness be evident to all. The Lord is near.

Philippians 4:5

When You Need Strength

The LORD is my strength and my song; he has become my salvation. He is my God, and I will praise him, my father's God, and I will exalt him.

Exodus 15:2

All his laws are before me; I have not turned away from his decrees.

2 Samuel 22:23

The LORD is my strength and my song; he has become my salvation.

Psalm 118:14

Surely God is my salvation; I will trust and not be afraid. The LORD, the LORD, is my strength and my song; he has become my salvation.

Isaiah 12:2

You armed me with strength for battle; you made my adversaries bow at my feet.

2 Samuel 22:40

It is God who arms me with strength and makes my way perfect.

Psalm 18:32

You armed me with strength for battle; you made my adversaries bow at my feet.

Psalm 18:39

May the words of my mouth and the meditation of my heart be pleasing in your sight, O LORD, my Rock and my Redeemer.

Psalm 19:14

The LORD gives strength to his people; the LORD blesses his people with peace.

Psalm 29:11

Sing for joy to God our strength; shout aloud to the God of Jacob!

Psalm 81:1

My flesh and my heart may fail, but God is the strength of my heart and my portion forever.

Psalm 73:26

A wise man has great power, and a man of knowledge increases strength.

Proverbs 24:5

Trust in the LORD forever, for the LORD, the LORD, is the Rock eternal.

Isaiah 26:4

He gives strength to the weary and increases the power of the weak.

Isaiah 40:29

But he said to me, "My grace is sufficient for you, for my power is made perfect in weakness." Therefore I will boast all the more gladly about my weaknesses, so that Christ's power may rest on me.

2 Corinthians 12:9

Summon your power, O God; show us your strength, O God, as you have done before.

Psalm 68:28

Finally, be strong in the Lord and in his mighty power.

Ephesians 6:10

When You Need Deliverance

My soul finds rest in God alone; my salvation comes from him.

He alone is my rock and my salvation; he is my fortress, I will never be shaken.

Psalm 62:1,2

Find rest, O my soul, in God alone; my hope comes from him.

He alone is my rock and my salvation; he is my fortress, I will not be shaken.

My salvation and my honor depend on God; he is my mighty rock, my refuge.

Trust in him at all times, O people; pour out your hearts to him, for God is our refuge. Selah.

Psalm 62:5-8

One thing God has spoken, two things have I heard: that you, O God, are strong, and that you,

O Lord, are loving. Surely you will reward each person according to what he has done.

Psalm 62:11,12

When it was almost time for the Jewish Passover, Jesus went up to Jerusalem.

John 2:13

If this is so, then the Lord knows how to rescue godly men from trials and to hold the unrighteous for the day of judgment, while continuing their punishment.

2 Peter 2:9

He reached down from on high and took hold of me; he drew me out of deep waters.

He rescued me from my powerful enemy, from my foes, who were too strong for me.

They confronted me in the day of my disaster, but the LORD was my support.

He brought me out into a spacious place; he rescued me because he delighted in me.

Psalm 18:16-19

In the shelter of your presence you hide them from the intrigues of men; in your dwelling you keep them safe from accusing tongues.

Psalm 31:20

I sought the LORD, and he answered me; he delivered me from all my fears.

Psalm 34:4

A righteous man may have many troubles, but the LORD delivers him from them all.

Psalm 34:19

To the Jews who had believed him, Jesus said, ''If you hold to my teaching, you are really my disciples.

Then you will know the truth, and the truth will set you free.''

John 8:31,32

When Jesus had called the Twelve together, he gave them power and authority to drive out all demons and to cure diseases.

Luke 9:1

He called his twelve disciples to him and gave them authority to drive out evil spirits and to heal every disease and sickness.

Matthew 10:1

I have given you authority to trample on snakes and scorpions and to overcome all the power of the enemy; nothing will harm you.

Luke 10:19

When evening came, many who were demon-possessed were brought to him, and he drove out the spirits with a word and healed all the sick.

This was to fulfill what was spoken through the prophet Isaiah: "He took up our infirmities and carried our diseases."

Matthew 8:16,17

The Lord will rescue me from every evil attack and will bring me safely to his heavenly kingdom. To him be glory for ever and ever. Amen.

2 Timothy 4:18

When You Have Doubts

Ignoring what they said, Jesus told the synagogue ruler, "Don't be afraid; just believe."

Mark 5:36

"If you can?" said Jesus. "Everything is possible for him who believes."

Immediately the boy's father exclaimed, "I do believe; help me overcome my unbelief!"

Mark 9:23,24

I tell you the truth, if anyone says to this mountain, "Go, throw yourself into the sea," and does not doubt in his heart but believes that what he says will happen, it will be done for him.

Therefore I tell you, whatever you ask for in prayer, believe that you have received it, and it will be yours.

Mark 11:23,24

Then the man said, "Lord, I believe," and he worshiped him.

John 9:38

But if I do it, even though you do not believe me, believe the miracles, that you may know and understand that the Father is in me, and I in the Father.

John 10:38

Do not let your hearts be troubled. Trust in God; trust also in me.

Believe me when I say that I am in the Father and the Father is in me; or at least believe on the evidence of the miracles themselves.

John 14:1,11

"You believe at last!" Jesus answered.

John 16:31

So the other disciples told him, "We have seen the Lord!" But he said to them, "Unless I see the nail marks in his hands and put my finger where the nails were, and put my hand into his side, I will not believe it."

A week later his disciples were in the house again, and Thomas was with them. Though the doors were locked, Jesus came and stood among them and said, "Peace be with you!"

Then he said to Thomas, "Put your finger here; see my hands. Reach out your hand and put it into my side. Stop doubting and believe."

Thomas said to him, "My Lord and my God!"

Then Jesus told him, "Because you have seen me, you have believed; blessed are those who have not seen and yet have believed."

Jesus did many other miraculous signs in the presence of his disciples, which are not recorded in this book.

But these are written that you may believe that Jesus is the Christ, the Son of God, and that by believing you may have life in his name.

John 20:25-31

After much discussion, Peter got up and addressed them: "Brothers, you know that some time ago God made a choice among you that the Gentiles might hear from my lips the message of the gospel and believe."

Acts 15:7

So keep up your courage, men, for I have faith in God that it will happen just as he told me.

Acts 27:25

And he received the sign of circumcision, a seal of the righteousness that he had by faith while he was still uncircumcised. So then, he is the father of all who believe but have not been circumcised, in order that righteousness might be credited to them.

Romans 4:11

(And for this we labor and strive), that we have put our hope in the living God, who is the Savior of all men, and especially of those who believe.

1 Timothy 4:10

And without faith it is impossible to please God, because anyone who comes to him must believe that he exists and that he rewards those who earnestly seek him.

Hebrews 11:6

And this is his command: to believe in the name of his Son, Jesus Christ, and to love one another as he commanded us.

1 John 3:23

It [love] always protects, always trusts, always hopes, always perseveres.

1 Corinthians 13:7

Then he said to Thomas, "Put your finger here; see my hands. Reach out your hand and put it into my side. Stop doubting and believe."

John 20:27

May the God of hope fill you with all joy and peace as you trust in him, so that you may overflow with hope by the power of the Holy Spirit.

Romans 15:13

When You Do Not Feel God's Presence

The LORD replied, "My Presence will go with you, and I will give you rest."

Exodus 33:14

And teaching them to obey everything I have commanded you. And surely I am with you always, to the very end of the age.

Matthew 28:20

Keep your lives free from the love of money and be content with what you have, because God has said, "Never will I leave you; never will I forsake you."

Hebrews 13:5

A man of many companions may come to ruin, but there is a friend who sticks closer than a brother.

Proverbs 18:24

Greater love has no one than this, that he lay down his life for his friends.

You are my friends if you do what I command.

I no longer call you servants, because a servant does not know his master's business. Instead, I have called you friends, for everything that I learned from my Father I have made known to you.

John 15:13-15

Have I not commanded you? Be strong and courageous. Do not be terrified; do not be discouraged, for the LORD your God will be with you wherever you go.

Joshua 1:9

Because a great door for effective work has opened to me, and there are many who oppose me.

1 Corinthians 16:9

The LORD is near to all who call on him, to all who call on him in truth.

Psalm 145:18

And without faith it is impossible to please God, because anyone who comes to him must believe that he exists and that he rewards those who earnestly seek him.

Hebrews 11:6

All that the Father gives me will come to me, and whoever comes to me I will never drive away.

John 6:37

Come near to God and he will come near to you. Wash your hands, you sinners, and purify your hearts, you double-minded.

James 4:8

Here I am! I stand at the door and knock. If anyone hears my voice and opens the door, I will come in and eat with him, and he with me.

Revelation 3:20

You will seek me and find me when you seek me with all your heart.

Jeremiah 29:13

The LORD is good to those whose hope is in him, to the one who seeks him.

Lamentations 3:25

When You Feel Like a Failure

I can do everything through him who gives me strength.

Philippians 4:13

No, in all these things we are more than conquerors through him who loved us.

Romans 8:37

For everyone born of God overcomes the world. This is the victory that has overcome the world, even our faith.

1 John 5:4

I will exalt you, O LORD, for you lifted me out of the depths and did not let my enemies gloat over me.

Psalm 30:1

Do not let this Book of the Law depart from your mouth; meditate on it day and night, so that you may be careful to do everything written in it. Then you will be prosperous and successful.

Joshua 1:8

But you are a shield around me, O LORD; you bestow glory on me and lift up my head.

Psalm 3:3

The LORD sustains the humble but casts the wicked to the ground.

Psalm 147:6

You, dear children, are from God and have overcome them, because the one who is in you is greater than the one who is in the world.

1 John 4:4

But thanks be to God, who always leads us in triumphal procession in Christ and through us spreads everywhere the fragrance of the knowledge of him.

2 Corinthians 2:14

I have been crucified with Christ and I no longer live, but Christ lives in me. The life I live in the body, I live by faith in the Son of God, who loved me and gave himself for me.

Galatians 2:20

Therefore, if anyone is in Christ, he is a new creation; the old has gone, the new has come!

2 Corinthians 5:17

But I have prayed for you, Simon, that your faith may not fail. And when you have turned back, strengthen your brothers.

Luke 22:32

Do not cast me away when I am old; do not forsake me when my strength is gone.

Psalm 71:9

My flesh and my heart may fail, but God is the strength of my heart and my portion forever.

Psalm 73:26

Now if we are children, then we are heirs — heirs of God and co-heirs with Christ, if indeed we share in his sufferings in order that we may also share in his glory.

Romans 8:17

If you belong to Christ, then you are Abraham's seed, and heirs according to the promise.

Galatians 3:29

But thanks be to God! He gives us the victory through our Lord Jesus Christ.

1 Corinthians 15:57

When You Feel Unusual Stress

Persecuted, but not abandoned; struck down, but not destroyed.

2 Corinthians 4:9

Not only so, but we also rejoice in our sufferings, because we know that suffering produces perseverance.

Romans 5:3

Who shall separate us from the love of Christ? Shall trouble or hardship or persecution or famine or nakedness or danger or sword?

Romans 8:35

Be joyful in hope, patient in affliction, faithful in prayer.

Romans 12:12

Who comforts us in all our troubles, so that we can comfort those in any trouble with the comfort we ourselves have received from God.

2 Corinthians 1:4

I have great confidence in you; I take great pride in you. I am greatly encouraged; in all our troubles my joy knows no bounds.

2 Corinthians 7:4

These have come so that your faith — of greater worth than gold, which perishes even though refined by fire — may be proved genuine and may result in praise, glory and honor when Jesus Christ is revealed.

1 Peter 1:7

Dear friends, do not be surprised at the painful trial you are suffering, as though something strange were happening to you.

1 Peter 4:12

But even if you should suffer for what is right, you are blessed. "Do not fear what they fear; do not be frightened."

1 Peter 3:14

I have told you these things, so that in me you may have peace. In this world you will have trouble. But take heart! I have overcome the world.

John 16:33

Therefore we do not lose heart. Though outwardly we are wasting away, yet inwardly we are being renewed day by day.

2 Corinthians 4:16

In the day of my trouble I will call to you, for you will answer me.

Psalm 86:7

The righteous man is rescued from trouble, and it comes on the wicked instead.

Proverbs 11:8

Do not be anxious about anything, but in everything, by prayer and petition, with thanksgiving, present your requests to God.

Philippians 4:6

In my distress I called to the LORD; I cried to my God for help. From his temple he heard my voice; my cry came before him, into his ears.

Psalm 18:6

In my distress I called to the LORD; I called out to my God. From his temple he heard my voice; my cry came to his ears.

2 Samuel 22:7

The king then took an oath: "As surely as the LORD lives, who has delivered me out of every trouble."

1 Kings 1:29

In my anguish I cried to the LORD, and he answered by setting me free.

Psalm 118:5

I call on the LORD in my distress, and he answers me.

Psalm 120:1

When You Have Bad Memories of the Past

Do not conform any longer to the pattern of this world, but be transformed by the renewing of your mind. Then you will be able to test and approve what God's will is — his good, pleasing and perfect will.

Romans 12:2

Therefore, if anyone is in Christ, he is a new creation; the old has gone, the new has come!

2 Corinthians 5:17

Brothers, I do not consider myself yet to have taken hold of it. But one thing I do: Forgetting what is behind and straining toward what is ahead.

Philippians 3:13

See, I am doing a new thing! Now it springs up; do you not perceive it? I am making a way in the desert and streams in the wasteland.

Isaiah 43:19

See, the former things have taken place, and new things I declare; before they spring into being I announce them to you.

Isaiah 42:9

See! The winter is past; the rains are over and gone.

Song of Solomon 2:11

God presented him as a sacrifice of atonement, through faith in his blood. He did this to demonstrate his justice, because in his forbearance he had left the sins committed beforehand unpunished.

Romans 3:25

In which you used to live when you followed the ways of this world and of the ruler of the kingdom of the air, the spirit who is now at work in those who are disobedient.

All of us also lived among them at one time, gratifying the cravings of our sinful nature and following its desires and thoughts. Like the rest, we were by nature objects of wrath.

Ephesians 2:2,3

To be made new in the attitude of your minds.

Ephesians 4:23

To make her holy, cleansing her by the washing with water through the word.

Ephesians 5:26

When You Want To Be Close to God

The LORD is good to those whose hope is in him, to the one who seeks him.

Lamentations 3:25

You will seek me and find me when you seek me with all your heart.

Jeremiah 29:13

Come near to God and he will come near to you. Wash your hands, you sinners, and purify your hearts, you double-minded.

James 4:8

But if from there you seek the LORD your God, you will find him if you look for him with all your heart and with all your soul.

Deuteronomy 4:29

He sought God during the days of Zechariah, who instructed him in the fear of God. As long as he sought the LORD, God gave him success.

2 Chronicles 26:5

One thing I ask of the LORD, this is what I seek: that I may dwell in the house of the LORD all the days of my life, to gaze upon the beauty of the LORD and to seek him in his temple.

For in the day of trouble he will keep me safe in his dwelling; he will hide me in the shelter of his tabernacle and set me high upon a rock.

Then my head will be exalted above the enemies who surround me; at his tabernacle will I sacrifice with shouts of joy; I will sing and make music to the LORD.

Hear my voice when I call, O LORD; be merciful to me and answer me.

My heart says of you, "Seek his face!" Your face, LORD, I will seek.

Psalm 27:4-8

As the deer pants for streams of water, so my soul pants for you, O God.

My soul thirsts for God, for the living God. When can I go and meet with God?

Psalm 42:1,2

O God, you are my God, earnestly I seek you; my soul thirsts for you, my body longs for you, in a dry and weary land where there is no water.

I have seen you in the sanctuary and beheld your power and your glory.

Psalm 63:1,2

The LORD is near to all who call on him, to all who call on him in truth.

Psalm 145:18

It was not by their sword that they won the land, nor did their arm bring them victory; it was your right hand, your arm, and the light of your face, for you loved them.

Psalm 44:3

Blessed are those who hunger and thirst for righteousness, for they will be filled.

Matthew 5:6

God did this so that men would seek him and perhaps reach out for him and find him, though he is not far from each one of us.

Acts 17:27

The Spirit and the bride say, "Come!" And let him who hears say, "Come!" Whoever is thirsty, let him come; and whoever wishes, let him take the free gift of the water of life.

Revelation 22:17

When You Do Not Feel Like God Hears You

Moreover, I have heard the groaning of the Israelites, whom the Egyptians are enslaving, and I have remembered my covenant.

Exodus 6:5

If my people, who are called by my name, will humble themselves and pray and seek my face and turn from their wicked ways, then will I hear from heaven and will forgive their sin and will heal their land.

2 Chronicles 7:14

You will pray to him, and he will hear you, and you will fulfill your vows.

Job 22:27

Those who know your name will trust in you, for you, LORD, have never forsaken those who seek you.

Psalm 9:10

You hear, O LORD, the desire of the afflicted; you encourage them, and you listen to their cry.

Psalm 10:17

The eyes of the LORD are on the righteous and his ears are attentive to their cry.

The righteous cry out, and the LORD hears them; he delivers them from all their troubles.

Psalm 34:15,17

Evening, morning and noon I cry out in distress, and he hears my voice.

Psalm 55:17

O you who hear prayer, to you all men will come.

Psalm 65:2

Again, I tell you that if two of you on earth agree about anything you ask for, it will be done for you by my Father in heaven.

For where two or three come together in my name, there am I with them.

Matthew 18:19,20

The LORD hears the needy and does not despise his captive people.

Psalm 69:33

Hear my prayer, O LORD; listen to my cry for mercy.

Psalm 86:6

He will respond to the prayer of the destitute; he will not despise their plea.

Psalm 102:17

The LORD is near to all who call on him, to all who call on him in truth.

He fulfills the desires of those who fear him; he hears their cry and saves them.

Psalm 145:18,19

Before they call I will answer; while they are still speaking I will hear.

Isaiah 65:24

Call to me and I will answer you and tell you great and unsearchable things you do not know.

Jeremiah 33:3

This third I will bring into the fire; I will refine them like silver and test them like gold. They will call on my name and I will answer them; I will say, "They are my people," and they will say, "The LORD is our God."

Zechariah 13:9

But when you pray, go into your room, close the door and pray to your Father, who is unseen. Then your Father, who sees what is done in secret, will reward you.

Do not be like them, for your Father knows what you need before you ask him.

Matthew 6:6,8

When People Think You Are Weird

For they loved praise from men more than praise from God.

John 12:43

No, a man is a Jew if he is one inwardly; and circumcision is circumcision of the heart, by the Spirit, not by the written code. Such a man's praise is not from men, but from God.

Romans 2:29

Therefore judge nothing before the appointed time; wait till the Lord comes. He will bring to light what is hidden in darkness and will expose the motives of men's hearts. At that time each will receive his praise from God.

1 Corinthians 4:5

Peter and the other apostles replied: "We must obey God rather than men!"

Acts 5:29

For you have spent enough time in the past doing what pagans choose to do — living in debauchery, lust, drunkenness, orgies, carousing and detestable idolatry.

They think it strange that you do not plunge with them into the same flood of dissipation, and they heap abuse on you.

1 Peter 4:3,4

If you belonged to the world, it would love you as its own. As it is, you do not belong to the world, but I have chosen you out of the world. That is why the world hates you.

John 15:19

Great Mothers of the Bible

Eve, First Mother —

Adam named his wife Eve, because she would become the mother of all the living.

Genesis 3:20

Mary, Mother of Jesus —

And Mary said: "My soul glorifies the Lord and my spirit rejoices in God my Savior, for he has been mindful of the humble state of his servant. From now on all generations will call me blessed, for the Mighty One has done great things for me — holy is his name.

His mercy extends to those who fear him, from generation to generation.

He has performed mighty deeds with his arm; he has scattered those who are proud in their inmost thoughts.

He has brought down rulers from their thrones but has lifted up the humble.

He has filled the hungry with good things but has sent the rich away empty.

He has helped his servant Israel, remembering to be merciful to Abraham and his descendants forever, even as he said to our fathers."

Luke 1:46-55

In a loud voice she [Elizabeth, mother of John the Baptist] exclaimed [to Mary]: "Blessed are you among women, and blessed is the child you will bear!"

Luke 1:42

Additional copies of
The Mother's Topical Bible
are available from your local bookstore
or by writing:

Honor Books
P. O. Box 55388 • Tulsa, OK 74155

THE INSPIRATIONAL GIFT SERIES

Leather Editions — $19.95

The Mother's Topical Bible
ISBN 1-56292-020-0

The Father's Topical Bible
ISBN 1-56292-021-9

The Businessman's Topical Bible
ISBN 1-56292-022-7

The Teen's Topical Bible
ISBN 1-56292-009-X

Image of Excellence
ISBN 1-56292-005-7

Our Life Together
Wedding Edition
ISBN 1-56292-751-5

Valentine's Day Edition
ISBN 1-56292-011-1

Dare To Succeed
Graduate's Edition
ISBN 1-56292-001-4

Business Edition
ISBN 1-56292-014-6

Paperback Editions — $5.95

The Mother's Topical Bible
ISBN 1-56292-015-4

The Father's Topical Bible
ISBN 1-56292-016-2

The Businessman's Topical Bible
ISBN 1-56292-017-0

The Teen's Topical Bible
ISBN 1-56292-018-9

The Businesswoman's
Topical Bible
ISBN 1-56292-029-4

Our Life Together
ISBN 1-56292-028-6

Christmas Town
Peggy Gilchrist

Published by Steeple Hill Books™

STEEPLE HILL BOOKS

Steeple
Hill™

ISBN 0-373-87048-5

CHRISTMAS TOWN

Copyright © 1998 by Peg Robarchek

Printed in U.S.A.

Lay not up for yourselves treasures upon earth, where moth and rust doth corrupt, and where thieves break through and steal. But lay up for yourselves treasures in heaven, where neither moth nor rust doth corrupt, and where thieves do not break through nor steal. For where your treasure is, there will your heart be also.

—*Matthew* 6:19-21

Dedicated with love and gratitude to
Lynne and Dianne,
who taught me faith by example.

Chapter One

All 122 pairs of eyes in the basement fellowship hall of the church watched in riveted silence as the black Lincoln glided down Main Street. The only pair of eyes that held even a tiny spark of hope was the honey-flecked brown pair belonging to Joella Ratchford.

When the imposing automobile was out of sight, all eyes returned to the institutional green room whose walls were decorated with construction-paper cutouts of turkeys and Pilgrims.

"Looks like the executioner has arrived," someone muttered.

"We can't give up," Joella said as forcefully as she could manage, although forcefulness wasn't her strong suit.

Joella looked for reassurance to white-haired Reverend Hatfield Martin, who had been there for Joella during all of the toughest times of her life. He smiled his reassuring smile—the one that always seemed to say she wasn't alone in whatever difficulty life was dishing up. Then she looked around her at the roomful of mill workers, most of whom she had known all her life. Some had wandered back to the circle of metal folding chairs, some remained beside the windows. All were dear to her.

Most of them weren't smiling, reassuringly or otherwise. Joella could see in their faces that they had already resigned themselves to an unwelcome future.

"Come on, everybody," she said, her tone close to pleading. "Don't any of you believe it when Reverend Martin says the Lord will provide?"

Only a few people would return her gaze. Joella wanted to cry. She had grown up in Bethlehem, South Carolina. Her father had worked for Scoville Mill as long as she could remember, until his death three years ago. Every person in this room was like a member of Joella's extended family. Surrogate aunts and uncles, cousins by marriage, best friends she'd played summer softball with. People she loved, all of them. Even the ones who got on her last good nerve sometimes, for that was the way with family.

Bethlehem was home, and Joella felt the loneliness of being the only one in town still willing to fight for it.

"Shoot-fire, Joella," Eben Ford finally said.

"What're we supposed to do? The Scovilles are outta money. That means the mill's outta money. The whole town's outta money."

"We're all as good as homeless," came Rutta Story's thin, creaky voice. Mumbling, grumbling voices joined Rutta's statement of doom.

"There's the retirement fund," Joella protested over the rumble, but no one listened. Weakly, knowing nobody heard, she finished, "At least we've got that to fall back on."

"Joella's right," Reverend Martin said, standing to capture the attention of the room. "The Scovilles may fail us. But the Lord never will. Faith will see us through this."

Some of the people looked sheepishly into their laps, but most of them kept right on complaining.

Joella swallowed hard and dropped into a chair, giving in to a wave of despair. Time was when her number-one goal had been to get away from Bethlehem as fast as she could. College in Asheville, North Carolina, then marriage to Andrew Ratchford, the high school valedictorian whose aspirations matched hers, had seemed the perfect plan. Then, two years later, Nathan was born and college put on hold for the more important job of motherhood. But Andy stuck with it, graduated with Joella's help and took a promising job with a major bank. Not long after, Andy told Joella his lawyer would be in touch. She didn't fit his plan any longer.

In the middle of all the hurt, old-fashioned and

soothingly familiar Bethlehem had seemed a safe haven.

But as much as Joella hated to admit it, Rutta and Eben and the rest were right. Their safe haven was on the verge of turning into a bankrupt ghost town. Joella looked around the church basement at the cracked plaster, the rusty legs on the chairs. Even the construction-paper turkeys made by the children's Sunday school classes had been cut out of faded, yellowing paper.

She looked for the one with Nathan's name on it and wondered if anyone would have enough holiday spirit left to replace them soon with herald angels and Nativity scenes.

"Don't know why we all act surprised." Fred Roseforte's strident voice carried over the rest of the rumbling voices. "This here's the only family-owned mill village left in the state. We're a dinosaur. The rest of 'em's already gone belly-up or sold out, long time back. We might's well quit our grousing and start looking to the future, too."

Fred stood then, and took a step toward the door. "I'm looking for work somewhere else, starting tomorrow."

Joella watched other heads nod, saw others rise. "Wait!"

"Wait for what?" Fred demanded, his voice revealing his impatience just as surely as his red face did. "Wait till they tell us they ain't got money to pay us for the last month's work we did? Wait till they cut off the power to our houses—excuse me, *their* houses—and ask us to clear out?''

"Wait for…'' Joella thought fast. There had to be something someone could do. "Wait till we hear what young Mr. Scoville has to say.''

Fred guffawed at that. "You might be too young to remember young Scoville, Joella. But I ain't. I'll wager most of us ain't. You saw that big, fancy automobile he just rolled into town in. He's not going to dirty his hands for long with a hundred or so grubby little mill families.''

A sense of loss settled into the pit of Joella's stomach, like too many sour green apples when she was a kid.

"Then wait till Christmas, at least,'' she pleaded. "It's only a month away. But if you start walking out, they might have to shut down now. Then *none* of us will draw a paycheck this month. What kind of Christmas will that be for our kids and grand-kids?''

She took heart when she saw a few heads nodding at that reminder.

"Let us all remember that this is a holiday for miracles,'' added the Reverend Martin.

"By golly, a miracle's just what it's gonna take,'' Eben Ford said.

"Won't be much Christmas, anyway,'' Rutta said. "What I hear is there's no money for the celebration.''

Joella didn't want to hear that, either. For more

than a century the Christmas celebration in Bethlehem had been Scoville Mill's gift to its employees. And a spectacular gift it had become over the decades. Hundreds of thousands of lights twinkled all over the village. Life-size Nativity scenes and painted plywood angels decorated churchyards and rooftops. Caught up in the spirit, residents each year dressed in Dickens garb and walked the village at dusk, carolling. The light-studded village drew visitors first from all over the state, then all over the South, then all over the country. Christmas Town, U.S.A., it was called. Year before last, a national magazine wrote up the story.

Losing the Christmas celebration would cut the heart right out of the town, that was for sure.

"Let's talk to them," she pleaded, hoping to keep everyone else from feeling the despair she felt at the prospect of Bethlehem without its celebration. "Sit down and at least make sure our voices are heard when they make their plans."

"Joella, you've got stars in your eyes, girl," Fred said. "They ain't worried about our future. All they're worried about is coverin' their own backs and cuttin' their losses."

"Still—" Eben spoke up "—she's right. Somebody ought to be there. Looking out for us. Sort of a union representative, you might say."

Fred's snort made his opinion of that obvious. "If we'd had a union before, we might not be in this fix now."

"Now, Fred, you know Mitchell and Truman always treated us right," Joella said. "The Scovilles are good men and—"

"Fine! You want to know what a good man their nephew is? *You* go sit down at the negotiating table with young Scoville. *You* ask him what kind of retirement we can look forward to. *You* ask him what we're gonna have for a lifetime making the Scovilles rich when he closes the doors the first of the year."

Again a brief silence descended. Followed by a loud rumble of agreement.

And that was how Joella got herself elected to represent the mill hands in the Scoville Mill bankruptcy proceedings.

Jordan Scoville surveyed his father's office and decided not to sit.

His father and his uncle Truman sat in the matching silk-striped chairs that faced the desk. He remembered his mother telling him, back when his legs were still too short to reach the floor, that those chairs were reserved for people who were reduced to asking a favor or listening to a lecture. Now Mitchell and Truman Scoville, once two of the most influential men in South Carolina, sat side by side in those chairs, feet crossed at the ankles, age-spotted hands clasped expectantly in their laps, hope shining in their eyes.

Clearly they'd left Mitchell's big leather chair behind the desk vacant for Jordan. But Jordan had no intention of taking on that burden for them. He was here to clean up their mess because that's what sons did when their fathers couldn't do it for themselves. But he would be granting no favors and delivering no lectures.

"Well, Jordie, your father and I—"

"Jordan." He interrupted his uncle. There would be no misunderstandings. Not about his role here. Certainly not about the fact that he was no longer a kid. "I'm not eleven any longer, Uncle Truman. Please call me Jordan."

Truman smiled uncertainly and looked at Mitchell, who didn't look back. The two men, one seventy-seven and the other seventy-nine, might have been twins. Both had flyaway white hair that floated atop their pink scalps in wispy tufts. Both wore round, wire-rimmed glasses and favored white buck shoes and seersucker suits, even in the winter, now that Jordan's mother was no longer around to exlain why white buck and seersucker could not be worn after Labor Day. The seersucker hung loosely on their rounded shoulders. Both had plump pink cheeks, and their razors tended to miss a gray whisker or two directly under their noses. Both were dreamers and people pleasers and entirely too soft-hearted to have been given the responsibility of running a business that had been in the family four generations.

The only significant difference between the two was that Truman had never married and Mitchell favored bow ties, although Jordan noted he had switched to the clip-on variety now that he didn't have Eugenia Jordan Scoville's nimble fingers to help with the tying.

Jordan had heard it said that Southern women were often the real backbone of the family. Considering the mess that had developed following his mother's death, he had no choice but to believe it. Steel magnolia, indeed.

Although as a child he'd always wanted a softer, warmer mother, Jordan was now grateful for all that Eugenia had been. For he was, thankfully, more like her than he was the Scoville side of the family, both in appearance and temperament.

Eugenia had been statuesque where her husband was stocky, golden skinned and dark haired where her husband was pale, assertive where her husband was tentative. She had been an aristocrat and her husband a man with the common touch. Growing up, Jordan had admired neither option. He'd hated being regarded as the little prince in the village where his parents were benevolent monarchs. But he'd been too much like his mother to play the role of the common man at his father's side.

In the end, he'd followed his natural inclinations. He supposed, after all, he'd become his mother's son.

Uncle Truman cleared his throat. "Well, then, Jordan. I see. That is, we're so glad you're home. For the holidays and all."

Jordan frowned. Another sore spot struck. All his adult life, Jordan hadn't been able to think of the holidays without thinking of Christmas Town, U.S.A. And as much as everyone else in Bethlehem had loved the elaborate celebration, it had done nothing for young Jordie Scoville but remind him that he didn't fit in. He'd hated the extravagance and the knowledge that it was bought and paid for by his parents, that it wasn't the product of anybody's real Christmas spirit.

Since leaving, he managed to find ways, each December, to concentrate on anything *but* the holidays. Big deals closed on December 24. Trips to scout property took place on December 25.

Jordan frowned and walked to the window overlooking Main Street. "I'm not here for the holidays, Uncle. I'm here to shut down the mill."

He heard the little hum of dismay that was his father's response and wondered if other sons could handle all this with more grace, more sympathy. And, if so, why couldn't he? Why did all this family stuff bother him so?

And why couldn't he manage to be tough enough that it really didn't matter?

"Well, of course, Jord…an. Of course. But it *is* almost December and we *will* all be together."

"Not all of us," Mitchell reminded his brother gently. "Not Eugenia."

"Well, I didn't mean that, of course. I'm not senile, Mitchell. I know the dear woman is departed. All I meant was—''

''Do you have all the records I asked for?'' Jordan interrupted, impatient with their prattle. Impatient with himself for his impatience. He couldn't stand seeing them like this, so helpless and so clearly in need of someone's help.

But there was no one but him, and that was out of the question.

Little wonder Scoville Mill was bankrupt. What had Eugenia been thinking, dying and leaving the family business in their care these past ten years? ''Is everything in order?''

''Oh, yes,'' his father said. ''To be sure. Venita has everything you'll need, doesn't she, Truman?''

Jordan shut out the sound of their cheery debate over who would summon the woman who had served as their secretary for as long as Jordan could remember. This was taking its toll on him already, dredging up memories he preferred to keep buried.

He studied the block-long Main Street of the town where he'd grown up, the town he'd left without looking back as soon as military school, followed by Duke University, offered an escape. He remembered Main Street as busy, like a midway at a rural carnival. People milling around, talking, in and out of the post office and the general mercantile and the diner. All the storefronts were still the same, except for being about fifteen years drearier. Few cars or pickups were parked along the street. No third-shifters moseyed along carrying out the day's errands. The yellow caution light at the end of the hill didn't even blink now, simply stared out dark and unseeing over the narrow, deserted street.

Just as Jordan had decided that Bethlehem was already a hopeless cause, with blessedly little left for him to dismantle, the door opened from the basement of the Little Bethlehem Baptist Church at the top of the hill. People poured out, talking, gesturing. In their denim and flannel they were more than animated, they were agitated. And all their agitation seemed directed toward one person at the very center of the frenzy.

The eye of this human hurricane was a petite woman, also wearing the requisite denim and flannel—snug jeans and a red-and-yellow-plaid shirt open over a red turtleneck. She kept shaking her head. They kept shaking their fingers at her. Finally she slapped a baseball cap on her short, dark hair and stalked away, dismissively waving them off. Without his realizing it, Jordan's lips curled into a small smile.

They can't push you around without your permission, he thought, remembering the words his mother had said to him more times than he could count. The woman in the baseball cap looked ill inclined to be pushed around, despite being heavily outnumbered.

The heavy oak door to his father's office closed with such determination Jordan knew at once that

Venita Tanner had made her entrance. He turned to her, his smile automatic. Surely, if there was anything left in this town to feel good about, it would be Venita.

She didn't disappoint him. She stood in the doorway like a tall, dark warrior, broad of shoulder and sure of stance. The turquoise of her suit lent a glow to her ebony skin. She still defied her black hair, now shot through with silver, to return to its natural waves by yanking it back in a knot so severe it had always made Jordan stand straighter, even as a boy.

After all this time, he noted, squaring his travel-weary shoulders, Venita Tanner was still a formidable woman. Although Venita was called secretary, Jordan knew she had run much of the show herself for years. He also knew the African-American woman would never have been hired for such a responsible position if not for his mother. Thirty years ago Eugenia had been adamant that this college graduate was a better choice than a local high school girl of eighteen, who could barely find the shift key on the old Underwood typewriter. Jordan believed that if Venita hadn't come of age at a time when black women didn't easily go far, Venita could have owned the world, or at least a substantial portion of it.

She didn't smile back, but he knew there was welcome in her big heart, even for the Prodigal Son.

"You always said you'd marry me when I was as tall as you," he said, hanging on to the small smile prompted by the petite woman at the center of the storm on Main Street. "I'm back to see if you'll keep your word."

She grunted. "As long as they're still selling four-inch heels, Jordie, you don't stand a chance."

"Oh, um, Venita, you see," Truman began, nervously, "he wants us to call him Jordan now. Of course."

She grunted again, hands on her generous hips. Jordan had the strangest notion she was waiting to see if he had enough human being left in him to hug the woman he'd spent more time with, growing up, than he had with his own mother. He didn't want to disappoint her. He tried to remember the last person he'd hugged. Really hugged, not one of those phony social embraces at cocktail parties when some client's anorexic wife remembers you from the last cocktail party.

By the time he'd made up his mind to give it a try, Venita had clearly grown tired of his indecision.

"Okay," she said briskly, thrusting a folder in his direction. "Here's what I've got. You better sit down."

Feeling more completely alone than he had only moments before, Jordan caught her eye as he took the thick file folder from her, one that looked identical to the one she retained for herself. She looked apologetic and resigned. If he'd seen an ounce of fight in Venita's eyes, he would have harbored some hope. Instead, he gave up any notion of salvaging anything from the wreckage that was the once-mighty Scoville Mill.

He'd hated this town and this company for so long, he couldn't even say he was sorry, except for what this would do to his father, his uncle, and Venita.

He gave in to the inevitable and dropped into his father's chair. From the corner, Venita pulled up a smaller, straight-back chair and opened her file folder. Jordan followed her lead.

"The first thing you should know is that—"

Mitchell's crumpled-paper voice interrupted. "Maybe Truman and I should leave. Let you two go through this first."

Jordan and Venita exchanged a look. Jordan's inclination was to have them suffer through the autopsy, but he relented at the recommendation for mercy in Venita's eyes. The two elderly men stood and shuffled toward the door, leaving behind another round of cheerful welcomes and their bright-eyed optimism for the wonders Jordan could accomplish, now that he was here.

Watching them leave, so defenseless and so rumpled looking, would have broken Jordan's heart if he hadn't become so good at steeling himself against such compassion.

At the door, just before it closed behind them, Truman stuck his head back in. "Um, Venita, my dear?"

"Yes?"

"Um, you don't... That is, will it be necessary...um...?"

"Yes, Truman," she said softly, her smile apologetic. "I think it will be quite necessary."

His brow deepened its furrows, but he merely nodded as he backed out the door and closed it at last.

Hurt squeezed Jordan's heart. He thought perhaps it was merely the bad chicken dinner he'd had at the country-cooking truck stop on the way in from Atlanta. "*What* will be quite necessary?"

Venita pursed her glossy mahogany lips and sighed deeply. "For you to know about the retirement account."

Jordan felt uneasy as he heard the words and sensed how deep her distress went. "What about the retirement account?"

She smiled, a sad smile that for the first time made her look all of her fifty-plus years. "I'm afraid we don't have one anymore."

Chapter Two

Nathan Ratchford scrolled through the E-mail file, hoping against hope that today he would find some sign from his dad.

Zip. Zilch.

Sulking, he pulled his feet up into Venita's desk chair and made a circle with his legs. He picked at a raveling thread in the seam of his jeans and wondered what a seven-year-old could do to get his bigshot dad to acknowledge his son's existence.

Nathan thought about sending another E-mail message. Maybe something had happened to the other message. Like maybe his secretary had accidentally, stupidly, moronically killed it out before his dad could see it. Or the humongous mainframe computer that ran the whole, entire bank where his dad was a big shot had crashed, paralyzing the entire banking industry of the Southeast. And if Nathan

the Wonder Kid came in and got the computer up
and running again, then even his dad would see
that...

The tantalizing fantasy momentarily wiped the
sullen expression off Nathan's face. Until he realized that if anyone was being stupid or moronic it
was one Nathan Ratchford.

"Yeah, I'll send you another letter," he muttered,
signing off E-mail to page through the directory of
other goodies available on Venita's computer.
"Dear Deadbeat Dad: In case it has slipped your
busy, important mind, you have a son, aged seven
years and eight-point-two months, who is growing
up without the bare essentials—a computer, a pair
of purple-and-teal high-top sneakers, or even one
measly ticket to a Charlotte Hornets home game.
Yours truly, Nathan the Half Orphan."

The brilliance of his memo cheered him again
briefly, and Nathan selected the Encyclopedia option
on Venita's computer directory. He had almost finished the *A*'s. The way he had it figured, if he
worked hard and kept to the schedule he'd worked
out, he could finish the *Z*'s by the end of the sixth
grade and sail right from elementary school to the
freshman class at Duke University. Do not pass Go,
do not stop at junior-stupid-high, do not collect two
hundred dollars.

Azimuth was snore-city, but Nathan figured the
Aztecs must be up next, so he plowed ahead. Keeping his mind on due northeasts was hard and he grew

impatient with Venita for being late. He kept thinking she'd come out of her stupid meeting soon, but she didn't. The old geezers had come out a long time ago and Venita was still locked up behind that big old door. Before he knew it, his mom would come after him and Venita wouldn't even get to help him with his new plan, the way she'd helped him find out about his dad's E-mail address. Venita knew stuff like that, especially stuff about Charlotte.

Venita knew more about Charlotte, North Carolina, than anybody in both the Carolinas, he supposed. Maybe in the world. Because she went to college there about a million years ago, back in the Paleolithic Era, circa 1965 B.N.

Before Nathan.

He'd taken his glasses off and placed them carefully in the middle of Venita's big desk calendar and was about to doze off over *Azoic Era* in the computer encyclopedia when the big old door opened. Nathan's eyes snapped open, but everything stayed blurry until he remembered his glasses.

He reached for his glasses, but not before a man followed Venita out the big old door. In that fuzzy, glasses-free instant, Nathan's heart flew to his throat and he thought he might fall right out of Venita's office chair.

Dad!

He realized it wasn't so the minute he got his glasses on, of course. Still, the man made him think of his dad, who was also tall and broad shouldered and wore suits the color of number two pencil lead and really, *really* white shirts and striped neckties, but whose most distinctive characteristic was the grim expression on his face. Intimidating. Nathan had learned that word in a movie and he had always remembered it, because he knew that was exactly what his dad was. Intimidating.

And so was this man Venita seemed to like. She was paying such close attention to him she hadn't even noticed Nathan. So he cleared his throat and rattled the middle drawer of her desk a little bit.

"Well, Nathan, hello." She looked, as always, pleased to see him, but she didn't look at him or talk to him in that cutesy way grown-ups usually did. She always acted as if she thought Nathan was as grown-up as anybody. Which, of course, he was.

"Hey, Venita. You're late."

"I know. And I am sorry. But Mr. Scoville and I had a lot of business to talk about today." She glanced at the man again. They both looked tired. "Nathan, this is Jordan Scoville. Mr. Mitchell's son. Jordan, this is Nathan Ratchford. He's the best office assistant I've had in…oh, I'd say about twenty-five years."

Nathan sat up straighter in the chair and offered up his hand for a shake. "Pleased to meet'cha, Mr. Scoville."

"Same here, Mr. Ratchford." And the man with the intimidating face took Nathan's hand, shook it grown-up to grown-up. "I'm always glad to meet anybody who's managed to impress Venita."

Nathan wasn't sure how to take that, and he didn't have time to think about it because he suddenly remembered who Jordan Scoville was and it kind of shook him up. Jordan Scoville was the man everybody said was coming to town to fire them all and put them out of their homes. *Wo!* Nathan was excited. A real, live, bad-to-the-bone business tycoon!

"Jordan only says that because I was impressed by *him* when he was your age," Venita said with the smile Nathan always thought she reserved just for him. For a minute that made Nathan a little jealous.

Then, he started to wonder if this was Venita's way of letting him know that what she always said was true. *Just because you're growing up on the mill hill doesn't mean you can't make something of yourself, Nathan. If you apply yourself.* Maybe Nathan, too, could grow up and be grim-faced and intimidating and wear pencil-lead suits and really, *really* white shirts.

He hoped so. Mom always said those weren't important things in life, but Nathan thought she might be wrong about that one matter.

"Get any word on the E-mail today?" Venita asked and the sound of her voice seemed to say it was truly insignificant whether he had or not. Nathan was glad of that, because then he could pretend it didn't matter, too.

"Nah." He shook his head and unfolded his bony legs. "I think I'm going to have to plan another strategy."

She nodded and dropped her files onto her desk. But before she could reply, the front door from the street opened and Nathan's mom walked in. Forgetting for a minute all about what kind of impression he would be making on Mr. Bad-to-the-Bone Jordan Scoville, Nathan dashed into her arms.

"Mom!"

And she gave him that big, old hug that made it not even matter whether his dad hated his guts for the rest of his life.

Jordan felt that hitch in his heart again when Nathan Ratchford and his mom lost themselves in a hug. Once more he blamed his truck-stop lunch, because that was easier than admitting what he was witnessing struck at something vulnerable inside him.

He'd had a lot of hugs from Venita when he was that age, but not too many from his mother.

He wondered, as he watched mother and son, what it would be like to have a mother who was tender and welcoming instead of regal and imposing. Apparently Nathan Ratchford thought it was pretty cool, the way he pressed his oversize ear against his mother's red flannel shirt. Jordan tapped the file Venita had given him and busied himself stuffing it into his briefcase.

Thank goodness he wasn't a lonely little outsider any longer.

He glanced up in time to see the boy's mother peer in his direction. It was then he really looked at her, and saw the short, dark curls peeking out from beneath a red baseball cap. The woman at the center of the brouhaha on Main Street.

Her arms loosened their hold on her son, while the rest of her stiffened visibly. "Oh. Come on, Nathan. Venita's got important work to do."

Jordan watched the soft expression on her face change as she took him in. No doubt she knew exactly who he was—little escaped the gossip mill in Bethlehem, unless things had changed drastically since he was a kid. Although the expression on her heart-shaped face grew a little timid, he also saw a certain pride. He studied her as Venita made the introductions. Joella Ratchford's sharp, dark eyes issued a challenge. Her chin came to a determined-looking point. Color rose in her smooth ivory cheeks.

"I'm glad for the opportunity to meet you, Mrs. Ratchford." He hated the way he sounded when he said it, like the king of the hill talking down to one of his subjects. His mother's voice. The one that kept everyone in town at arm's length.

"You mean before we all get put out on the street, Mr. Scoville?"

Jordan saw Venita's eyebrows rise as she turned to study the effects of Joella Ratchford's comment.

He saw Nathan punch his glasses higher on his nose and stare at his mother in surprise. Jordan hoped he revealed nothing, because what he had to reveal was an enormous well of guilt and anxiety. It was hard to remember that he didn't have a thing to be guilty about. This mess wasn't *his* fault.

In fact, he was as inconvenienced by this as anyone else. Here he was, every penny he had tied up buying property that would—that might—be the location for a football stadium, if the National Football League ever got off dead center and made up its mind. And with all that going on, he had to drag himself away from the action to baby-sit the family business. He'd fought against being dragged into the family business all his life and now, with his future hanging in the balance, here he was. Back in Bethlehem. And finding out that everything was way more complicated than he'd imagined.

Mrs. Ratchford and her friends weren't the only ones unhappy with the way things were going.

"I understand your dismay over the closing of Scoville Mill, Mrs. Ratchford," he said, knowing how cool and heartless he must sound to a woman who was afraid of finding her family on the street. He wondered if anyone in town had any way of knowing just how realistic such a fear might be. If he'd been a praying man, he would have been praying for all he was worth right this minute that Joella Ratchford and her neighbors had no idea what was going on behind closed doors at Scoville Mill.

"I'm glad to hear that, Mr. Scoville." If Jordan could have closed his eyes, he could almost imagine this mill hand dressed in a power suit and shaking a leather briefcase at him. She had a firmer voice than that initial hint of timidity had indicated. "I might as well let you know now that the townfolk have asked me to represent them in these bankruptcy proceedings. If it's all right with you, I'd like to sit down with you and see what we can expect to happen this next month."

A lesser man might have choked on apprehension, but not Jordan. "I can assure you, that won't be necessary. The interests of all our employees will be first and foremost in our minds. I promise you that."

He could see right away that she was no more ready to have him push her around than she'd been to have those townspeople push her around earlier in the afternoon.

Her eyes narrowed as she said, "I appreciate that, Mr. Scoville. But the townfolk have asked and I figure I owe it to them to do what I can to set their minds at ease. Don't you believe that's so, Mr. Scoville?"

Jordan's grip tightened on his briefcase. He knew only one thing. There was no way anybody from the mill was going to sit in on meetings about closing the mill. Not until Jordan had figured out a way to cover up the things that needed covering up.

Otherwise, Mitchell and Truman Scoville would

spend their last years in prison. And that was not going to happen while Jordan had any say about it.

"I'll certainly do all I can to keep everyone apprised of our progress in this matter," he said. "I'm certain no one expects you to spend your valuable time listening to a roomful of lawyers and businessmen throwing around legal and financial jargon, Mrs. Ratchford."

"I appreciate the fact you're thinking about my valuable time, Mr. Scoville. I really do." Based on her tone of voice, Jordan doubted she appreciated a word he'd said. "But these folks—I've known most of them all my life, you know—have trusted me with something and I guess I'll do the best I can. Even if it means having to listen to a bunch of fast-talking lawyers."

Then she took her son by the hand. "Come on, Nathan. We've got to get supper on the table. I'll be in touch, Mr. Scoville. So long, Venita."

And they walked out the front door.

Venita let out a low whistle. "You've got problems, Jordan Scoville."

"I can handle it," he said.

Venita just grunted.

Joella had to call Nathan twice after she set the butter beans and cornbread on the table, he was so engrossed in lettering his signs for the grocery-delivery business he wanted to launch. Joella had tried to dissuade him, gently explaining that money would be tight in Bethlehem over the coming weeks. People might not have money for extras.

But he was that much like his father. Blind to anything but his own confidence in whatever he set out to achieve. Andrew Ratchford had gone far that way; no reason to suppose Nathan couldn't do the same. Although it did bother her sometimes to think of sweet, serious Nathan turning into a hard-edged, unfeeling businessman. People like that—like Jordan Scoville, for example—scared her.

She smiled as she peered into the tiny living room and saw Nathan's dark head bent over his poster board, a bold purple crayon clutched in his fingers. "Even budding entrepreneurs have to eat, Nathan."

"Just let me—"

"Now."

His shoulders slumped and he released his grip on the purple crayon. He dragged himself to his feet and headed for the table, making sure his disappointment was eminently readable in his body language.

"You'll have plenty of time to finish your signs after supper," she said after Nathan finished saying the blessing.

"I'll bet Jordan Scoville doesn't have to stop for supper."

Joella frowned. She hated the notion that even a seven-year-old could see the difference between the Ratchfords and a man like Jordan Scoville. Breeding and power were written all over his face, were apparent in every inch of him, from the way he carried

himself and the way he spoke, to the way he looked
right at home in that suit. Why that suit was probably worth more than every single item Joella possessed, including her grandmother's antique sleigh
bed, the only thing she owned with any monetary
value at all.

"You're right about that," she conceded.

"I knew it. If you want to be successful, you can't
let things like supper stop you," Nathan proclaimed.
"You've got to—"

"Rich folks don't eat supper," Joella interrupted.
"Rich folks eat dinner."

Nathan paused to consider that. "They do?"

"Yep. About six courses. First they get soup."

"What kind of soup?"

"Not chicken noodle. Something like turtle or ox-
tail, maybe."

"Oh, yuck! Mom, that is so gross."

"Well, you want to be hoity-toity like Mr. Scoville, you better start cultivating a taste for turtles
and oxtails."

He screwed up his thin, freckled face and stared
into his plate for a moment. "What else? For dinner,
I mean."

"Then you have to eat salad."

"Okay. I'll take potato salad. No onion."

"That's not upper-crusty enough, either. You'll
probably have to have avocado stuffed with arti-
choke hearts. How's that sound?"

He responded by pointing his finger down his

throat and making a gagging sound. "I'll bet *real* rich people just eat peanut butter and jelly whenever they want it."

Joella had a hard time imagining the Scoville heir eating peanut butter and jelly. "You think so?"

Nathan thought about it and apparently had the same problem with his imagination that she was having. "Naw. Maybe not." Then he giggled. "All that grape jelly'd probably just squoosh out all down your tie and your really, *really* white shirt and boy would you be in trouble then."

Joella laughed with him, despite the pang in her heart as she was once again struck by fear. What was she going to do? With the mill closing, how was she going to take care of Nathan?

The Reverend Martin would tell her—had told her many times—that all she needed was faith that God would meet her needs. But she'd tried that these past four years and look where it had gotten her. Living in a tiny little mill village house with butter beans and cornbread for dinner, and facing the day when even that little bit might be out of reach.

Having faith would be easier, she thought, if she had only herself to worry about.

If push came to shove, she'd have to humble herself and let all those social services people take Andrew to court for child support, the way Venita had been telling her to for years. Then Andy would think he'd been right all along when he said she didn't have the brains to take care of herself.

All these years she'd been dead-set determined to prove him wrong. It hurt like crazy to think she might have to swallow her pride and let him know she couldn't make it on her own, after all.

"I thought he was Dad, at first," Nathan was saying.

"What? Who?"

"That Mr. Scoville."

"Why in the world would you think that?" she asked, but she didn't have to hear his answer. In all the superficial ways a child would notice, Jordan Scoville was exactly like Andrew Ratchford. Tall, imposing, well dressed, with that precise way of speaking that you didn't hear much in a small town like Bethlehem.

"You know, Mom. 'Cause he was intimidating."

That he was. Her reaction to him had felt like full-scale panic—heart racing, knees shaking. Joella had no idea how she was going to make him take her seriously over the next few weeks. Maybe she ought to call Fred Roseforte right now and admit she was no match for Jordan Scoville.

Then she tried to picture prickly-pear Fred up in Jordan Scoville's face and knew precisely how much that was likely to gain the hardworking folks of Bethlehem. No, as long as she was the only one who believed the Scovilles would treat them right, had every intention of taking care of them, she needed to keep Jordan Scoville away from people like Fred Roseforte.

"'Cept he didn't intimidate you, did he, Mom? You stood right up to him."

"Well, I have to admit, I was a little…scared."

Nathan grinned. "I knew that. 'Cause your hand was sweaty when we went out the door."

"You scoundrel. What're you trying to do, catch me in a fib?"

"Yeah." He laughed so hard he almost slipped out of his chair. Then his mirth vanished as quickly as it had appeared and he turned his serious young face in her direction again. "Mom, when are we gonna get a Christmas tree?"

Joella looked down at her plate. "Um, I'm not sure, Nathan. I was thinking…maybe we won't exactly have a tree this year."

"Why not?"

"Well, you know I was telling you how money's going to be tight. I was thinking, maybe we'd spend that money on other things, instead of a tree that we'll have to throw out the first of the year anyway."

"What things?"

She heard the challenge in his voice and knew she was treading on thin ice. She dared not say what she was really thinking. Things like bread and milk or one more month of paying the heating bill. No, that would never do. "I don't know exactly, but… Christmas things, maybe."

Nathan flattened a crumb of cornbread under his thumb, then drew it thoughtfully to his mouth. "I

liked it better before Patsy Kelley told me Santa
Claus didn't bring the presents.''

Joella sighed. He was growing up so fast. Too fast
to suit her. ''I know. Me, too.''

''So, when is the town going to turn on all the
lights and stuff?''

The ice she trod grew thinner yet. Explaining to
the children of Bethlehem that there might be no
lights this year would be just as bad as explaining
there was no Santa Claus to bring their hearts' desire. This year the Grinch was truly in danger of
stealing Christmas, at least here in Bethlehem, South
Carolina.

''Sweetheart, I don't know the answer to that yet,
either.'' But she kept praying that the miracle of
Christmas would come to Bethlehem one more time
before the village rolled up its sidewalks for good.
''But you know that lights and presents aren't what
Christmas is all about anyway, don't you?''

He ignored her question. ''You only call me
sweetheart when something's wrong. Something's
wrong about Christmas, isn't it? I mean, something
besides the money being tight.''

Joella stifled another sigh. Raising a son alone
was hard enough without having to raise one who,
to all appearances, was too smart for his own good.
''Finish eating, Nathan. You've got all those posters
to finish before bed.''

He put his fork down on his plate and stared at
her with the unyielding look that was his father all

over. "They're not going to celebrate Christmas this year, are they?"

She sighed. No fibs allowed. "I don't know, Nathan. Maybe not. Nobody's sure yet."

"It's that Mr. Scoville, isn't it?"

"It isn't that, Nathan."

"It is, too! Just look at him. If Patsy Kelley hadn't already told me there wasn't a Santa Claus, he'd tell me himself. He doesn't believe in Christmas and he doesn't care if anyone else does, either!"

"Now, Nathan, you don't know that. You're doing exactly what everybody in this town is doing, getting all worked up over something that may not even happen."

"I'm not all worked up." But Joella saw the glimmer of tears in his eyes before he picked up his plate and cleared it from the table. "But I don't see why Mr. Jordan Scoville has to come in and ruin Christmas for everybody. It's not fair!"

Seven wasn't old enough to hear the explanation that life was seldom fair. So all Joella knew to do was pull Nathan close to her and give him a hug that she hoped would wipe away a little bit of his frustration. "Nathan, we don't need the Scovilles' lights to have a wonderful Christmas."

"Yes, we do," he mumbled against her chest. "If we don't have lights, we won't have any Christmas."

"We sure will, sweetheart. I promise you. We'll

have the best Christmas ever, even if we don't have a single light.''

She wasn't sure how she was going to keep that promise. But she'd raised her son to know that one of the things he could count on was that his mom wouldn't fib to him. As she ran a sinkful of hot, soapy water, she closed her eyes and whispered, ''God, I know You've got a lot more important things to worry about. But please don't let me be fibbing this time, either. If it means changing Jordan Scoville from the Grinch into jolly old Saint Nick, please help me see to it that my boy gets his fill of Christmas joy our last year in Bethlehem.''

Chapter Three

Jordan was glad, as he drove up to the Scoville estate on the edge of Bethlehem, that he had chosen to stay in one of the family's smaller houses near the center of the village. He could deal with the massive stone Tudor in small doses. But he didn't feel up to coping on a daily basis with the suffocating rigidity it symbolized to him.

The circular driveway gave off impressions of darkness and isolation as he pulled the black Lincoln to a stop. The single round window in the carved wooden door glared forbiddingly and the tap of his heels on the marble entryway echoed of solitude. The feeling shivered around him and through him, the memory of his childhood.

Now thirty-four, Jordan thought he'd long since put those memories to rest. It disconcerted him to discover they merely lurked in quiet corners of his heart, waiting.

He shouldn't have come back. He knew it. If he'd had another choice, he wouldn't have.

Dinner hour had just begun at the Scoville estate, so Jordan joined his father and his uncle in the dining room. He'd already eaten his microwaved chicken-and-vermicelli frozen dinner while standing, the morning's newspaper spread across the kitchen counter, open to the business pages. He read of stock options and interest rates while devouring the low-fat, low-salt, low-taste food. It had settled heavily in his tension-knotted gut, and sat there still as he accepted the glass of tea his uncle Truman offered. Truman's hand trembled, the spout of the pitcher tinkling against the rim of the crystal goblet like chimes in the breeze.

"So, my boy, are you getting settled in?" Nerves gave Truman's voice a quivering quality not much different from the sound of crystal against crystal.

"Yes, thank you."

"I truly don't understand why you feel you have to stay over there, anyway," Mitchell added, and paused for an explanation that didn't come. Eventually he jabbed his fork in the direction of his half-eaten veal chop. "We would have fed you, you know."

"I'm accustomed to feeding myself," Jordan said, and instantly despised the stuffy chill of his voice. As a little boy, how many times had he sworn he'd never let himself sound that way? He tried to soften his words, his tone, but couldn't be sure he'd succeeded. "I don't eat heavy dinners much anymore."

They ate and he sat, sipping his tea, wondering how they managed to force food down their throats while waiting for the ax to drop.

You have to understand, Venita had said, *they were only trying to help. It made all the sense in the world to them.*

He waited for them to finish. He listened to their small talk about the men at the club he might remember, and who had broken eighty last summer. Truman rhapsodized that with the mill closing, giving him more time on the greens, perhaps he could shoot his age next summer. Jordan couldn't keep his mind on their words. His thoughts kept straying to Venita's revelations—and the slow-voiced, soft-eyed woman who wanted him to reassure her about the future of Bethlehem's families.

The sweet tea tasted sour on Jordan's lips.

At last they finished their meal—including an excellent trifle made from one of Grace's original recipes, although the cook from Jordan's childhood had passed away about fifteen years ago, before his mother, even. Jordan felt the past tug at him again. Grace, with her big, soft arms and the broad expanse of her comforting embrace, had always been fragrant with homey spices. Between Grace and Venita, he'd gotten all the hugs a little boy needed.

The feeling welled up in him again, that needy feeling that had swept over him when he'd watched Venita's young friend, Nathan, engulfed in his mother's hug. Needy and empty.

Shrugging it off—again—he followed Mitchell and Truman into the drawing room.

Lambs to the slaughter.

Ornate Art Deco lamps with their tasseled shades cast a soft, golden glow over the dark-paneled room. Leather-bound books and crystal growing dull beneath a film of long-standing dust set the tone for the room. Truman poured coffee. Mitchell accepted, Jordan declined.

"Well," Mitchell began cheerfully, "I hope you and Venita resolved this whole issue of the Christmas lights. You know, people have grown concerned, but I kept telling them, wait until Jordan arrives. He will know exactly how to take care of this little situation."

"Oh, yes," Truman added. "Rightly said."

"We've resolved the issue," Jordan said. "The lights will be dismantled as soon as possible."

"Dismantled?" Truman's withered shoulders straightened a tad beneath the seersucker. "But surely not now. Not right before Christmas."

"Oh, surely not."

Jordan set his jaw and refused to be moved by the dismayed confusion in his relatives' voices. "We've been approached by a buyer. Some sort of theme park. Some of these decorations are antiques. Quite valuable, it seems. Venita tells me if we act quickly, we can get a good price."

"A good price? But, son, these decorations, they're...well, they're...priceless."

"And lest we forget, they belong to the town, you know."

"They belong to the *mill*," Jordan corrected his uncle. "Like everything else in this town. And like everything else in this town, those decorations are going to have to be converted to cash if we're going to keep you two out of prison.''

"Out of—!'' Mitchell's hand jerked, sloshing his coffee onto the arm of the striped velvet chair that had always been ''his'' chair. A Brugge lace antimacassar soaked up the brown liquid, another minor indiscretion that would go unnoticed now that his wife was gone.

"Prison? Oh, my!'' Truman leaned over and very carefully, using both hands, set his china cup on the Duncan Phyfe side table that was no longer highly polished. "Surely, my boy, you don't mean that.''

"I'm afraid that's exactly what will happen,'' Jordan said, doing his best to soften his boardroom voice. Why was he using his boardroom voice at all? Why had he found himself despising his actions so many times in these few short hours since he'd been back in Bethlehem? "Unless the two of you have a very good explanation for the four-point-six million that's disappeared from the retirement trust fund over the last nine months.''

"Oh, that!'' Mitchell looked up, his eyes much brighter now. "Why, son, that's simple. Tell him about that, Truman.''

Truman clasped his hands between his knees and leaned forward earnestly. "Oh, of course. That was all very aboveboard. And unfortunate. I can do no more than admit it was an unfortunate circumstance. But there was nothing...I cannot stress it to you enough...there was nothing...the least bit...dishonest. I can assure you of that.''

Despite himself, Jordan felt something he could only call hope stirring beneath the dread in his heart. Perhaps Venita didn't know the whole story. Maybe, just maybe, there was some reasonable explanation and all this potential scandal would disappear. "Where is the money, Dad?"

"Why, it's gone, of course. It was just as Truman said. Unfortunate. Most unfortunate."

Jordan felt his flicker of hope give way to anger. He tried to keep it in check by reminding himself that these two men were not one whit like the near-scoundrels he did business with every day. These men were not land speculators and wheeler-dealers. These men were his befuddled but kindhearted father and his bemused but sweet-tempered uncle. These men were the last of the Scovilles to live off the labor of others, and naively expect gratitude in return.

"What happened to the money, Dad?"

"Well, we met this nice young man. At the club. Last…when was that, Truman? Last spring? Was it that Easter weekend at the member-guest or was it… Yes, that was it. The member-guest. I remember because Curtis was my partner and…"

"The money, Dad." His voice, finally, was soft, the sound of his heart breaking for two old men he still loved with the devotion of a child. Yes, this was the feeling he'd tried to shield himself against since he'd arrived—heartache. He pursed his lips to keep them from trembling.

"Yes, of course. The money. Well, he told us about this deal. Something to do with stocks, if memory serves. And, well, we knew even then that the mill was in trouble. And when he told us what kind of profit margin he expected... Well, we knew if we invested with him we could save the mill. But the only money we had..." He shrugged.

"The retirement account."

Mitchell smiled, clearly gratified that his son could see the wisdom of this decision.

Jordan sighed, but willed his face to remain composed and expressionless. Why hadn't someone told him the senior Scovilles had reached such a state of irresponsibility? Why had they been allowed to go on? Why hadn't Venita realized, and called him?

When he'd asked her that very question earlier in the day, she had stared hard at him through narrowed eyes. "How many times have you been home in the last ten years, Jordie? How many times have you even returned their calls when they left messages for you?"

And the answers to all his questions were clear to him. The responsibility had been his. Venita had little, if any, real authority over the senior Scovilles. And the retirement account wasn't under her jurisdiction, anyway. Saving Mitchell and Truman from themselves wasn't her job, although she'd done it more times than any of them knew, of that Jordan was certain.

No, saving the family honor was Jordan's job. And if he hadn't been willing to do it at the right time, then it fell to him to figure out how to do it after the fact.

He must keep his father and his uncle out of

prison. He must make sure no one ever knew the
real story—especially the woman with the preco-
cious son and the baseball cap, who was determined
to gain an audience with him. Yes, he must save the
family name. He must stay away from Joella Ratchford. And he must find four-point-six million to
cover the loss. At exactly the time when he was on
the verge of losing every penny of his own in a risky
scheme.

The very idea was almost laughable.

Ho! Ho! Ho!

Joella knew there must be a law against stalking,
but she didn't see where Jordan Scoville was leaving
her much choice.

He'd been in town almost an entire week now.
Six days, to be precise, since she'd met him unex-
pectedly in Venita's office the day she went after
Nathan. In those six days she'd called the Scoville
executive offices and asked for an appointment with
him no less than twelve times. Once the first day.
Twice the second and again the third. Three times
on the fourth day and… Well, at any rate, the calls
added up. And had accomplished absolutely nothing.

Jordan Scoville thought he could ignore her. To
him, Joella—and every single soul in Bethlehem,
she'd be willing to bet—was no more than an ant
in his picnic.

Joella had never been one to believe the Scovilles
thought themselves high and mighty, although
plenty in Bethlehem did. The old gentlemen were

always gracious and friendly whenever she chanced
to see them at the Independence Day fireworks or
the Labor Day pig-pickin'. But now that Jordan Scoville had taken over the big office, she might be
changing her mind on the matter of the high-and-
mighty Scovilles.

She would pray for patience. But first, she would
remember that God helped those who helped themselves.

The first place she tracked him to was the grocery
store. Thompson's SuperMart stayed open late on
Tuesday and Thursday nights and she followed him
there after he left his office.

A man in a suit was such a rarity in Bethlehem
that it wasn't hard to keep track of him, even in the
busy store. Even though the workday had ended for
a man like Jordan Scoville, he didn't take his suit
coat off. He didn't loosen his tie. Not one single
thing about the man relaxed a bit. He even grabbed
his cart and plowed down the aisles like a man on
a deadline. He also walked with a sure stride, like a
man who owned everything in his path. Which,
come to think of it, was pretty much the case.

Joella bypassed a cart for herself and followed
along, wondering if anyone would see anything
strange in her actions. If so, it would be all over
town tomorrow, sure as sunup, that she'd been seen
skulking around behind Mr. Scoville like some
country girl with a crush. Still, she kept her eyes on
his broad back and moved a little faster. She even
pretended not to hear when Mavelle Lingerfelt
called out a greeting, because Mavelle did not know

how to exchange two words when two hundred could be swapped instead.

He didn't pause until he got to the long refrigerator cases in the middle of the store. Then he stopped and began to toss frozen dinners into his cart. A Yankee pot roast and a sweet-and-sour chicken and a linguini with clam sauce. Then breakfasts. Joella wrinkled her nose at the thought of frozen scrambled eggs and link sausage, then felt herself overcome with something a lot like pity for a man who cared no more for himself than to indulge in a steady diet of frozen dinners.

The image of him standing in front of a microwave, waiting for it to ding at him, almost made her turn away.

Goose! she chided herself. *He's got the money to cater in a gourmet dinner every night if he wants to. He doesn't need your sympathy.*

So she marched right up to him just as he put his hands on frozen doughnuts. It would be neighborly to tell him about the fresh ones at the diner every Wednesday and Saturday morning. Instead, she stood smack in front of his cart and chased every notion of neighborliness right out of her head. "Mr. Scoville, you've been avoiding me."

He dropped the carton into his cart. "Have I?"

"Yes, you have. I've called you twelve times this week and you haven't called back yet."

He put his hands on the handle of his cart and backed away. Right here under her nose, he was trying to get away!

"I intend to see you, Mr. Scoville."

"You're seeing me now, Mrs. Ratchford." And he began moving down the aisle. Toward the checkout. "If you have something to say, why don't you do it now?"

"I don't think you understand." She scampered along to catch up, trying to stay ahead of him so she could look back and stare him straight in the eye. "The people of this town have elected me to represent them. And I intend to do that."

"Isn't it a little late to start a union, Mrs. Ratchford?"

He pushed his cart up to the checkout line and started unloading his frozen cartons. She glared at his back.

"I think you'd better take this seriously, Mr. Scoville."

He stopped long enough to turn and look her straight in the eye. His eyes were dark and bottomless and set her heart scurrying. It was that intimidation thing Nathan had mentioned, of course.

"I do take it seriously. Seriously enough that I know it's only going to slow things down having a woman who doesn't know anything about law or finance questioning every step we take. We want this to be as painless as possible for everybody, Mrs. Ratchford. Don't make it any more complicated than it has to be."

She felt short of breath, but she would not let him see it. "When do you meet with the lawyers again, Mr. Scoville?"

"I don't think you're listening to me, Mrs. Ratchford. It's really none of your concern when I'm meeting with the company lawyers."

"You're the one who isn't listening. I want an audience with you. And if you don't play nice with us poor, dumb mill workers, you'll find out we know how to play dirty."

Joella had no idea what she meant by that, but it sounded good and she knew it was time to talk tough, despite her racing heart and wobbly knees. Besides, Nathan had already warned her that would be the only way to get Mr. High-and-Mighty's attention.

"Are you threatening me, Mrs. Ratchford?" He turned and put his hands on his hips. He looked about as intimidating as anything Joella had ever seen and she figured she was melting a lot faster than the stuff in all his little cartons. "Threatening me, right here in plain view of half the town?"

With that, he waved his arms and Joella realized a fair-sized crowd of folks had rolled their grocery carts around for a better view of the ruckus.

"No," Joella said, putting her hands on her hips and knowing full well her faded jeans and sweatshirt were no match, intimidation-wise, for his charcoal suit and red-striped tie. She sent up a silent prayer for courage and for a voice that wouldn't wobble and give her away. "I wouldn't dream of threatening one of the powerful Scovilles. All I'm doing is appealing to you as a gentleman. I know all the Scovilles are gentlemen. So, I'll be in your office one hour before first shift starts tomorrow, to discuss how you're going to include me in your planning from now on.''

Then she saw the frown crease his forehead and she smiled. ''A fine gentleman like you wouldn't dream of disappointing a lady, now, would you?''

He sighed and pulled out a money clip, passing on a stack of bills to the cashier. ''Okay. How's this, Mrs. Ratchford? I'll keep you informed. In writing. Formal memos, every week.''

Joella's heart pounded. He was negotiating. With her. ''Every day.''

He took his change without glancing at it, shoved it into his pocket and hoisted two bags into his arms. ''Tuesdays and Fridays,'' he countered, walking away.

She followed. ''Okay. It's a deal.''

''Good.'' He dropped the bags into the front seat of his car and slid into the driver's seat. He moved with a grace that men in pickup trucks didn't seem to have. As if money somehow oiled his joints, smoothed the rough edges.

She put a hand on the car door before he could close it. ''And you'll talk to me *before* you make any major decisions.''

He looked exasperated. ''Mrs. Ratchford—''

''If you'll just agree to talk to us ahead of time, I'll promise not to make a pest out of myself.''

She could tell right away that was her trump card and she'd played it just in time.

''We have a deal, Mrs. Ratchford.''

She took her hand off the door to shake on their

deal, but he slammed the door instead and drove off before she could open her mouth.

But they had a deal and she couldn't wait to tell Fred Roseforte that Jordan Scoville would be forwarding memos on the bankruptcy proceedings every Tuesday and Friday. With God's help, she'd stood her ground. David against Goliath.

She had to remind herself that smugness wasn't an admirable trait.

Chapter Four

Joella looked once again at the too-brief memo in her lap, the one with Jordan Scoville's bold signature across the bottom.

The signature was the only thing that really told her much. The signature said the author of the memo was self-assured and important and far too busy to waste much time on memos to the masses. All the memo said was that no decisions had been made about the future of Scoville Mill, although further discussions were planned.

Of course, Joella had done her best to make the memo sound more significant than it was, when she read it for the gathering in the church fellowship hall. No one had been fooled and the church was now empty, the grousing now only a disturbing memory. The only ones remaining were Hat Martin and Claire Denny, who was helping fold the chairs and stack them against the wall.

"I guess I'm no match for Jordan Scoville after all," she said, stuffing the memo into her back jeans pocket.

"Let it be." Claire picked up her coat as the last of the chairs found its place against the wall. "You've got enough to worry about. Let Fred Rose-forte take on the Scovilles. He'll enjoy the tussle."

Joella was tempted. Her best friend, the only other single mother in Bethlehem, was right. Joella had her hands full just staying one step ahead of Nathan; how could she hope to keep up with Jordan Scoville, too? She looked at Hat Martin, who held out her corduroy parka so she could slip her arms into the sleeves. Her watch caught on the torn sleeve lining. She kept meaning to mend it, but there never seemed to be time. She supposed she'd have plenty of time soon.

She also supposed she'd look pretty shabby job-hunting in her old coat.

"Have you tried asking for help?" the minister asked as he switched off the lights and the three of them walked out into the nighttime chill. "A little assistance in softening Mr. Scoville's heart?"

Claire chuckled. "That's going to take more help than Joella's going to find around here."

Joella glanced at Hat, saw his gentle smile and knew exactly what he meant. Had she prayed about it, he wanted to know. Had she asked for a little help from above?

"I have to admit," she said, "I've been thinking this is something I can do on my own."

Hat nodded. "Ah. That so often gets me in trouble. I hope you have better luck than I when it comes to taking charge of things all by myself. I typically find myself woefully inadequate on my own."

The three of them started down Main Street on foot. The street was quiet. The night was crisp and cool, the kind of perfect night that late autumn often brought to the South. The trees were already bare, the velvet blanket of the sky studded with stars. Joella left her parka open, let her bare hands swing at her side.

"It's a shame everything can't be as perfect as this night," she said wistfully.

"Maybe it is," Reverend Martin said. "Maybe God's plan for us is as perfect as this beautiful night, but we just can't see it as clearly."

Joella tried to bite back the words that came to mind. But she'd known Hat Martin so long that she'd long ago given up keeping her thoughts to herself. "I know we're supposed to have that kind of faith. But it sure would be easier if God could see fit to let me in on His plan."

Claire rolled her eyes, but Hat Martin just chuckled.

"If it was all plain as day, Joella, they wouldn't call it faith, now, would they?" He put his hand on her shoulder. "Maybe this is another opportunity for you to learn to leave things in God's hands."

"I learned that lesson a long time ago," Joella protested. "But—"

"But we never get it perfect," the minister said. "We always have a new opportunity to learn the lesson at a deeper level."

Joella sighed. "You're right. But I still say it's one thing to have faith in God's plan and another thing entirely to put any kind of faith in Jordan Scoville."

Reverend Martin paused at the corner that would lead him to the parsonage. "No one is suggesting that you have faith in young Mr. Scoville."

Joella nodded. "I'll pray about it."

"You do that," the minister said. "Put Jordan Scoville in God's hands, see what happens."

The two women continued the three blocks to their little houses.

Claire shook her head, her golden curls lifting on a whiff of cool breeze. "I say leave Jordan Scoville in Fred Roseforte's hands. That would serve him right."

Joella laughed. "Nobody deserves that."

"That's always been your problem, Jo. You think everybody's good at heart."

Joella thought of the man who had fathered her son then walked out on them both, and knew that wasn't true. She thought of the drunk driver who had robbed Claire and her two boys of their husband and father, and knew it wasn't true.

"I think everybody *could* be good at heart," she clarified for her friend. "We're all God's kids, after all."

"Yeah, well, some of God's kids ran away from home and don't even call on holidays," Claire said.

"I know."

Was Jordan Scoville one of those? It certainly appeared so. The Reverend Martin was right, the only thing that had a chance of working was to leave the man in God's hands and hope for a miracle.

"What are you going to do, Jo, when they shut down?"

Joella heard the hushed whisper of fear in her friend's voice, mirroring what was in her own heart. The two of them had grown up in this town, spent virtually their entire lives here. What did they know but Bethlehem and Scoville Mill?

"My brother said I could stay with him."

"I guess big brothers do come in handy from time to time."

"He thinks I ought to go to the technical college." J.T. had plenty of ideas about turning his younger sister's life around. He always had. *Get out of Bethlehem,* he'd been saying for years. *Make something of yourself.* Maybe he was right. He had a good job at the cement factory in Spartanburg, a nice little house with a low-interest mortgage payment, a new pickup truck every couple of years. And what did Joella have?

"I was thinking of that, too," Claire said. "I could get nurse's training. What do you think about that?"

Joella thought it sounded scary, starting over. She wondered what Claire would do with her boys and how she would get by financially if she decided to go to school. How would she manage a new town with traffic and strangers and more living expenses? The same fears Joella had for herself. She remembered starting over, and she didn't want to go through it again.

"That sounds exciting," she said. But she knew she hadn't managed to work much enthusiasm into her voice. A glum silence hung in the air for a moment. "And scary."

"Yeah. That's what I thought."

They reached Claire's house first. Claire paused before turning into her sidewalk. "It's not always going to be this hard, is it? We're not always going to be struggling just to get by, are we?"

"Of course not," Joella said softly, remembering how she'd clung to her faith after Andy left her. And God had seen her through it. "Things will look up."

"Right. And you're going to whip Jordan Scoville into line."

Joella grinned. "He's quaking at the thought."

Jordan replaced the phone in its cradle and looked across the desk at Venita. "Okay. It's a done deal.

They'll be here in three weeks to start dismantling the Christmas decorations.''

The barest of creases marked her forehead, but her eyes were full of censure. "Correct me if I'm wrong, but did you not promise Joella Ratchford to inform her before you made any major decisions concerning the town?"

"This is not a major decision," he countered.

Venita's fingers tightened on her pen. "You may change your mind when you see how the people in this town react."

"I've got two weeks to get them accustomed to the idea." Jordan held her gaze, although it wasn't easy. He wondered if she would go back to Atlanta with him when this was over. With her managing his offices, nobody in town would stand a chance against him. "When they realize that sale will keep them in paychecks through the end of the year, they'll be grateful."

"They'll string you up."

"They're reasonable people."

"This is Christmas Town, U.S.A. Trust me, Jordie, there's nothing reasonable about it."

"It's all in how you present it to them."

Venita grunted, but she never had a chance to respond.

"You *are* the Grinch!"

Nathan Ratchford. Jordan recognized the voice instantly and closed his eyes. He was sunk.

"What's he doing here?"

The little boy hovered in the open doorway, then strode across the room and planted himself right in front of Jordan. "You're stealing Christmas, just like everybody said."

Jordan drew a deep breath and reached out to put a hand on the boy's shoulder. "Nathan, can we—"

Nathan jerked away from his touch. "My mom's not gonna like this."

Every word the boy said was true, and Jordan couldn't figure out a single graceful way to excuse himself. He was robbing the town of Christmas. And despite his rationalizations to Venita, he knew that this particular deal was exactly what Joella Ratchford had had in mind when she'd asked him to talk with her before he made any major decisions. But what was he supposed to do? Let some sentimental woman keep him from making a fortune off the town's obsession with Christmas, when that fortune might help keep his father and uncle out of hot water? Bring more grief onto his head by trying to have a businesslike discussion ahead of time, when he knew that wouldn't be possible?

Besides, he didn't want her getting the idea that he owed her the details of his negotiations on behalf of Scoville Mill. He didn't want her getting the notion he was going to do one thing any differently because of what she or the townspeople wanted.

Jordan had a job to do, and sentiment didn't enter into it.

Try explaining that to Joella. Or to Nathan, for that matter. Judging by the grim expression on Venita's face, even she was having a momentary loss of common sense.

"Can we discuss this man to man?" he asked the boy.

Nathan thumbed his glasses back up his nose and eyed Jordan warily. "I don't make deals with crooks."

"I'm not a crook." Jordan knew he sounded testy. He couldn't help it. He wasn't accustomed to being called a crook. He wasn't accustomed to justifying his decisions for a child. "I'm a businessman. Businessmen have to make tough decisions."

Nathan considered that. "My dad's a businessman."

This sounded promising, a possible common ground. "I'll bet he has to make tough decisions sometimes, too."

"I don't know. He divorced me."

The matter-of-fact words jerked a knot in Jordan's gut. For just a moment a hint of hurt little boy lingered in Nathan's eyes. Jordan identified, felt himself sinking.

"I'm sorry he did that," Jordan said.

"But when I grow up, I'm going to be a businessman, too. That way, he'll know he made a mistake. Divorcing me, I mean."

Jordan was in way over his head. Discussions about divorce and absent fathers and things of an emotional nature were way beyond his area of expertise. He decided to retreat to an area where he had more confidence.

"Listen, Nathan, if you want to be a businessman someday, you have to learn one thing. It's not our job to make everybody happy. It's our job to keep people working as long as we can."

"You mean if you sell all the Christmas stuff, you won't have to fire everybody in town?"

Jordan hesitated. It seemed suddenly important that he not give this young man another opportunity to think of him as a crook. "Not right away, anyway."

"Oh."

"You see, Nathan, Christmas lights won't mean much to people in Bethlehem if they don't have paychecks."

Nathan's glasses slipped down on his nose, but he seemed to be thinking so intently about what Jordan had said that he didn't notice.

"So you're really doing something nice by selling all our Christmas stuff. Is that it?"

Venita cleared her throat, but Nathan's gaze didn't waver. His brown eyes demanded the truth.

"Not everybody's going to see it that way," Jordan admitted.

Nathan nodded, caught his glasses in their downhill slide. "They'll be mad at first. Like I was."

"That's why it would help if I have a chance to explain this to everyone myself. At the right time."

"What you mean is, I should keep my mouth shut."

"It would make things easier."

"What's in it for me?"

The boy had a bright future; Jordan could see that already. "What did you have in mind?"

"A job."

"A job?"

"I make deliveries. Like groceries. Or stuff from the hardware store. In my wagon. Or I can run errands. You know, deliver important messages and stuff."

Jordan strained to keep from smiling. What a kid. Smart and tough and ambitious. He had a momentary pang over what he would have to do to this kid's life before all this was over. But that was out of his hands. He wasn't here to be this kid's savior. He glanced up at Venita, saw the hint of amusement in her eyes, too.

"Venita, how soon can we get Nathan on the payroll?"

"I can have that taken care of by tomorrow."

"Can you start tomorrow?"

Nathan's eyes lit up. "Sure. Right after school."

"Then we have a deal. You now work at headquarters, and that means anything you learn here stays here. No leaking information."

"No leaks."

Then Nathan thrust his hand in Jordan's direction. A gentleman's agreement, sealed with a handshake.

Jordan hesitated, feeling suddenly squeamish that his motives might not have been entirely gentlemanly. He took in the boy's square chin, the bright eyes, the mop of thick, dark hair. He took the hand he was offered and shook, man to man. Nathan's grip was strong, even if his hand felt small in Jordan's.

He turned back to the desk, but couldn't keep himself from looking up as the boy walked out, Venita's hand on his shoulder.

Divorced.

He thought of the way Joella Ratchford's eyes spit fire at him when she felt pushed around, the way she stood up to him even when she had to know that women in flannel and denim don't have a lot of leverage against men like him. He supposed a woman in her circumstances had to have a lot of fight in her.

Especially if she had what it takes to raise a shrewd kid like Nathan.

Jordan grinned. He liked Nathan. He might even like the annoyingly persistent Joella. His grin faded. Liking anyone in Bethlehem wasn't going make any of this one whit easier.

The office door closed. He looked up. Venita stood there, legal pad across her chest like a shield. "You will not manipulate that boy."

He hadn't heard that particular tone of voice for almost twenty years.

"That's not a question, that's a warning."

"I noticed."

"He's a good boy, and his mother's a good woman."

"I suppose you have instructions for me regarding her, as well."

She smiled and approached the desk. "Since you ask…"

"Venita, you know I'm going to have to do certain things that nobody in this town is going to like."

"Nobody understands that any better than me. But those certain things don't include using anybody, tricking anybody or deceiving anybody."

"You think I need to tell Mrs. Ratchford."

"I think she can be your ally or your enemy. Your choice."

"And you think she'd make a formidable enemy."

"Maybe, maybe not. But *I* would."

Indeed.

"Jordan, every soul in this town is about to lose its future, its dreams, maybe even its faith. How you handle things could go a long way toward saving some of that for them."

He didn't like the feeling that he held the future of all those souls in his hands. He was prepared to say so, when Venita continued.

"You might even recover a little bit of your own soul in the process."

He was prepared to protest that, as well, but she

had already turned toward the door. He stared after her, fighting all the feelings she'd stirred. When the door closed again and he was alone, he tossed his pen onto the desk and said, "Okay. I'll talk to her."

Jordan couldn't remember ever having been in the sanctuary of the little church at the top of the hill; his family had always made the trip to one of the fancy churches in one of Charlotte's ritzier neighborhoods when he was a boy. Since then, he hadn't been in many churches, period. A wedding here and there, when it was good for business. Mostly, he steered clear of churches. Things spiritual didn't seem to have much place in the real world.

But this is where Venita said he would find Joella Ratchford on a Thursday evening after work, so here he was.

Lightning didn't strike when he walked through the door and made his way up the aisle.

The piano sounded tinny, but the voices coming from behind the pulpit were rich, moving even. Soaring sopranos and strong tenors blended, raising the hairs on his arms. He shivered beneath his all-weather coat and slipped into a pew near the middle of the church.

He felt nervous. Nervous about his surroundings, yes. And nervous about facing Joella with his news, which struck him as funny considering how tough it was to rattle him in his dealings with far more formidable opponents than this gamine-faced single mother who spent her spare time rehearsing Christmas carols with the church choir.

He spotted her, third from the end on the front row. Her hair glistened in the harsh overhead light, a dark, shining cap with auburn highlights that he hadn't noticed before. She looked intent on the music, and he wished he could single out her voice from the others.

No sooner had he wished than it was granted. The other voices in the choir grew hushed and soft, leaving one voice soaring in solo. Her voice. A pure but powerful soprano, she sent the words of the Christmas miracle heavenward, an angel sent just for him. For the second time in minutes, Jordan found himself caught up in the music, and in her glowing, glorious face as she sang.

For an instant Jordan felt that glow, as if she had bestowed it upon him with her voice. Then it vanished, and he felt more alone than he had ever felt in his life.

He wanted to get up and leave, to escape before the singing ended. But he had made up his mind to talk to her. Besides, the voices continued to enchant him, keeping him tied to his seat. The enchantment wasn't as strong as that moment when Joella had raised him with her voice, but it was strong enough to keep him when a part of him simply wanted to get away.

She spotted him when the rehearsal ended, and broke away from the others.

"We could use another baritone," she said. He'd never seen her eyes looking so merry.

"Your voice is beautiful." That wasn't what he'd meant to say. Where had that come from?

She looked down, shyly. There was nothing coy about the look. "I'm glad you liked it."

He helped her with her coat, noticed that the corduroy looked worn at the elbows. "You must be proud of your talent."

"Proud?" She looked at him oddly. "No. I wouldn't say that."

"You wouldn't?"

They walked back down the aisle.

"I could only be proud if I thought I had something to do with it."

"Well, you certainly can't think a small-town choir director could teach you to sing that way."

She smiled, a kind smile that seemed to say he was missing a very important point. "No. I know who's responsible for my voice. It isn't the choir director, and it certainly isn't me."

He got it then, and pushed open the heavy front door of the church. The breeze had kicked up, swirling dried leaves along the lawn and sidewalk. "I see. You're giving credit to the man upstairs."

Again, that kind smile. "My voice is just one of the gifts I've been given."

Like her smile, he thought, and her eyes. Those soft lips and those intense eyes. "And what are my gifts?"

Another inane comment out of the blue, one he wished he could call back.

"I don't know yet," she said, shuffling her feet through a pile of dried leaves to create a noisy rustling. It was the action of a child and it seemed one more thing designed to make her appealing. Too appealing. "Maybe the chance to come home and make things easier for a whole townful of people is a gift you've been given."

"If it's all the same, I think I'd rather be a terrific soprano."

She laughed, a delighted sound that pulled a chuckle out of him, too.

"I'm not sure that's an option, but I suppose you could pray about it."

"The man upstairs probably only listens to dark-eyed women with beautiful singing voices."

"You'd be surprised."

That was an understatement, but he had no desire to pursue this line of conversation with her or anyone else. She had faith; so did he—in himself.

"Your son was by the office today." He would ease into the real purpose for walking her home. "He asked for a job."

"Oh, Mr. Scoville, I'm—"

"I'd rather you call me Jordan. Whenever anyone calls me Mr. Scoville, I look over my shoulder to see if my dad or uncle are around."

"All right then, Jordan. I'm sorry he's bothered you. I'll talk to him as soon as I get home."

"No need. He's a bright boy. I told him he was on the payroll."

She paused and he stopped to look down at her. The streetlight was half a block away and the moon was only a sliver in the sky. But he could see her troubled expression. "You don't have to do that."

"I know I don't."

"That's very kind of you."

Now, he thought. Now he should tell her. Get it out in the open. He tried to think of a way to broach it gently. "I'll have to do a lot of things before this is over that won't seem kind at all."

"We all know that. Still, taking time for a little boy, that is kind." She resumed walking. "I think he's fascinated by you. He has big dreams, you know."

The opportunity was slipping away. He had to move now, steer the conversation back around to his purpose. "You don't sound happy about his ambitions."

"He thinks…he thinks if he's successful, his father will pay attention to him one day."

The admission accentuated the hollow feeling in the center of Jordan's heart. "But you don't think so."

"It's been four years. I don't think Andy has any intention of complicating his life with a son from a mill hill."

Jordan couldn't sort out the unpleasant brew of emotions her words created. He'd like to believe that even he couldn't completely abandon his own flesh and blood, no matter how complicated it made things. "He doesn't know what he's missing, Mrs. Ratchford."

She turned to him with a broad, grateful smile. "No, he doesn't. And you have to call me Joella."

He realized then that he'd made a mistake. He'd let things stray to a far too personal footing with this woman who represented the entire town he had no choice but to betray and destroy. They were on a first-name basis. He knew how her eyes could shift from merry to morose in a flash. He had laughed with her and he had already let her son wiggle his way into his heart. He felt himself awash in emotions—no, not emotions, just physical reactions, he chided himself, a little minor attraction for a natural beauty.

He had to tell her. Now. That would destroy any inclinations toward romance their moonlit walk might have created.

"This is it," she said, gesturing. "I'm home."

He looked toward the tiny house, where a dim light brightened the porch. He saw the flicker of a television through a front window.

"I appreciate your walking me," she said. "And your interest in Nathan. That means a lot to me."

Her smile was sweet, he realized all over again. It wasn't sultry or seductive or alluring or suggestive or any of those things that he'd often thought made women's smiles so fascinating. It was simply sweet.

And that made it more captivating than any smile he'd seen in a long time.

He wondered what it would be like to kiss an open, warm woman like Joella.

"I told them you'd be just as kind as Mr. Mitchell and Mr. Truman," she said. "And I was right."

He couldn't kiss her. He couldn't even tell her what he'd come to tell her. With that misguided pronouncement, all he could do was shove his hands deep into the pockets of his all-weather coat and watch her walk up the cracked and buckling sidewalk to her house.

She waved at the door. Her smile was still sweet.

Yes, Jordan was in way over his head.

Nathan eased out of the living room, where Claire and her two sons were watching television with him while his mother went to choir practice. Like he needed a baby-sitter. He tried to humor them.

He didn't turn the lights on in his room, but sprawled across the bed and stared out the window. He wished for a telescope, so he could see the stars up close. But he knew that wasn't going to happen, not now that he understood why his mom was so worried these days.

She was going to lose her job.

He pulled on his lower lip and wondered what would happen to them then. Would they go live with Uncle J.T.? Or maybe in Florida, where his grandma lived with her twin sister every winter, and he could learn to bodysurf and talk to dolphins. They might even have to find his dad. And who knows, maybe his dad would be stricken with remorse and realize how much he had lost when he divorced them and vow to make it up to them every day for the rest of his life.

He saw that in a movie once. It had been kind of barfy in a movie, but it had possibilities in real life.

The only thing he knew for sure was that he was going to work real hard for Mr. Scoville and on his grocery delivery business and make enough money so that his mom had one last super fantastic Christmas before they got the boot.

He could do that much for her.

The couple coming up the sidewalk in the dark startled him. He'd been looking for his mom, alone, but this looked like her with—

Mr. Jordan Scoville.

Wo!

He edged closer to the window. They stopped at the front gate, talking. His mother was smiling and Mr. Scoville looked for just one minute as if he might lean right over and plant a big one on his mom.

Nathan's heart raced. He held his breath, not wanting to do a thing to disturb what was happening on the sidewalk in front of his house. But before anything serious could happen, his mom walked up to the house and Mr. Scoville stood there looking at her the way they always looked in movies right before they fell in love.

Nathan rolled over on his back and stared at the ceiling. Could a rich man like Mr. Scoville fall in love with his poor mom? Nathan wasn't so dumb that he thought things like that happened much outside of movies. But he knew what he'd seen.

He was going to have to keep an eye on things. He was going to have to make sure his mom didn't get hurt, even if it did mean he'd never have a telescope or cool sneakers or season tickets to the Charlotte Hornets.

Chapter Five

The National Football League was delaying its decision on expansion teams—again.

Jordan groaned into the telephone. "No. Not again. They can't do this to me."

His partner, who kept enough deals cooking that one falling apart was no reason for panic, chuckled. "Hey, it's not like we're talking about your golf game going south. It's only business. You win some, you lose some."

Everything hinged on the NFL awarding an expansion franchise in southern Georgia. Every penny Jordan had managed to put together during his ten years as a successful commercial real estate broker was tied up in this deal. If everything fell into place, he was a multimillionaire. The land he and Les had invested in was the prime location for a stadium, plus plenty of acreage left over for restaurants, hotels, an amusement park and a golf course, all of which could be extremely lucrative *if* professional football came to the area.

If, instead, the NFL deal fell through, the land was worth less than he'd paid for it and he was ruined. Starting from square one.

At the moment, everything was going wrong.

"Les, every time they do this, I can hear my money going down the drain."

"Don't sweat it. We don't even have the land locked up yet."

"Don't remind me."

The office door creaked and Jordan looked up to see his uncle Truman's bright eyes peering in at him. When Jordan held up a finger to indicate he would be a minute, Truman walked through the door, nodding.

"Yes," Truman said. "One minute. That's all I'll need, Jordie. Then I'll be—"

Jordan interrupted his partner's update on efforts to purchase one final site squarely in the middle of the thousands of acres of south Georgia farmland he and Les now owned. Without that final site, they'd be lucky to build a truck stop and all-night diner, even if the NFL showed up in Georgia tomorrow. Les didn't seem distressed. Neither did Truman.

"So sorry to interrupt, Jordie, but that nice man from Columbia who sells us our chemicals just called from the club and wants to know if we can join him for lunch."

His uncle looked happily expectant. He couldn't seem to grasp, even now, that soon there would be no more business lunches, no more calls from people hoping to curry favor and pitch products.

"Not today, Uncle Truman."

"Oh, but he specifically said he hoped to meet you, Jordie. I mean, Jordan."

"You'll have to tell him no," Jordan said, growing impatient with trying to hear what Les was rushing on to say and fend his uncle off at the same time. "No, not you, Les. Do whatever you think is right. I—"

"Jordie?"

"Yes, uncle."

"He's been very good to give us an extension on our account."

Swell. "What time, Truman?"

The worry dropped from Truman's face. "Twelve-thirty. Oh, Jordie, this is so good of you. I…"

Jordan nodded and turned his attention back to Les, although Truman continued to croon his gratitude all the way back to the door. Jordan brushed off the beginnings of a warm feeling that stole through him at his uncle's obvious delight.

"So what you're telling me, Les, is that if the widow doesn't sell, we're sitting on thousands of worthless acres. Am I getting it straight?"

"I wouldn't call it worthless. We could always plant a peach orchard."

"Not funny, pal."

Les laughed anyway. "I told you this was going to take some patience."

"I know. And nerves of steel."

The door opened again, and a face nearly identical to the previous one in both features and hesitant hopefulness peered in. "Son, if I could trouble you for just a moment."

Jordan sighed. What had happened to the confident man who'd driven here from Atlanta a week ago, a man who had both patience and nerves? "Les, charm the widow. Get the land."

"Charm is your area of expertise, not mine. Why don't you break away at the end of the week and we'll drive down to…"

Mitchell seemed oblivious to the fact that his son was on the telephone. "It's the, um… That is… Oh, dear. Well, it seems I've forgotten precisely the problem. But they've had to shut down the production line. Fred Roseforte, he's a difficult sort sometimes, but very capable, Mr. Roseforte said we're going to have to make some repairs, but I remembered you said there's no point in making repairs at this point and I just couldn't be sure what you'd want me to say to Fred. Fred can be difficult. Did I say that already? I wondered if you'd like to talk to him yourself. I can, of course, but…"

"Not this week, Les."

"But—"

"I'll get back to you."

He stood as he was hanging up. He wished he were going to charm the widow. He hated the mill and all its problems. He felt their weight so heavily, pressing down on him. "Okay, Dad. What's going on?"

Mitchell smiled his beatific smile and explained again in his own vague way. Jordan tried not to resent the fact that an equipment problem at a company that wouldn't even be operating two months from now was taking even more time away from the deal that he'd been waiting for all his life. Wasn't it enough that he was here, in Bethlehem, when he should be in Atlanta lining up financing, reviewing architects' concepts, meeting with contractors, courting the power brokers at the NFL and, yes, figuring out what it would take to get this widow in rural Georgia to part with her twenty acres of parched red clay farmland? He was on the verge of losing everything, and here he sat doing his duty for a lost cause.

He resented the lousy timing. He resented this town's intrusion on his real life. He resented feeling like a scoundrel in the eyes of everybody in town when all he was really trying to do was save his dad and his uncle from prosecution.

Of course, Venita was the only one who knew that. Thank goodness.

It kept coming to him that he could tell Joella Ratchford, too. That letting her in on the secret would take the heat off. She was too softhearted to want anything bad to happen to Mitchell and Truman Scoville. He barely knew her, but he knew that. Her compassion, her understanding shone on her face, in her eyes.

Yeah, maybe. Or maybe he was more interested in her lips. In her shining eyes. Maybe he was romanticizing her, building her up in his mind into some kind of small-town earth mother just to distract himself from the fact that he was attracted to her in a way that was totally inappropriate, under the circumstances.

But even if he could trust her to understand, he couldn't risk it. He also couldn't put that kind of burden on her shoulders. He knew how much it was weighing him down. He wasn't about to do that to someone as nice as Joella.

He frowned. He didn't need to be worrying about her. He didn't need to be even thinking about her in terms of whether she was nice or compassionate or understanding. That was dangerous. Joella was nothing more than one more person in this town who expected more from him than he could possibly deliver.

But she was pretty. And sweet.

Oh, boy! Where had his good sense vanished to?

He shrugged into his suit coat and trailed after his father, who was on the phone assuring someone named Roseforte that Jordan was on the way. Now all he needed was a telephone booth, so he could

change into his blue tights and his red cape, Jordan
thought. Superman to the rescue.

But before he could get out the door, Venita
called after him. "Did you square things with
Joella?"

He halted in the doorway. "Tonight. I'll do it
tonight."

Venita didn't make a sound. Jordan didn't have
to turn around to imagine the expression on her face.
At least *she* didn't think he was Superman.

Fred Roseforte apparently didn't think Jordan was
Superman, either, based on his attitude. But between
the two of them they figured out how to get the
production line up and running again without the
expense of a service call.

Jordan found it tough to get himself back on track
for the remainder of the day, mostly because he kept
remembering the face he'd seen in the break room
at the mill.

Joella.

She was drinking a canned soda and sharing a bag
of chips with a table full of mill employees. She was
oblivious to his presence, as she had been the night
before in the choir loft at the church. She laughed a
lot, and it looked to Jordan as if her cheerfulness
coaxed laughter out of the others. He knew she had
a seven-year-old son, so he would have pegged her
age at somewhere between twenty-five and thirty.
But despite that, she looked guileless, alive with the

innocence of a child who hasn't yet experienced the world's cruelties.

He knew better than that, too. Her own son had let him in on that. She was divorced, so she must have known pain and sadness.

He wondered how she'd come to look so...so...serene?

Her eyes had swept the room at that moment and, through the big plate glass window that sound-proofed the break room, her gaze had landed on him. He'd been staring at her and he supposed that was why her gaze had stalled and locked on him. His heart had begun to beat a little faster. It had been warm in there. Too warm. He'd wanted to loosen his starched collar. Instead, he'd looked away.

But he hadn't been able to shake the way her attention had rattled him.

So he found himself standing on her front stoop before heading home for dinner, knocking, heart beating so hard he thought surely it must be as noisy as the equipment in the mill. He'd buttoned the second button on his suit coat. Too stiff? He unbuttoned it, wondered if he should have left it in the car. It was too late. The door opened. Nathan stared at him, then broke into a grin.

"Hey, Mom, it's my boss!"

Then he ran in the direction he'd called, leaving Jordan standing uncertainly at the open front door. Jordan was rarely uncertain of himself, rarely at a loss for what to do next. He didn't like the feeling.

"My goodness, Nathan, ask him in!" She appeared at the door, opened the screen. "I'm sorry, Mr. Scoville. Nathan forgets himself when he gets excited. Please come in."

He hesitated. What was he doing?

Coming clean. You're here to come clean with her.

He felt a sinking in his gut.

He followed her into the living room, accepted when she offered coffee, because she seemed as nervous as he suddenly felt. Maybe acting normal, maybe acting out the niceties, would ease the jitters for both of them.

The house was spotless and tidy, except for the coffee table, where Nathan had spread out notebooks and pencils and a book opened to pages of simple addition. The house smelled nice, too, like home cooking.

But the more closely he looked, the more the house made Jordan uncomfortable.

For starters, he realized it was the first time he'd set foot in one of the mill houses. If that wasn't enough, he was suddenly struck by the realization that the house belonged to him, to the Scovilles. On close inspection it seemed pitifully little to offer people who sweated for his family forty hours a week. The living room was small, a square box with a stingy front window and room for one couch, one chair and one TV on a rickety stand. The walls were white, with a few cracks running along the plaster near the corners. An overhead light glared at all of it, offering no soft shadows in which to hide.

This was how poor people lived, Jordan realized. This was how Joella Ratchford had to raise her son, because Scoville Mill offered no way up, no way out.

The mug in which she brought his coffee didn't match the one from which she drank. The spoons were stainless steel. But Joella served it with as much dignity as he'd ever seen in Eugenia Jordan Scoville.

That didn't ease his conscience. Somehow, her dignity made it worse.

So did all the soft touches that marked Joella Ratchford's determination to turn this little box into home. A wall of family photos, dressed up in dime-store frames. A bright, fluffy afghan and two big, cross-stitched throw pillows. A collection of bells— silver, brass, crystal, ceramic—were grouped on a shelf over the television. A rustic basket on the floor, beside the armchair filled with colorful balls of yarn in peach and fern green.

The room was as pretty as a limited budget and unlimited imagination could make it, he supposed. It struck him that Joella deserved more. That he wanted more for her.

Nathan sat cross-legged on the floor, but hadn't turned his attention back to his homework. "How come you're here, Mr. S?"

"Nathan." His mother's voice was a warning.

"Maybe you should take your homework to your room."

"Aw, Mom. You know, he's probably here to see me. About work." He looked at Jordan expectantly.

"Ah, actually, Nathan, I did want to make sure you'll be in tomorrow. I've got a big delivery I'll need you to make."

Nathan's thin face lit up. "See, Mom."

Joella smiled. "I see. Now, why don't you tell Mr. Scoville what time you'll be in tomorrow, then take that homework into your room."

Nathan looked at Jordan, a man-to-man look that said women will never understand the things that a man has to do. Jordan nodded his silent agreement, then watched as the boy shoved his school things back into his book bag. They agreed on a time and Nathan trudged out of the room.

Jordan was alone with Joella. He had been alone with her before, in the moonlight. She looked as lovely in the glare of a hundred-watt bulb as she'd looked bathed in moonbeams.

He thought of telling her that. He could imagine her response. He kept his mouth shut.

"You're very kind to my son," she said.

The praise made him feel awkward. With so much to apologize for, behaving like a human being around a seven-year-old boy seemed a meager contribution to the world. "I like him."

Her eyes grew soft.

"I don't know much about kids, but he seems...special."

"All mothers like to believe that," she said.

She was silent again and Jordan knew this was where he was supposed to explain why he was here. This was where he talked about Christmas in Christmas Town, U.S.A. About economics and harsh reality and two softhearted old men who had ruined the future for hundreds of families.

He glanced at her, then stared into his coffee. Her eyes were so bright, so expectant, the hint of a smile so open to confidences. The worst of it was, he knew she would understand.

But he couldn't do it.

"One of the attorneys will be in town tomorrow," he said, his courage slithering away on the whisper of her smile. "I thought maybe you'd like to come. In case you have questions."

The hand that held his coffee mug gave a nervous jerk as the words spilled out, the words intended to compensate for his cowardly inability to tell her the truth. What was he thinking, inviting her to sit in on a meeting with an attorney? Inviting her to ask questions? He'd lost his mind.

"Oh, Jordan, you don't know how much it will mean to everybody in town."

Her soft, trusting voice rubbed against his guilt, aggravating it. He forced himself to look her in the eye as he set his mug on the table. "It'll be boring. I doubt if there's much to report right now."

"That's okay. Just being able to tell everyone how forthcoming you are, that's what really matters."

Oh, boy. "Joella…"

She placed her mug on the table, too, and leaned forward with her elbows on her knees. She was close enough to touch, close enough that he could brush her cheek with his knuckles, if he dared.

If he sat there a moment longer, he might just dare.

Then where would he be?

He stood abruptly. "I should be going."

"Oh. Well, of course." She stood, too, and followed him to the door.

He stood on her front stoop, waiting for something. Waiting for the moment to pass, or for the courage to act on his feelings. Neither happened.

"Good. Then…tomorrow afternoon."

"Thanks again. For everything. For Nathan, I mean. And everything."

When he reached the front sidewalk he turned back, but she had already closed the front door and disappeared into the tiny home. Light glowed from the windows and he remembered how warm it had felt in her presence.

In one of those windows he saw that he, too, was being watched. A small boy with big round glasses stared at him, Jordan hurried off, but he couldn't leave behind his uneasiness. How was it he'd managed to dig himself a little deeper into the hole that was ultimately going to bury him?

Joella barely understood a word of the conversation between Jordan and the well-dressed attorney from Atlanta. And apparently no one expected her to understand. No one asked her questions, no one turned to her to see if she wanted more information, no one seemed to remark her notice. So she made notes as swiftly as she could and prayed she could find someone who would help her decipher them once she escaped.

The one thing she took particular notice of was the difference between this Jordan Scoville and the one who'd sat in her living room the night before.

That one had seemed almost human, saying nice things about her son and paying no notice at all to the sad state of her secondhand furnishings. She'd felt so…strange. A way she couldn't quite describe. Comfortable and yet…agitated…all at the same time. It was silly, really, the way she'd reacted to that man, when she remembered who he was.

Still, it was hard to think of him as the same man sitting here now. This one wore a stern expression on his face, grunted out brusque replies and jumped up periodically with ill-disguised impatience to make sure a call from Atlanta hadn't come in.

"I know where you are, Jordie," she heard Venita say the third time he inquired. "If the call comes in, I believe I can probably remember how to buzz you.''

He hadn't replied, and came back with a frown deeper than it had been forty-five seconds earlier.

Despite her eternal optimism about people, Joella was about ready to write off Jordan Scoville when the office door opened and Truman Scoville—or was it Mitchell?—peeked in. When he saw the gathering, his cheerful smile faded.

''Oh, dear,'' he said, ''I've interrupted. Oh, my, this isn't about the—''

''What is it, Uncle Truman?''

Joella hurt for the old man, but he seemed oblivious to his nephew's sharp tone. He eased into the room and looked around. ''Oh, my. And it's young Nathan's mother, if I'm not mistaken. Mrs. Ratchford, so good to see you.''

Joella felt herself blush. She'd liked it better when no one in the room seemed to remember she was around. ''And you, Mr. Truman.''

''Well, this is lovely. Just lovely.''

''Uncle?''

''Yes? Oh, of course. I've interrupted. Well, I was just…um…that is… Actually, I seem to have forgotten.''

Now the old gent did look acutely embarrassed.

''When you remember, you could let Venita know,'' Jordan said, his voice marginally more gentle.

''Oh, that's a fine idea, Jordie. Jordan. I'll talk to

Mitchell." Truman turned his smile on Joella. "Mitchell is younger by two years, you see. I'm afraid his memory is better."

Joella smiled. *What a dear.* "I understand."

He backed out of the office, muttering about his failing memory. Joella's heart ached for him, and for the coldness with which his nephew had interrupted him and deftly gotten him out of the way. Who, she wondered, was the real Jordan Scoville?

And as the meeting wrapped up an hour later, Joella made up her mind to find the answer to that question.

"I have an idea, Mr. Scoville," she said as he walked out the front door with her.

"I thought you were going to call me Jordan?"

There it was again, that flip-flop in his attitude. Two minutes ago he had been a block of ice, rigid and cold. Now he sounded downright human again. Well, she had an idea for figuring out what kind of man he really was. Maybe she should pray about this first, but she had an opportunity now. And she was praying about things. Every day. Maybe this whole idea had popped into her head courtesy of God.

"One of the things I heard you say—" and one of the few things she'd understood "—was that you were going to need a lot more information before you could make some of the decisions you need to make."

"That's right."

"I'd like to help you with that."

"I'm not sure—"

"Just give me the rest of this week, Mr. Scoville. A few hours each afternoon after I finish first shift at two. I promise, you'll have a lot more information than you have right now. Information that will help you make your decisions."

"If I had just a little more..." He paused and smiled. "Information. About what you have in mind."

She smiled back. "Trust me, Mr. Scoville."

He looked as if he didn't know how to get around that. He agreed, if reluctantly. As she walked home, Joella hoped the rest of the week wouldn't prove what everyone else in town already believed about Jordan. She liked believing there was good beneath the tough surface he showed the world.

Chapter Six

Jordan was overdressed and outmaneuvered. He figured that out quickly. What he couldn't figure out was how to weasel out of his agreement without damaging Joella's opinion of him.

Her opinion of him shouldn't matter. He knew that as surely as he knew how many points up the market had finished the day before. But just as surely, he knew that her opinion did matter. Way too much.

So he went along with her scheme and tried to harden his heart against what she was attempting to do.

Their first stop when she came by for him after lunch the next day was a little house at the end of Main Street. It was neat and well kept, its shiny green window boxes filled with pansies. Joella didn't knock. She walked in, taking him by the hand when he hesitated.

"Inez? Inez, it's just me, Joella. Mind if I come in?"

"Come right ahead, sugar."

Jordan followed Joella into the kitchen, where the thin voice had come from. Most of the extra space in the sparkling clean kitchen was taken up by the wheelchair occupied by a birdlike black woman with a smile that seemed to sparkle more than the scarred but spotless countertop.

"And you've brought your fella," Inez said. "Sugar, I didn't even know you had a fella."

"Now, Inez, you know I don't have a fellow," Joella said, finishing the sandwich the old woman had been making. "This is Mr. Jordan Scoville. Young Mr. Scoville. He's hear to help Mr. Mitchell and Mr. Truman. And he's interested in meeting everybody in Bethlehem, so he can figure out how to help us all now that things aren't going so well at the mill."

Joella looked at him with a triumphant smile, as if she knew full well that he couldn't dispute what she said in the face of this frail old woman.

"Is he, now? Well, isn't that a fine thing, to meet an old woman like me."

The way she studied his expensive suit made Jordan squirm, mentally. How many different ways could this woman use the exorbitant amount he'd spent on this custom-tailored suit? He squelched an urge to defend himself.

"Jordan, this is Inez Withers. She's the oldest retiree still living in Bethlehem."

Then the Oldest Retiree Still Living put out her hand, which shook as it hung in the air, waiting for him. He took it quickly, gently. Her fingers were knobby and trembling, her skin as fragile as old newsprint.

"It's an honor to meet you, Mrs. Withers."

Her ancient eyes sparkled. "I remember when Mr. Mitchell was still in knee pants, you know."

He had to laugh at that. "Do you, now?"

"Indeed I do. He still have freckled knees, young Mr. Scoville?"

"Well, I can't say that I know the answer to that. But I'll do my best to find out and report back."

That seemed to tickle her, too.

"I worked in spinning. Started when I was twelve."

"Twelve?"

She nodded. "Young'uns didn't much stay in school those days. The family needed the money."

And still do, he speculated. Had Scoville Mill ever paid its employees a living wage?

"You take good care of me. Pay all my doctor bills. Give me a good retirement check. Let me stay here in this house where I've lived since way before you were born. I'm grateful for the Scovilles," she said simply.

Jordan felt as if he might choke on the woefully inadequate words, but he forced himself to respond. "And we're grateful for you, Mrs. Withers."

When they left the house—after looking at an album in which Inez Withers had preserved dozens of photos of the mill and its workers from earlier in the century—Jordan stopped on the sidewalk.

"It's not going to work," he said.

Joella smiled faintly. "What isn't?"

"You're trying to make me feel guilty."

"No, I'm not."

"What do you call it, then."

She put a hand on his forearm. Even through his coat, the electric shock of her touch startled him. His throat grew tight and his pulse grew quick.

She dropped her hand. "I want you to see that what's happening here is more than shutting down a bunch of noisy machines."

"I know that. I—"

"I want you to know that this is about people."

Which was exactly what he didn't want to see. "I don't have time for this."

"You promised me."

"You…misled me."

"No, I didn't."

She was too rational. That was her problem. And she made him forget that he needed to be, too.

"Okay. But no more centenarians in wheelchairs."

She smiled. It was dizzying. He needed to remember not to make her smile.

"I think Inez is the only one."

"Thank goodness."

That didn't make the rest of the afternoon any less poignant, however. She took him to the mill and introduced him to people during second-shift breaks. He met a woman whose hearing had been damaged by the mill equipment, which had been far worse when she started work thirty-five years earlier. He met a couple who had put three sons through college by scrimping and saving. And he met Randy, a young man with Down's syndrome who thought the simple tasks he did each day were the most important things going on in Bethlehem.

"When's it gonna be Christmas, Mr. Jordan?" Randy asked, shaking out a garbage bag, his excitement infectious.

Jordan felt the hitch in his gut that was becoming his instinctive reaction to most of what he encountered in his hometown.

"Soon," he said, telling himself it wasn't a lie. Christmas would roll around whether Bethlehem decorated or not. But he knew the absolute truth. It wasn't going to look much like Christmas for people like Randy. And Jordan was the one responsible for that.

The second day was worse than the first.

He met a little girl with sunshine in her eyes and a pronounced limp, and learned that she might never have walked if his uncle Truman hadn't insisted on personally paying for whatever the specialists in Charlotte recommended, after the insurance company said no to experimental treatments. He met a family that had worked at Scoville Mill for six generations and the old man with the unbelievably real, snowy beard who dressed as Santa every year. He visited the elementary school, and saw the bulletin board that had been decorated with children's drawings and essays on textiles in the Carolinas. Pride showed in their work, a poignant testimony to their feeling of connection to their heritage.

"Enough," he said at last. "I've seen all I can take."

"One more thing," Joella said.

And he couldn't say no. Where Joella was concerned, he had finally been forced to admit that he couldn't say no. Of all the things he'd had to look at these past two days, that was the hardest, recognizing that he was losing his ability to harden his heart any longer.

But he could make today the last day. He could do that much. Then he could lock himself back in an office, fortify himself behind a big wooden desk and lock up his emotions once again.

Except that meant locking Joella out, too.

Right now, as he followed her to the edge of town without even questioning where she was leading, he wondered if he could lock her out. If he would chose to even if he could.

He wasn't sure of the answer. She lightened his spirits, even in the midst of all his guilt over the people of Bethlehem. She made him want to believe in possibilities—and impossibilities—including the remote one that she might unearth some goodness of spirit beneath the calculator it sometimes seemed substituted for his heart. She also warmed him, inside and out.

He wasn't the only one who reacted so powerfully to Joella, either. One of the things that struck him so during their journey through Bethlehem was the wholehearted affection everyone seemed to have for Joella Ratchford. People might start out glaring at him with suspicion, but that didn't last long with Joella around. She melted even the hardest of hearts.

He was proof of that.

He told himself, as she chatted about the quilting circle she wanted to visit the next afternoon, that he was simply interested in her. That he would enjoy holding her in his arms, kissing her, feeling her warmth, being with her with no messy emotions involved. That had always been enough for him, no matter who the woman. But he knew, even as he tried so hard to convince himself otherwise, that it was a lie.

He was interested in her physically. But it was more than that. As impossible as it was, what he felt for Joella skirted dangerously close to being real emotion.

He should weasel out of tomorrow. Either that, or

insist that they start with a picnic, so he could gaze into her eyes and have her melodious voice all to himself.

When he looked up to see where she had led him, he realized they were at the cemetery. "What now?"

She took him by the hand. Hers was soft, despite the hard work she did each day. It felt warm in his. "This way."

Jordan hadn't been to his mother's grave for years; it had been too hard, had stirred too many emotions that he didn't really want dredged up. But he recognized it right away. A low iron fence laced its way around the Scoville family plot, and a graceful spire marked the plot of ground where Eugenia Jordan Scoville rested. The spire was visible from here.

He halted.

"I don't want to do this."

She didn't let go of his hand. "You need to see this."

"Why?"

She fell back beside him then, and linked his arm through hers, as if sensing that he needed her support. "Because I want you to see how much love there is in this town."

One more time, he followed her despite his misgivings. His heart hammered; there was nothing calculating about that part of his anatomy after all, it appeared. And when he turned a corner in the cemetery and saw the family plot, he sucked in a startled breath.

The patch of ground beneath the spire was covered with fresh flowers.

Not an elegant spray designed by the best florist in town, but a mound of potted poinsettias and countless little bouquets of mums that were now fading for the season and pansies that were just beginning to show their bright faces. As if half the town had come the day before to pay its respects to a woman who had died four years earlier.

Jordan wanted to weep. He wanted to touch the petals and see if he could find the softness of heart he'd longed for so desperately as a child. So desperately that he'd eventually learned how to deny ever wanting it.

"You had them do this," he said gruffly.

"It's like this all the time," she said.

He turned to her. "No."

She nodded. "Oh, yes, it is. You should see it in the summer. People bring cuttings from their gardens all year round. And plant mums and pansies every fall, so it's nice through the winter."

"But...why?"

"Because they loved her. And they love Mr. Mitchell and Mr. Truman."

Jordan shook his head, felt a leap of something like anger in his heart. "But they're poor, and we're the ones to blame. Their whole lives, they've never had enough, while the mighty Scovilles had everything. We've cheated them out of a decent life. How…how can they forgive that?''

Joella leaned over the low iron fence and plucked a blossom from one of the bouquets. She tucked it into his lapel and smiled at him.

''They don't see it that way. All they can see is how much you've done for them. Feeding their children, paying for doctors, providing a good school, a roof over their heads. To them, the Scovilles have always been their benefactors. They want a reason to keep believing that.''

''But if they're wrong?''

She looked at him with a faith that tore his heart out. ''That's up to you, isn't it?''

The only way she could get him to accompany her for one final day of her tour was to agree to start their afternoon with a picnic. At least, she believed that was her motive.

She'd prayed this whole week that her motives were right, that she was simply working to touch his heart in some way.

Sometimes, even in the middle of her prayers, she found herself stalled, staring right ahead. Wondering if there were other reasons she was taking all this time with Jordan Scoville.

She was to meet him in the town park, a block off Main Street and overlooking the pond at the foot of the hill. Late autumn this far south could be beautiful, and this was one of those Chamber of Commerce days. Bright, sunny, a day when the sky stretched out forever, cloudless and blue. She was sitting in one of the swings, nudging herself back and forth with the toe of her sneaker and wishing for something to wear this afternoon besides her old work clothes. A soft, full skirt maybe, with little flowers on it, and a sweater. In yellow, maybe. *What a thought!* A little ashamed of her vanity, Joella wondered once again what was going on with her this week. That was when she saw him.

He'd left his suit coat behind, although his trousers were still sharply creased and neatly cuffed. He wore a white shirt, open at the collar, sleeves rolled up to reveal his wrists and forearms, and a luxurious-looking sweater vest in a shade of maroon that made him look regal. As if he needed help with that. His thick, dark hair ruffled a bit in the November breeze. She smiled faintly. This was as casual as she'd ever seen him. In one hand he carried a large sweetgrass basket, like the ones woven in the South Carolina Low Country by generations of African-American women. In the other, a quilt.

He dropped the quilt onto the ground and deposited the basket beside it. She touched the ground with her foot to stop the swing. She felt the breath catch in her throat at the look she imagined in his eyes.

You're seeing what you want to see, she told herself.

''Hungry?'' he asked.

You're not Cinderella, she warned herself, *and there's no glass slipper in that basket.*

Oh, but he certainly looked like Prince Charming. Joella tried to remember the last time she'd developed a crush on anyone, and couldn't. She might have known she'd save it all up for the Scoville heir. Silly her.

"Starved," she said.

She helped him spread the quilt. Then he insisted she sit while he unpacked the basket.

"Crab salad," he said. "Do you like crab salad?"

"I don't know. My budget doesn't stretch to cover crab."

He studied her with those piercing brown eyes and she wished that, just once, she didn't have to be so honest.

"You will," he promised. "With crusty sourdough, a selection of cheeses, some fruit and a little sparkling water. The picnic of kings."

She'd been right. There was no glass slipper in the basket. And if there had been, it probably wouldn't have fit her big, clumsy foot.

"It's lovely," she said as he filled a plastic plate for each of them. "You went to a lot of trouble."

"I'd like to take credit," he said. "But I'm afraid I'm not this clever. I had it delivered from the deli in Greenville. My repertoire is rather limited."

She nodded. "Frozen dinners, if I recall."

"Guilty as charged."

She took a bite of the crab salad, found it sweet

and tender. "I'm ruined for fried catfish. It won't do for me to develop a taste for the good life, young Mr. Scoville."

"Home cooking is the good life," he said. "Deli takeout is what you do if you can't get the real thing."

"My idea of home cooking and yours are probably two different things," she said, more to remind herself than to inform him.

"Perhaps. I'm willing to test that theory sometime."

Her instinct was to duck her head and avoid looking him directly in the eye, but she forced herself to overcome that bit of timidity. Was he playing games with her? Had he seen something in her face—the fascination she had tried to hide, a longing for things that only happened in fairy tales—and decided to string her along? She couldn't see those intentions in his dark, probing eyes, in his smile that was almost solemn. What she saw, what she'd seen these past two days, was something vulnerable in him, an uncertainty and need that the fairy tales never mentioned.

And that's because he isn't your Prince Charming.

"I'm sure we could arrange country-style steak and mashed potatoes any number of places in Bethlehem," she said. "You haven't met the Linebergers yet and—"

"Oh, no." He smiled wryly. "The tour is over today. I'm convinced."

"Are you? Of what?"

"That Bethlehem is a charming little town full of warm, deserving people. That their livelihood should be preserved at all costs."

She put down her plastic fork. "Please don't treat it lightly."

"I'm not. I don't mean to, anyway. Everything I've seen has touched me, Joella. I...I've hated this town for a long time and...what you've shown me has made a difference."

"Hated Bethlehem?" She couldn't imagine it. "Why?"

He looked at her as if her question was as unfathomable to him as his comment had been to her. He sat in silence for a long time; Joella had to fight the urge to jump in and say something to cut through the discomfort she felt.

"It was a hard place to grow up. For me." He busied himself putting away their picnic. "I was always the outsider. Everybody...the other kids...they either hated me for being rich or wanted to be my friend because I was rich."

He looked up and smiled as if to minimize what he'd said, but she recognized the forlorn look in his eyes and knew he'd revealed more than he usually did. She saw, for a moment, exactly how difficult it must have been being who he was. A normal childhood would have been little more than a distant dream, she supposed.

"I never thought of it that way," she said. And she should have. She'd heard the way certain people in town had talked about the Scovilles this past month, the ill-disguised hostility, the jealousy that lingered just below the surface. She'd been careful to keep him away from that these past two days.

But he'd known about that part all along.

"This week, I think I've felt like a human being in this town for the first time in my life."

Joella's heart filled for him. No wonder God had led her to what had seemed like such a crazy, futile idea. She fought the urge to touch the sharp edge of his jawline, felt clear down to her toes the need to touch him with tenderness. "Oh, Jordan, I—"

"Mom! Mom!"

Joella jerked around in the direction of the frantic shouts. Her son should be at school, but she would know that voice anywhere. She felt a moment of panic.

Sure enough, Nathan was barreling across the park in their direction, his dark hair flying. "Mom, you've got to come. Right away!"

He skidded to a halt at the edge of the quilt, winded and flushed. Joella put a hand on his chest, felt the wild beating of his heart.

"What is it, Nathan?"

"A bunch of guys with a truck. They're tearing

down all the Christmas stuff. Mom, you've gotta come.''

Joella's momentary anxiety turned to a chill, filling her from head to toe. She turned to Jordan, saw the guilt in his eyes.

"I'm sorry. I—"

She jumped up and took her son by the hand. "Come on, Nathan. We'll have to see for ourselves what's really going on in our town."

Chapter Seven

Jordan followed her, abandoning the quilt and the basket and the remnants of their picnic. He followed reluctantly, like a man shouldering a burden. He knew what he would find and he wanted to walk back to the office as if it didn't matter.

But he couldn't turn and run. Not now. Not any longer.

His heart sank as he turned the corner onto Main Street. The usually deserted street was overflowing with people, and more continued to pour in from the side streets, even from the direction of the mill. Workers, storekeepers, homemakers, children, old people.

The entire town had always turned out for Christmas. Why should this morning be any different?

But it was different. This morning the streets were filled with an angry buzz, a low rumble that was growing louder. Jordan sighed and stood on the fringes, taking it all in.

A truck from the resort had backed up to the building where most of the Christmas decorations were stored eleven months of the year. A couple of men were going back and forth between the building and the back of the truck, ignoring the angry shouts from the crowd as they loaded crates into their truck. Another couple of men were carefully stripping off the strings of lights that had already been put up along the storefronts and trees along Main Street.

It wasn't supposed to happen this way. He'd been promised more time. More time to find a way to break the news to the people of Bethlehem. For one weary moment he thought of stopping them, of telling them he'd return their check, that the decorations weren't for sale any longer. But it was too late. He'd already spent the money to pay off creditors.

Worse, he'd already disappointed Joella.

Beneath the buzz of angry words, Jordan heard something else, another sound. The sound of people crying. Women and children. He looked around. This afternoon he recognized too many of these devastated faces. He'd met them, he knew who they were. They were real people to him. And thanks to him, they were not only losing their livelihood and their homes, they were losing one last month of peace and goodwill to all.

He had to do something. He was Jordan Scoville

and he had to find a way to reach them, to explain it to them, to help them.

Except that the only way to explain this away was with the truth about why Scoville Mill was so desperate for money. And that was the one thing he could not give them.

He started through the crowd in the street, thinking surely something would come to him. He was smart. He'd run into plenty of business crises in his life, and he'd managed to come out smelling like a rose in all of them. But the difference this time, he realized, was that this wasn't a business crisis.

This was a people crisis. And when it came to people, Jordan Scoville had no tools, no answers, no clue.

"And Merry Christmas to you, too, Mr. Scoville!" someone shouted as Jordan elbowed his way through the crowd.

"Scrooge!" came the cry from another direction.

Jordan began to wonder if the crowd would turn on him, if things might really get ugly. He had to do something, but what?

Another person stepped out in front of him—Randy, the young man with Down's syndrome whom he had met just this week. He had tears in his eyes, but he was smiling at Jordan. "I told 'em you'd come. I told 'em you'd fix it, Mr. Jordan."

Jordan looked into the trusting eyes and had to fight to keep his own eyes from misting. "I wish I could, Randy. I wish I could."

Randy looked confused. Jordan kept walking. Where was the armor that had kept him from caring all these years? Torn down. Stolen. By a woman with trusting brown eyes.

Before he reached the truck, the crowd began to spread apart, revealing Joella. She was reaching for the hands of those around her. Her eyes were closed. There was no anger in her face.

"Pray with me," she was saying to the people around her. "It's the only thing we can do. Our anger can't make a difference, but our prayers can."

And as people along the street linked hands, the shouts and the mumbles began to die down. Quiet spread through the crowd, a wave of peace rolling gently from person to person. Soon, Jordan realized as he stood in their midst and turned in a circle, the anger had been diffused. The noise was stilled.

The entire town of Bethlehem was praying, hands linked, voices stripped of their rage. Jordan heard the familiar words. *Deliver us from evil.*

Anger swept through him. He supposed he was the evil they all hoped to be delivered from. How could he even blame them for believing it? He wanted to shout at them. He wanted to tell them it was going to take a lot more than prayer to fix what was wrong in this town. Frustrated and filled with guilt, he stalked over to Joella. Her eyes were closed, her face serene.

"It's not going to work, you know," he said. "Your God isn't going to change my mind."

She opened her eyes and looked at him. He didn't like what he saw in her eyes, didn't even have the courage to label it. "I'm not praying for God to change your mind. I'm just praying for God's will to be done."

Then she closed her eyes again and resumed her prayers.

Humiliated, wondering how he'd ever be able to hold his head up in Bethlehem again, Jordan turned and walked back to the office.

God's will. As if that God of hers could make something good come out of this whole ugly mess.

Nathan was subdued at suppertime. Joella worried about him. She worried about them all.

She ruffled his hair as she cleared their plates off the table. He squirmed away from her touch. Who could blame him? Hadn't she promised they would have a good Christmas this year?

"I'm sorry, Nathan," she said softly. "But I won't let you down. We'll still have a good Christmas. You'll see."

He got up from the table and walked back into the living room without a word. It occurred to her that he might be disappointed with Jordan Scoville, too. He had admired Jordan; Jordan had let him down.

Her heart ached for a little boy with one more man in his life who couldn't be depended upon.

And as crazy as it seemed, her heart ached for

Jordan Scoville. She thought about the things he'd said about growing up in Bethlehem. Mostly, she thought about the look in his eyes when he'd said those things. His eyes had spoken to her of sadness and loneliness. And later, standing on Main Street with the air full of prayer, she had seen something that distressed her even more. Hopelessness.

She couldn't shake the feeling that Jordan Scoville had given up. On himself, on others, on all the gifts and blessings of life.

That broke her heart.

But she didn't have time to dwell on it now. She would pray for Jordan—as well as for herself, for strength to resist these powerful feelings she was having for him—later. Compassion was one thing, but romance had no place in her relationship with Jordan. She had to admit that romantic hope was precisely what she'd felt, sitting there in the park with him, watching the sunshine play in his dark hair, aware of the fullness of his lips.

Later. She would ask God's help with that later.

Now she had more important problems to deal with. Her son was grumpy and hardheaded. Just forcing him to do his homework and get ready for bed took all her time and effort. When he was finally tucked in, he lay there with his hands behind his head, staring up at the ceiling. She watched him for a moment, praying for guidance.

"Tell me what you're thinking," she whispered, walking over and kneeling beside his bed.

He shrugged. *Men.* Even the little ones, it seemed, knew how to shut a woman out.

"If you won't talk to me, will you talk to God about it?"

A scornful expression flickered across his face. Seeing her little boy look that way frightened Joella. She couldn't let skepticism take root in the heart of a seven-year-old child. She just couldn't.

"God doesn't care," he said, so faintly she almost missed it.

"God cares about everything," she said, trying to remember everything Hat Martin had ever said to her when things were at their worst. "But sometimes God sees answers that you and I can't see. Our vision is limited, so we can't see how God can use things that seem awful to us today to make good things happen tomorrow."

Nathan flounced onto his side, turning his face to the wall. "I know what's gonna happen, all right. We're not gonna have Christmas and we're all gonna end up living on the street and it's all Mr. Rat-Face Scoville's fault."

Joella smiled. At least he was talking. Feeling angry. That didn't worry her nearly as much as having him bottle things up. The way he bottled up things about his father. He never talked to her about his father, but she saw feelings dance across his face sometimes when other kids talked about their dads.

"That's your boss you're talking about." She patted his shoulder. "I'd think twice about calling him that to his face."

"I don't want to work for him anymore."

She thought about how much he'd talked about Jordan this past week. Every day after school he had come home full of stories about hauling things around in his wagon for Mr. Jordan. He was overflowing with it. "That's up to you."

"Good. Then I resign."

"We could all turn our backs on him because he did something we don't like. But I wonder if that's what God really wants us to do."

"Aw, Mom. You mean like loving our enemies and junk?"

"That's exactly what I mean. Loving our enemies and junk."

He turned back to her then. "Do *you* love Mr. Jordan?"

Joella's heart leapt at the question. She knew what Nathan meant, of course. Did she love Jordan Scoville the way they were supposed to love all their neighbors? But that wasn't the question her heart heard, or answered.

Was she in love with Jordan Scoville? That was the real question.

The answer trembling in her heart terrified her.

Jordan drove around a long time before he returned to the house in town that night.

The rural countryside of northwest South Carolina

was peaceful once you strayed off the interstate highway. Narrow highways with only the occasional car or truck were lined with farmhouses, peach orchards, tobacco fields now fallow for the winter. Most of the towns were nothing more than the proverbial wide spot in the road, a gathering place for a service station, a hamburger stand, a church, a post office. Some of the houses had already been dressed in Christmas finery. Strings of lights encircled rooftops, lampposts had become candy canes and evergreen trees winked from picture windows.

The world was preparing to make merry.

Jordan wondered if he should pick up his bags and drive straight back to Atlanta. He could be back in his condo before midnight, in his own office at a reasonable hour the next morning. From there, he could call the shots surrounding Scoville Mill's bankruptcy proceedings without having to stare down a bunch of sentimentality and emotional garbage. Without having to worry about what would happen to a couple of foolish old men.

Without having to look into the disappointment in a pair of lustrous brown eyes, and knowing he deserved every recrimination he might see there.

Actually, it might be easier to go back to Bethlehem if he were facing recriminations. But the silence in the streets, the quiet assurance on Joella's face—that had been more than he could stand. He wondered how one fought back against faith and forgiveness.

More betrayal didn't seem like the right answer, but for the moment it was all he had.

He was still debating whether to simply return to Atlanta when he pulled up at the house in town later that night. The front light was on. Someone must've come by trying to find him and left the light on for him. But when he let himself into the house, he discovered his father sitting in one of the armchairs in the living room, staring into the empty fireplace. Jordan shivered against the chill in the room.

"You should have made a fire," he said.

Mitchell smiled wanly at his son. "Oh, well, I suppose I could have, couldn't I?"

Jordan dropped into the chair facing his father. It still startled him to realize how old his father looked. Especially now, it seemed, even the spark of naive exuberance that had exasperated Jordan so in both his father and his uncle appeared to have vanished, leaving Mitchell Scoville a lifetime older.

"We really have put you in a pickle, haven't we, son?"

Jordan thought of how, just days earlier, he'd wanted to take them both by their shoulders and shake them until they realized the enormity of the problem they'd created. Now he would have given most anything to give his father back the veil of denial.

"It'll work out."

Hope brightened Mitchell's face. "It will, won't it?"

Jordan wondered how Joella's God felt about this particular kind of dishonesty. "Of course it will."

Mitchell folded his quivery hands across his belly. "But today was not a good one."

"No, it wasn't. I'm sorry it had to be that way. For everyone."

"But there was no other way." Jordan heard the question in his father's voice.

"No, I'm afraid not."

"I've been thinking.... What would Eugenia do? You know, your mother always had the most wisdom about these things."

Jordan had always thought of his mother as shrewd. But he remembered the mound of flowers at her grave site and wondered now if there were things he hadn't fully understood about his mother. The shrewdest of businesswomen didn't inspire that kind of loyalty and affection.

"And what did you decide?" he asked.

Mitchell shook his head. "Now, there's the problem, you see. Eugenia, you see, she was a woman of strong faith, and I think that made her wise. But I'm not that wise. What sounds so clever to me ends up causing no end of additional difficulties." He smiled. "Like using the retirement fund. I thought surely Eugenia would have liked that idea. And now…"

They sat in silence. The clock over the mantel chimed the half hour. There wasn't a sound from the silent streets outside. The little town lay still and quiet, far removed from the turmoil in Jordan's heart.

"Tell me about Mother."

Mitchell looked surprised. Jordan knew it wouldn't do his father one bit of good to hear his son's impressions of Eugenia as he was growing up. Mitchell obviously still worshiped his wife; Jordan wanted to know why.

"Tell me about falling in love with her."

Even in the dim light, Jordan saw his father's cheeks grow pink.

"Oh. Well. I see. Falling in love with Eugenia. That's... Gracious, that was a long time ago, Jordie."

Jordan watched the worry fall away from his father's face as the old man traveled back in his mind, back to a simple time when the son of one good family could fall in love with the daughter of another good family and everyone rejoiced.

"Her grandfather, Prescott Jordan, was the king of cotton in South Carolina," Mitchell said, his eyes growing soft and distant in the dim light. "A very powerful man. Of course, I didn't know that when I first met Eugenia. It meant nothing to me, cotton and textiles and money and power. She was simply the most beautiful thing I'd ever seen. Fourteen, I think, and leading her granddaddy around by the nose already."

Mitchell laughed softly and so did Jordan. He could picture it almost as vividly as his father did.

"She already wore her hair up, which wasn't done. Not at fourteen. She should've still been in braids. But Eugenia was a big one for having her way." He pulled off his wire-rimmed glasses and polished the lenses with a starched linen handkerchief he pulled from his breast pocket. "She paid me no more mind than she paid the litters of kittens all over the Jordan farm.

"I never did know what happened. We turned nineteen and she seemed to look up one day and realize I was there. Amazing. Most amazing. I never cut a dashing figure, you see. But Eugenia, she was like a queen. The most beautiful woman in South Carolina. Someone said she should have been a beauty queen, and she could have been. But you should have seen the look on Eugenia's face whenever someone suggested that." He chuckled. "'I have a greater mission in life than to decorate some man's arm.' That's what she'd say."

"And her mission?"

"Why, to help those who didn't have the means to help themselves. To give them work, which she always said gave them dignity. And if you give them dignity, she always said, the next generation wouldn't need as much help." Mitchell sighed happily. "I think she was right, you know. The young people in Bethlehem today, they're going off to college. Isn't that grand?"

Jordan thought of Joella, bright, wise Joella, living in her little box of a house raising a boy so bright he would never need to labor in a mill. The image wrapped itself warmly around his bruised heart. Maybe it was grand.

"Everyone loved her," he said.

"Oh, yes. I think they all knew that nobody worked any harder to put a roof over their heads than Eugenia."

Jordan wondered, for a moment, how he could have failed to see so much about his own mother. How blind he had been.

He listened for the next hour as his father talked about the woman who had kept Bethlehem strong in an era when mills were being gobbled up by huge conglomerates. In Eugenia's mind, those megacorporations would never care about the people who depended on them as she, as her family, did.

She was right, Jordan supposed. What she hadn't counted on was a son who would walk away from it all. A son who had the mentality of a megacorporation, not the heart of the father and mother who had raised him.

When he saw his father off in the early hours of the morning, Jordan thought about the question Mitchell apparently asked himself with regularity. What would Eugenia do?

When it came to the question of letting Mitchell and Truman accept responsibility for squandering the company's retirement fund, there was no doubting the answer.

Jordan would have to shoulder the blame himself.

Chapter Eight

The hardest person Jordan had to face the day after the lights were dismantled was Nathan Ratchford.

That was only because he didn't see the boy's mother.

Before he even reached the office, he'd had to confront the consequences of selling the town's holiday decorations. The waitress at the diner brought him cold coffee and biscuits that might have been left over from the day before. From the glare she gave him, he supposed he would consider himself lucky if his breakfast didn't turn out to be laced with arsenic. He stopped by the post office and the window slammed shut before he could even request an envelope for overnight mail. The guy at the garage said it would be two weeks before he could work him in for a brake job.

Jordan was beginning to think the only business

in town where he could count on receiving cheerful service was the funeral home.

Even Venita had given him a piece of her mind. He didn't get past her desk before she was on her feet and on his heels.

"You didn't tell her, did you?"

"I thought I had another week," he said.

"An excuse, Jordan. A very poor excuse. You were with her every day and couldn't be bothered to tell her."

He looked at the woman whose opinion had always mattered to him more than anyone else's. He realized that was still the case, with maybe one exception. He wanted Joella Ratchford to think well of him. So far, he was batting zero.

"I was afraid to tell her."

His confession seemed to take Venita aback. She opened her mouth, gaped for a moment, then closed it. He walked into his office.

"Good," she called out. "Maybe there's hope for you after all."

He sat at his desk. He sensed her walking into the room. "What should I do now?"

"You mean now that you've got everything in a royal mess?"

"You're so good for a man's ego, Venita."

"Most men's egos don't need one little bit of help," she said sharply. Then her expression softened, as if it occurred to her that Jordan's ego might not be all that it appeared on the surface. "I'm sorry, Jordie. I know you stepped into the middle of this."

He picked up the marble paperweight naming his father 1976 South Carolina Businessman of the Year. No wisdom emanated from its cool weight. "I can't see any way out."

She studied him, then nodded. "Sometimes that's where we have to get with a problem."

"And when we do?"

"When we finally give up, we sometimes get willing to see solutions we don't really want to see."

"What does that mean?"

She hesitated, then laughed. "Maybe it just means I can't see any way out, either."

He set the paperweight back in its place beside the framed photo of his mother. For a moment he glimpsed her as the girl his father had described the night before. It raised in him a hunger to know her that way, and the way the rest of the town had apparently known her, too.

"What would Eugenia do?" he said softly, staring into the serious eyes in the photo. "Okay, Venita. They haven't whipped us yet. Let's beat the bushes one more time. There has to be somebody out there interested in giving us a fair shake in a buyout."

"The only ones we've found so far want to buy us out at rock bottom, take the equipment and shut things down."

"So maybe since yesterday a starry-eyed dreamer

has appeared on the horizon.'' He caught the skeptical look in her eyes. "I know, I know. That's going to take a miracle.''

"Well, if you put it that way…''

As they set to work, it irritated Jordan to realize he'd used the term *miracle*. That was the kind of thinking that had gotten Mitchell and Truman in trouble. The kind of thinking that brought a glow into Joella's eyes. But it wouldn't do for Jordan. Jordan knew how the real world operated—on guts and hard knocks and harsh realities. Not sentimentality or faith, and especially not miracles.

He would have settled for a miracle, though, when Nathan walked through his office door not five minutes after the school bell rang at two that afternoon.

Nathan stood in the doorway, a sneaker untied, book bag dangling off one arm, with his glasses sitting slightly askew on his freckled nose and a sullen expression on his face.

"You're a rat.''

Jordan flinched. He'd been called worse—a lot worse—by some of the sharks he'd bested. But this seven-year-old made him flinch.

"You knew this was coming," he said.

"Yeah. But it still stinks when you see it happening. Even if you knew. And most people didn't even *know*.''

Venita looked up from the ledgers spread out on the conference table. "I think I hear the phone.''

And she disappeared, leaving Jordan to face the disgruntled boy alone. He leaned on the edge of the conference table and racked his brains for a plausible excuse for letting the town be taken by surprise. None presented itself. He gave up.

"Yeah. You're right. I'm a rat."

Nathan blinked. "You are?"

Jordan nodded. "I've been trying to think of some way around that conclusion since yesterday afternoon. But everybody I've seen since then thinks I'm a rat. It's beginning to look like a unanimous conclusion."

Nathan let his book bag slide down his arm and land on the floor at his feet. "So lots of other people have been telling you you're a rat, too?"

"No. You're the only one brave enough to say it to my face."

Nathan grinned. He walked over to the conference table, climbed up in a chair and studied the disarray of paperwork. "So, what're you gonna do about it?"

Jordan grinned, too, and sat to bring himself to eye level with the boy. "I don't know. What do you think I ought to do?"

Nathan sat back on his knees and folded his hands over his narrow chest. He pursed his lips and frowned, a perfect imitation of a businessman engaged in some serious decision making. If it hadn't been for the cowlick at his temple, Jordan might have been fooled.

"You could take out an ad in the county newspaper and tell people you're sorry you were a rat and you won't do it again.''

"A possibility.''

"But you'd have to buy it with your own money. Not company money. So that might not work, unless you have plenty of your own money.'' Nathan pushed his glasses up on his nose. "Or you could give the guys with the trucks their kazillions of dollars back and make 'em bring back the Christmas stuff.''

"That's really not an option, Nathan.''

He didn't miss the disappointment that flickered across the young face. "Yeah, that's what I figured. Say, you didn't sell Mr. Feemster's Santa outfit, too, did you?''

"Ah, yes. I'm afraid the Santa suit is gone, also.''

"Man. You really messed stuff up, Jordie.''

Nathan hid his smile. "As my adviser, you're not being much help.''

"Yeah, well, Mom says God helps those who help themselves. That means I can't just run around doing bad stuff and whine when I get caught and expect God to bail me out every time.''

Jordan had heard enough about God to last him quite a while, thank you. He fished a five-dollar bill out of his pocket. "How about this? You make a soft-drink run, and we'll take a look at this from every angle.''

Nathan jumped up. "Sure.''

"Unless it's not a good idea for you to be working for me right now. Public opinion and all that."

Nathan put his hand out for the money. "A businessman's gotta face a little unpopularity. Goes with the territory."

Jordan put the money in Nathan's fist, catching a whiff of little-boy scent—the smell of school gymnasiums and chalk dust and bubblegum. His insides lurched in response. If this boy were his, he would never walk away.

If the boy's mother were his, he would never walk away.

His certainty on both counts was fierce. So was the certainty that neither would ever happen. He cleared his throat. "What about your mom? She might not approve."

"She'd probably say it's okay to love the sinner but not the sin."

The boy's impish grin said that he loved the opportunity to label his boss a sinner. Jordan sent him on his way, surprisingly unperturbed by the boy's words because of the mischievous smile that had accompanied them. He turned his attention back to the ledgers and files and the stack of telephone messages that he needed to return. His heart had felt so heavy all day, but Nathan's smile had lifted some of the burden from his shoulders.

Most of it, however, remained. The part that was his fears about what was going to happen when everyone discovered that there was no money in the retirement fund. And the part that knew Joella must still think badly of him—and would think even worse before it was all over. That part still weighed particularly heavy.

Although he dreaded seeing Joella again, Jordan found it hard not to relax the next few days as he spent more time with Nathan.

He found out about the boy's plan to educate himself using Venita's computer encyclopedia, and thus avoid junior high and high school. "I'll be ready to support my mom by the time I'm sixteen," he said. "Pretty cool, huh?"

He watched as Nathan completely ignored the disheartening evidence that his delivery service might never fly in a town like Bethlehem. Every day, Nathan posted more flyers and offered more advantageous deals to people all over town. He never lost heart. "They'll come around," he predicted. "You can't ignore progress."

Jordan saw, no matter how surreptitious Nathan tried to be, the boy count his money almost every afternoon. The little stack of wrinkled bills did seem to be growing, thanks primarily to Jordan's tendency to tip generously whenever Nathan ran vital errands to the general store for cold soft drinks or afternoon snacks.

He also saw the boy studying a map of Charlotte one afternoon when everyone else was out of the office. He couldn't, however, entice the cagey youngster into explaining what he was doing with a map of the largest city in North Carolina.

"I have a plan," he said, folding the map and tucking it into the zippered compartment on the inside of his book bag, where he also kept his money. "That's all I can divulge at this time."

For days Jordan managed to be deeply engrossed in something whenever it was time for Joella to drop by for Nathan. From the safety of his office, he heard her voice plenty of times, soft and melodious, sometimes laughing over something Nathan or Venita said. Jordan longed to join them, to laugh with them, to see the light in her eyes.

He longed for her, simply and purely. And because of that he couldn't bear to see the disappointment in her eyes. The longer he put off seeing her, the tougher it became. The deeper the ache. Sometimes, thanks to Nathan, he could set aside that ache and pretend it didn't exist. Or pretend, at the very least, that the ache would evaporate quickly once he got out of this town, back to his own territory.

"No wonder you spent so much time with me," Jordan said one day after Nathan left. "Kids are fun."

"You were never a kid."

"What's that supposed to mean?" He walked to the front window and watched Joella and Nathan. The boy didn't seem to mind one bit walking down Main Street with his mother's arm around his shoulders.

"That means what was fun about you was watching you try so hard to be a grown-up." She joined him at the window. "That was also the sad part about watching you."

"Don't go soft on me, Venita."

"I've always been soft on you, Jordie. It's nice seeing *you* go soft on somebody for a change."

"I don't know why he gets to me."

"Don't you?"

Joella reached down to pull a knit cap out of her son's coat pocket and snugged it down over his unruly hair. The motherly act roused Jordan's own needs to protect them both, and to have someone want to protect him in that same way.

"No." He turned abruptly away from the window.

"Maybe it's because he's trying so hard to be a grown-up."

"You think he's like me."

"You're a smart fellow. You figure it out." She walked back to the calculator and began to punch out numbers. "Or maybe it's not Nathan you're soft on at all."

His heart grew still for a moment.

"You may think you know everything," he said, "but you don't."

She laughed. He ignored her.

Joella rummaged in her locker, dragging out her old corduroy coat and the leather handbag her

mother had given her for Christmas four years earlier. She tried not to think about how close Christmas was. She had to think what to do, not just about
the holiday but about the rest of her life. But thinking about the future just made her tired.

"Chin up." Claire nudged her. "Things'll look
up."

They walked toward the mill exit, part of the
trickle of first shifters leaving their jobs in the hands
of the second-shift crew.

Claire had a job lined up in Spartanburg, in one
of the little dress shops at the mall starting this Saturday. She would work weekends during the holidays, then start full-time after the first of the year.
"I'm looking at apartments in Spartanburg this
weekend after work. Want to come?"

Claire thought they ought to be roommates, share
expenses and child care and housekeeping. It might
make school possible, and then they could look forward to better things in the future, she said. Joella
supposed it was a good idea, but just thinking about
it made her sad. She couldn't imagine not living in
Bethlehem. She couldn't imagine a little apartment
complex where you lived elbow-to-elbow with
strangers instead of people you'd known all your
life.

She was being silly and ungrateful. She'd talked
to God about her attitude every night for weeks, but
so far she hadn't had a change of heart.

"Not yet," she said, walking out into the drizzle with her friend.

"It'll be easier once you've started actually making plans," Claire said. "Once you let go of stuff here."

That was it, of course. She had to let go of Bethlehem. Joella fought the tears that prickled her throat. "I know. But I'm not ready yet."

They paused to button up against the damp and the chill. Joella avoided looking up at the sky, which was as gray as her heart this afternoon. She hadn't bought a single Christmas present for Nathan yet, either. Maybe she should go into Spartanburg with Claire this weekend, start her Christmas shopping before her paycheck got eaten up by the electric bill and the laundromat. Nathan *would* have a good Christmas if she had to hock everything she owned.

Nathan. Thinking of him made her smile despite her own disheartened emotions, despite the dreary December afternoon. Nothing dragged him down for long. Each afternoon when they walked back to the house together, he was full of stories about his day. Full of stories about Jordan Scoville. Joella supposed she should be concerned about the time her son was spending with the man who had betrayed them all so heartlessly. But she wasn't.

Because she knew Jordan wasn't heartless, no matter what his actions implied. She remembered the things he'd said, the vulnerability she'd seen in his eyes those few days they were together. She trusted her instincts about Jordan. Deep down, he was a good man. He might not know it yet, but she did.

She waved goodbye to Claire at the corner where the pharmacist was packing up to close the doors of the drugstore one week from today. Claire turned toward the day care, Joella toward the offices of Scoville Mill.

Today, as every other day, she wondered if she would see Jordan.

She wiped her feet on the welcome mat, shook the raindrops out of her hair as she walked through the front door. Venita's office was empty. The door into the office where Jordan had been working stood open. Joella heard voices, his and her son's. She followed the sound, her heart beginning to pound.

Her son and the man who was deciding the fate of her town sat cross-legged on the lush carpet, playing a board game. Neither of them noticed her.

"So some guy with a lot of money who used to be a big-shot quarterback is throwing his weight around at the NFL," Nathan was saying.

"That's about the size of it," Jordan said, moving a piece on the game board.

"And if the NFL guys like him better than they like you, you lose your shirt."

"Your grasp of business astounds me, Ratchford."

Joella chuckled softly. Jordan looked over Nathan's shoulder and saw her standing there. He froze. His guilty conscience was written all over his face. She wondered how he managed to get anywhere in business with such a transparent face.

"Then what you need to do," Nathan said, "is ask God to make the deal go through for you. I'll bet that rich old quarterback isn't praying."

Joella cleared her throat, capturing her son's attention. He, too, looked guilty when he looked around to see her standing there. "Mom."

"I'm not sure your mother considers it proper use of prayer to ask God to waste time making me a millionaire, Nathan."

Joella smiled. "Your grasp of spirituality astounds me, Mr. Scoville."

He nodded, looking sheepish. "I don't doubt that."

"Come on, Nathan. Let's see if we can get home before the drizzle turns into a downpour."

"But Mom, one more turn and I'm going to beat his socks off."

"Now, Nathan."

He jumped off the floor and went into the front office, where she heard him packing up his book bag. Jordan stood, leaving the game on the floor. He looked different, not so imposing, although he was still tall and broad shouldered and his dark eyes still unsettled her. But there was something new, something almost boyish, as if Nathan had rubbed off on him while they sat on the floor playing a board game. Joella felt her heart reach out to him.

She also felt the physical tug of his nearness. Wistfully, because she knew it was no more than a fanciful daydream, she wondered about kissing him, felt a swirl of unsettling sensations taking her over.

She shook herself free of the feelings. "I'll have him pick it up before he leaves." Her voice sounded a little breathless.

"Nah. We'll pick up tomorrow where we left off."

She should go now. Turn and leave. His gaze wouldn't release its hold on her. She felt her mouth go dry. "If he gets in the way when you need to be working—"

"No. I like having him around."

Now his voice had wrapped itself around her. "Okay. If you're sure."

She forced herself to turn.

"Joella?"

She paused. He walked around to face her again. She wished he hadn't. How could a man with so much power, so much money, look so unsure of himself? But the look of uncertainty in his eyes didn't diminish his powerful hold over her one bit.

"I'm sorry," he said.

She nodded, not trusting her voice.

"I'm trying to figure out a way to make it up to…everybody."

"Do the best you can, Jordan."

"Maybe I should be praying."

He intended it as a joke, she could tell from his

expression. It broke the spell, reminding her who he was and what was at stake here. This was the wrong man. This was Andrew all over again, another mistake waiting to happen. She sent up a fleeting prayer to be strong enough to resist the temptation he presented.

"Yes, praying would be a good idea," she said stiffly.

He frowned when she said that, and she left his office. Nathan stood by Venita's desk, watching them, taking it all in. She put her hand on his shoulder and started for the front door. Jordan's voice captured her as she opened the door onto the dreary day.

"Joella? I...uh...I'll see you soon."

Something about the tone of his voice frightened her, dampened her spirits. She didn't suppose for a moment that he meant it, but she could almost hear in his wistful tone that it was what he wanted. And that was enough to worry her. For she wasn't sure she was strong enough to resist the temptation of a man like Jordan Scoville.

Yes, praying would be a very good idea. She would ask God—again—for the strength to keep from making the same mistake all over again.

He did see her soon, however. Later that night, after choir practice, in fact.

She saw him when he came in, her voice almost faltering when he settled on a back pew to listen as they worked on the numbers for the Christmas program. His presence was so powerful she could almost feel it, physically, even across the expanse of the empty church.

That frightened her, too. She was definitely pinning too much hope on this. When it came to Jordan Scoville and her silly notions, she was weak, weak, weak. She repeated her plea to God for strength to resist the attraction of this man and the way his presence made her heart sing.

After rehearsal was over, he wanted to walk her home. She felt powerless to turn him down. Her excuses were lame and when he linked arms with her, she leaned into him, certain in her head it was wrong, but unable to resist the call of her heart.

The rain had stopped, but the bare branches overhead splattered them from time to time.

"I've missed you, Joella," he said.

She couldn't say it back, although it would have been the truth.

"But I've been too ashamed of myself to come out of the hole I dug for myself."

"We do dig our own holes, don't we?" She mused on the one she was digging for herself.

"Thank you for letting Nathan hang around with me. I could understand if you didn't want him to."

His words softened her further. "He enjoys it. I trust you with him."

"Why?"

She didn't want to answer that, either. She was

grateful the wind chose that moment to rattle one of the branches overhead, showering them with raindrops. She laughed, began to wipe her face. But he stopped her. She told herself it wasn't too late to back away, but it was. Far too late. She held her breath.

He touched her damp cheek with the silky scarf he wore around the collar of his overcoat, drying the raindrops on her cheek. Then he touched her other cheek. Joella felt her breath go shallow, her heartbeat begin to thunder. His touch felt so tender. The same way his eyes looked.

If she hadn't known that this was young Mr. Scoville and she was nobody but a first-shift worker in his family's company, she would have thought he intended to kiss her.

That, of course, was ridiculous.

And then he did, a soft kiss that warmed her from the inside out and sent every bit of good sense she'd ever possessed flying right out of her head. What use was good sense when the caress of a man's lips felt so tender, so right?

Chapter Nine

Joella was sitting beside the pond at the foot of Main Street when the two cars with out-of-state license plates drove by slowly and stopped.

The day was clear, the shallow pond especially blue, its center reflecting the cloudless sky overhead, its edges mirroring the scruffy pines growing up along the opposite bank. Those pines, for as long as Joella could remember, had been wreathed in twinkling, multicolored lights at this time of year. The drive downhill from Main Street after dark was magical, thanks to the lights glittering back from the surface of the still water.

Hunching her knees to her chest, Joella coached herself out of the funk that sometimes came on her when she looked around and realized that this year there would be no magic.

The best way to elevate her mood, she had discovered, was to remember that Jordan Scoville had kissed her, with lips so soft and warm the very memory had the power to melt her heart. She tried not to indulge in that particular memory too often, but it was such a pleasant place to go.

Sometimes it seemed to her that God must have put her and Jordan together just so everything could work out perfectly, a fairy-tale ending for Bethlehem, for the sad-eyed Jordan, for herself and her fatherless son. After all, she'd prayed so hard to be strong that maybe her very weakness proved that being with Jordan was God's will. Most of the time, however, Joella knew that such a fanciful idea was all in her head and probably had little to do with what God wanted for her.

After all, if God had wanted her to have a rich, powerful businessman for a husband, wouldn't she still be with Andrew?

Joella groaned at how easily she could rationalize her crazy thinking by calling it God's will. God had never once promised to bring her another man to round out her life or her son's life. Certainly not Jordan Scoville, no matter how sweet and tempting his kiss.

And the kiss had been sweet, especially when it was over and she saw that stunned, shy look on his face, as if he couldn't quite believe how lovely the moment had been.

As she heard a car door close from the drive circling the pond, Joella wondered if the expression on

Jordan's face had merely been her wishful thinking. Had she brought about a reflection of her own emotions just as the lake duplicated its surroundings?

"Excuse me, miss? But is there some problem this year?"

Reluctantly turning away from her reverie, Joella looked over her shoulder into the concerned eyes of a grandmotherly woman in a shiny red-and-green jogging suit. She stood beside two vans with Tennessee license plates. "About the Christmas festivities, I mean. Where are all the decorations?"

Joella's heart sank. "Oh, dear."

This caravan of senior citizens might be the first disappointed people looking for an explanation, but Joella doubted they would be the last. December was going to be a long, cold month.

Jordan stood at the window overlooking Main Street, as he had that first day weeks ago. The quiet town had looked like a stranger to him then, something long forgotten from his childhood. Now it looked too familiar. Almost like a place where he belonged.

That, he knew, was an illusion.

He now knew most of the people he saw scurrying up and down the streets, from post office to supermarket to laundromat. He knew which directions they would turn when heading for home, which cars or pickup trucks they would drive away. He knew who had kids still at home and who had already shipped teenagers off to college.

Joella Ratchford was to blame for all of that.

She was to blame for the way he felt about it, too, guilty and hopeful all at the same time. Because of Joella, it was through different eyes that he was beginning to see the town he'd always hated. Through her eyes, he supposed. Eyes tempered by a gentleness of spirit he couldn't quite define. Because of Joella, he was even beginning to see himself a little differently. Just for a moment, the other night, he'd thought of himself as the kind of man who could kiss a woman like her. The man he'd been for years—a man driven by ambition, a man who orchestrated his life around amassing money, a man who viewed women as one more sign of success— wouldn't have looked twice at the simple good-heartedness of a woman like Joella.

And a good thing, too. She deserved better.

Nevertheless, he didn't regret the sweet surprise of her lips on his. A gift of softness and warmth lifting his heart.

As he stood at the window, another unfamiliar car crept slowly down Main Street from the direction of the highway. Another tourist, he supposed, looking for Christmas Town, U.S.A. And all they would find would be the dying hometown of a modern-day Scrooge. They'd been pouring in all week, listening with stunned expressions as they heard that this year there would be no Christmas in Bethlehem.

Jordan sighed heavily. The town needed a name change.

He was turning away from the window when he saw a slight figure dashing along Main Street at breakneck speed. It was Nathan in a mad rush, barely noticing the oncoming vehicle, screeching to a halt at the curb only when the Reverend Hatfield Martin managed to snag him by the shoulder at the last minute. When the car passed, Nathan darted off again, stumbling in the middle of Main Street when he remembered to turn and wave to the minister.

Moments later the front door of Scoville Mill opened with a bang. Jordan smiled and turned toward the office door, anticipating the whirlwind that was Nathan.

"Guess what!" Nathan's eyes were wide and wild. He hadn't even bothered with his coat. It was looped through the straps of his book bag, which he dumped unceremoniously onto the floor. "You won't believe it! It's, like, too cool! They never did this before and I don't know why they're doing it now. 'Cause there's nothing here now. But they're here and—"

"Slow down, Nathan. What in the world are you talking about?"

"About all the tents!"

"What tents?"

"The ones in Mr. Exley's tobacco fields! You oughtta see 'em! Monday I only saw two. By yesterday, I counted five. And now—" He gulped. "I'll bet there's two dozen! And a van with TV cameras. And I've got the only grocery delivery service in town! I could be rich! I've cornered the market!''

Now the boy really had Jordan's attention. ''A TV crew? Nathan, what's going on out there? Who's in these tents, anyway?''

''Visitors. Christmas visitors. Just like every year. Except this time, they're staying.''

The hill on the other side of the highway overlooked Lyle Exley's farmland. Jordan reached the crest of the hill in five minutes, although he didn't keep up with Nathan's excited trek back to the scene of his newly discovered market.

The view from the hilltop stunned him.

Just as Nathan had said, a dozen or more tents and campers dotted the fallow field where Lyle Exley planted a small crop of tobacco each spring. A few children who weren't yet school age played, throwing sticks for a brown-and-white collie. Older people sat outside their tents in folding chairs, tending camp stoves or tinkering with binoculars. A long-haired man with a video camera on his shoulder followed a woman in a red suit as she thrust a microphone in one face after another. Three more cars topped with luggage racks were wending their way down the rutted tractor path from the highway.

Joella stood in the middle of a small knot of townspeople at the crest of the hill. Most of the people pulled away when Jordan moved in, as if afraid of being infected with his lack of spirit. Joella didn't move away.

"What's going on here?" Nathan said.

"I don't know." Joella shook her head. "Let's find out."

She started down the hill and he followed. She took the dips and ruts gracefully, like someone accustomed to roaming the countryside. Jordan kept forgetting this wasn't a paved city sidewalk; he lurched along after her, admiring her grace and bemoaning his clumsiness.

You don't fit in her world, he told himself. *And that means you have no business kissing her. Ever.*

The first two tents they reached were pitched close by one another. Two men who were past middle age but not yet ready for retirement were going through tackle boxes, squaring away their fishing gear. The two women who were apparently their partners sat in folding chairs beside the front of the tents, one knitting, the other making notes in a journal.

"You're still here," Joella said to one of the women. Her voice was bright with cheerful greeting. "I thought you'd be back in Tennessee by now."

"Oh, look, Myrtle, it's that nice young woman from the lake in town." The woman with the journal marked her place with her fountain pen. She smiled at Joella. "The one who told us they wouldn't be having Christmas in Bethlehem this year."

"Why, how nice of you to come out for a visit."

Jordan felt irritation growing as the couples exchanged introductions with Joella. They might have been sitting around Joella's parlor. Except that Joella didn't have a parlor, of course.

"So, you see, we decided to stay," Myrtle was saying. "We've started our holiday here in Bethlehem every year since our firstborn was old enough to understand all the excitement. And, well, I guess we just have faith that things will work out."

Joella looked moved by the woman's words.

"It's not a matter of faith," Jordan said brusquely. "It's a matter of economics."

The four older people exchanged amused glances, the kind children receive when they explain about finding baby brothers under a cabbage leaf. They clearly considered Jordan's explanation to be simpleminded.

"The decorations have been sold," he persisted. "Christmas Town, U.S.A is over. It's not coming back."

Delores the journal-keeper humored him. "Why, of course not."

"You know," Myrtle said to Joella, gesturing with her knitting needles, "you really should talk to the Conkels. That's them over there in the camper. They come all the way from Arizona every year. And they have the dearest little girl. They're an inspiration. They really are."

Joella headed off in the direction of the Conkels from Arizona. Jordan, having no better plan in mind and no desire to discuss fly-fishing with the spouses of Myrtle and Delores, followed.

The Conkels were younger, closer to Jordan's age. They had a look of peacefulness.

"We just couldn't bear to leave, even after we heard the news," Mrs. Conkel said in response to Joella's inquiry. Her husband reached over and took her hand. "Bethlehem is...well, it's just meant a great deal to us."

"And to Andrea," Mr. Conkel added.

"Andrea? That's your daughter?"

They nodded.

"She's inside napping," Mrs. Conkel said. "She...she had a stroke, you see. When she was just a little thing. Right after we left here one Christmas. Oh, she loved this place so—"

Her voice broke. Her husband picked up. "Andrea had great fun here, that last Christmas before her stroke. After the stroke, nothing seemed to reach her. She...she wouldn't respond to anything. So Judy thought of bringing her back to Bethlehem for Christmas the next year."

Backhanding a tear on her cheek, Judy Conkel nodded. "So we did, and that's when she started turning around. She absolutely lit up when we topped the hill on Main Street and she saw the village spread out below her. It was like a miracle."

Jordan wanted to stalk off. He didn't know who had orchestrated this little charade designed to trigger his guilt. Even Joella wouldn't have gone this far, would she? He didn't like being manipulated like this one little bit. Kindly older couples and seriously ill children, for goodness' sake. As if he would change his mind over a sappy greeting-card moment.

Joella, however, seemed totally caught up in the story. Tears glistened in her eyes. He opened his mouth to protest, but Mr. Conkel finished the story.

"She still has a long way to go, but she's made a lot of progress. And it all started here. Now, every year when the weather turns cool, she starts asking about Bethlehem."

"We haven't figured out how to tell her there won't be any Christmas village this year," Judy Conkel concluded. "So we just decided to wait it out with the others. Everybody says something will happen, that things will turn around."

Joella stayed to talk with them a little longer, but Jordan had to get away. He wandered through the small but growing village of camping pilgrims. Despite the less-than-comfortable conditions, they were all cheerful and friendly, talking with one another as if they'd been lifelong neighbors. He overheard plans for a joint effort to prepare a community dinner of soup and fresh bread, which someone assured them could be made in skillets over a campfire. He heard laughter. The only unpleasantness he heard came from the woman in the red suit, who finally thrust her microphone in his face and said, "Mr. Scoville, I understand you are the one responsible for stealing Christmas this year in Bethlehem, South Carolina. Would you care to comment?"

Then she turned her best smile in the direction of the video camera and waited for Jordan's comment.

Jordan tried to remember what his partner always told him to do if confronted with a hostile member of the media. He was certain there had been nothing in Les's advice about wrestling the camera away from the camera crew and smashing it underfoot. But that was the only response that came to mind.

"No," he said. "No comment."

Then he remembered. No comment, his partner always said, was the moral equivalent of I'm guilty, as far as the American public was concerned.

"But surely you owe the public some explanation," the reporter said, her camera-ready smile artfully etched onto her flawlessly made-up face.

"No, I don't," he said, knowing he was only digging a deeper hole but completely at a loss for how to back down now. "This is private business and—"

"What Mr. Scoville means," came a gentler voice at his shoulder. Joella's voice. Both microphone and video camera immediately shifted to her face. Jordan almost groaned. The phrase lambs to the slaughter came to mind. "What he means is that this is a very difficult time for everyone in Bethlehem. No one wants to see the town and the holiday tradition survive any more than the Scoville family."

Joella glanced up at him hopefully. He couldn't help but remark the contrast between her fresh, shining face and the artificial face of the woman wielding the microphone. The TV reporter looked exactly like most of the women he escorted around Atlanta. At the moment he couldn't imagine anything less appealing than the idea of spending time with Miss Film-at-Eleven. Not when a woman like Joella existed in the world.

It occurred to him that Joella might be the last woman of her kind in the world. That if he didn't act soon, she would be gone, too. He felt a moment of panic at the thought of missing out on Joella, on the opportunity to have her in his life.

"That's right," he said automatically. "That's exactly right."

Nathan saw it all on the TV news that night. His mom and the way she saved Jordan Scoville from looking like the Grinch that stole Christmas. And the way Jordan looked at his mom, with that mushy look in his eyes. He supposed everybody saw it, although nobody else said a word and he supposed it was possible that grown-ups get so wrapped up in grown-up stuff like paying bills and wiping up kitchen spills before they turned into mounds of permanent crud that they couldn't see what was right under their noses.

Like the way his mom and his boss were falling in love.

Nathan wasn't sure how he felt about that.

He liked Jordan Scoville. They had lots of fun together, now that Jordan had learned how to be a good sport when Nathan wiped him off the face of the earth in a video game. But Nathan had to be realistic. Deep down, he knew that Jordan Scoville was just like Nathan's dad. And that was bad news in the long run, both for Nathan and his mom. Because one day Jordan would get in his big black car and drive back to Atlanta and forget that Nathan and Joella Ratchford even existed.

Nathan had seen that routine before. He didn't want to go through it again.

In the meantime, though, his mom seemed to feel happier, maybe because of the way Jordan Scoville looked at her and maybe because of the nice people in the tent village. She'd talked about them all through supper.

And, best of all, his grocery delivery business was really taking off. He'd made $17.34 hauling groceries back to the campers this afternoon alone. It would have been eighteen dollars, but he'd needed the sixty-six cents for a soft drink. Hauling that wagon full of canned chili and tuna fish was hard work.

That brought his venture capital up to sixty-one dollars and change. Soon he would have enough to hire someone to drive him to Charlotte. Once there, he had no doubt he could smooth-talk his way in to see his deadbeat dad.

And who knows what might happen once Andrew Ratchford realized what a totally cool kid he had.

Chapter Ten

A few weeks before Christmas it was sunny and bright, but Joella felt as if the town was in the midst of a storm.

That storm would only get worse at the town meeting scheduled for that evening, Joella was sure of that.

Bethlehem was overrun with visitors. It seemed that almost everyone who came for the annual celebration stayed once they learned what was going on. Lyle Exley's tobacco field was full, and the overflow had now spilled into the vacant lot where the truck stop had shut down a year ago. Joella visited the tent village whenever she could; hearing their stories about how Bethlehem had boosted people's spirits and restored their faith over the years kept her spirits up, too. And, on a more practical level, business at local shops and stores was booming.

Scoville Mill was stirred up, too, but not because business was booming. The mill barely had enough work to keep two shifts going through until year's end. The supervisors weren't pushing for higher productivity because everybody knew that once these jobs were finished, they'd reached the end. Machinery would clatter to a halt, the doors would close and the final paychecks would be passed out.

Even Joella's heart wasn't still these days. And no matter how often she told herself that her future didn't lie with a man like Jordan Scoville, her foolish heart wouldn't listen. Didn't believe.

The meeting in the church fellowship hall had already begun when someone brought up recent gossip that the people of Bethlehem could buy the mill themselves. The mood in town had soared as the idea spread the past couple of days. Joella had tried to keep a level head; buying the mill sounded so improbable to her. But, like everyone else in town, she was here tonight because she was hungry for any dim ray of hope.

"So I say we buy the company ourselves." Fred Roseforte ended his pitch with a stubborn thrust of his chin. "We know more about running a mill than the Scovilles."

"That's a fact," someone said.

"It's also a fact we don't have that kind of

money," came another voice. "Fred, you're losing your marbles."

"You always were a sour old coot, Marv," Fred countered. "We pool our money and the bank loans us the rest. That's the way rich folks've always done it."

Joella wasn't sure, but she suspected every penny that could be pulled together in Bethlehem would be only a fraction of what would be needed to float a loan to buy Scoville Mill. But for a few minutes she heard the enthusiasm and excitement ringing through the fellowship hall and hoped she was wrong.

She even walked up to the front with the rest and gave Fred Roseforte the meager figure that she could contribute to the effort.

The total that Fred announced sounded pretty dismal to her, but Fred refused to let go of the idea.

"Some of the tent people have said they'd invest, too," he said. "Some of those folks are rich, you know."

Joella had heard those rumors, too, and she listened now as people speculated that a commitment from the visitors was simply wishful thinking.

"Besides," the town's pharmacist said, "they want to invest thinking that'll bring the celebration back. We'll be doing well to keep the mill running. Where would we get the money for a Christmas celebration, too?"

Joella's head buzzed with all the talk. She didn't

know who was right, but with every day that passed
she had leaned more toward the side of pessimism.
She knew miracles were possible, but it seemed
clearer every day that God had no intention of saving their town or their jobs. For some reason, it must
be God's will for Bethlehem to die.

She was tempted, sometimes, to stop praying for
God's will. She wasn't sure she liked the looks of
God's will these days. She would have to talk to Hat
Martin about that.

"When they settle our retirement money on us,
we'll have a small fortune if we all throw in together," Fred said.

"But that's all we've got to fall back on!" Marv
sounded alarmed. "We can't afford to lose that."

"He's right! Besides, if the Scovilles can't figure
out how to make a profit, how are we going to do
any better? You ain't a businessman, Fred. None of
us are."

During a barrage of similar comments, Fred
searched the crowd for a friendly face. His angry
eyes landed on Joella and he raised his voice over
the others ringing through the fellowship hall.

"Where's your all-fired optimism these days,
Joella? Don't you think God could provide us with
a little business smarts?"

All eyes turned to Joella, and she couldn't figure
out what to say. She couldn't figure out what she
believed, and that frightened her.

''Or has young Mr. Scoville convinced you *he's* going to take care of you?''

The sly accusation in Fred's voice was the final straw for Joella. Maybe he was right. Maybe her daydreaming over Jordan Scoville had managed to distract her from her faith; maybe she'd grown too eager to make a man like Jordan her higher power, seduced by the idea that he would provide everything she needed. She'd made that mistake once, and maybe she'd done it all over again. Her eyes filled with tears. She turned and ran out of the fellowship hall before they spilled down her cheeks and confirmed what Fred had intimated.

From his shadowy hiding place in the hallway outside the fellowship hall, Jordan listened with mounting anger as Fred Roseforte turned his frustration on Joella. He was ready to march right in and tell Roseforte a thing or two, then realized that trying to rescue Joella right now would simply reinforce what Roseforte had hinted.

He was standing in the darkened hallway, seething in his indecision, when Joella ran out of the church basement and swept past him without noticing his presence. He followed, catching her at the top of the stairs.

''I'm sorry,'' he said, putting a hand on her shoulder. The contact was like an explosion in his chest.

She was sniffling into a tissue and frantically

swiping tears from her eyes. "You've got nothing to be sorry about."

Shrugging away from his touch, she exited the building. He went after her, refusing to accept her rebuff. The night was bitterly cold, pinching his cheeks and nose. He thought of her worn parka and doubted she was warm enough for the walk back to her house.

"Let me drive you," he said.

"No, thank you."

He drew a long breath. "Please."

"So you won't feel guilty?"

"So your nose won't get frostbitten," he said, hoping for one of her smiles. No such luck. "And so I won't feel so guilty."

"I'll do it for my nose."

His car warmed up quickly, but he noticed that Joella didn't relax into the seat. She kept her parka zipped, her hands crammed into her pockets, her shoulders tensed against something that was no longer the cold.

He pointed the car out of town.

"This isn't the right direction," she insisted stiffly.

"It's the right direction for where I'm going."

"I can walk."

"Let's ride. You can calm down before you go home."

She finally murmured her agreement and he picked up speed as the car hit the highway. He thought of turning on the CD player, but the silence felt comfortable and comforting. That might be a first, he thought, and knew it had to do with Joella.

He drove automatically, the way he'd driven this highway almost twenty years earlier, before he left for military school. Every curve of the back entrance to the family estate felt familiar, and at the moment that didn't feel as suffocating as it had when he first arrived in Bethlehem. Very little, he realized, was the same as it had been then.

The private driveway was harder to spot than it had been years earlier, more overgrown now. He knew what that meant. No one came out here anymore, now that Eugenia Scoville was gone. At the end of the long, winding driveway, he pulled the car to a stop and killed the engine. The moon was only a sliver in the sky. If he hadn't known so intimately what lay ahead, Jordan realized, it would have been hard to figure out what he was seeing. Figures glimmered in shadow and faint light.

"What is it?" Joella asked in a whisper.

"My mother's sculpture garden."

"A sculpture garden? Right here in Bethlehem?" She sounded delighted, as if the surprise had managed to wipe away the unpleasant scene in the church. "Can we get out?"

"It's cold." *Too cold for your thin coat.* But he couldn't say that.

"Not long enough for frostbite," she said.

He liked the teasing that had returned to her voice.

She walked through the opening in the woods reverently, reaching out to touch the pieces of marble and granite and limestone that his mother had collected and cherished in her lifetime. She ran her hands lovingly over the cheeks of cherubic children, the flanks of a deer. She laughed over imps and a playful lion cub that had been one of his mother's favorites.

It was like seeing everything for the first time, through her delighted eyes.

"This is wonderful," she said.

He nodded. "When I was a kid, I called it the Enchanted Forest."

"That's exactly what it is."

"I haven't been in years. Thanks for giving me a good excuse."

"I don't see how you can stay away."

"Staying away's been easier than coming back. Actually I've only been able to come back since you took me to the cemetery. I... That's helped me see a different side of my mother."

"I'm glad."

He followed her gaze. She was staring at the Scoville estate through the trees.

"I've never seen it this close before," she said. "It's...gloomy looking."

"That's what I always thought. That's why I got away as quickly as I could." The shadows were too deep for him to see her face, but he sensed her lack of comprehension in the quizzical tilt of her head.

"You've never run away from anything, have you?"

She looked directly at him. Her ivory skin caught what little light there was, like the smooth surface of the marble statues. Her dark eyes were deep with shadow and with concern. He wanted to touch her the way she had touched the sculptures, reverently, with a bit of awe that anything so lovely could tolerate his caress.

"I suppose I ran away when I came back to Bethlehem after...my marriage ended."

"Were you running away or running to? There's a difference, you know."

"Is there?"

"Running away is cowardly. Running to takes courage."

"Then I must have been running away. I didn't have much courage in those days."

"Then you've changed."

She shook her head slightly. "Courage is just fear that's said its prayers."

"Then there's my answer," he said lightly. "I don't have much faith."

"It doesn't take much."

"That's right. A mustard seed's worth. Isn't that what it says?"

"That's enough to make a start." She turned back to the lion cub sculpture. "Jordan, I know you won't be staying when...everything's finished. But what about Mr. Mitchell and Mr. Truman? What will they do? Where will they go?''

With a sinking heart, Jordan realized he hadn't asked himself, or anyone else, that question. He'd been so focused on untangling the mess his father and uncle had created that he hadn't given a moment's worry to what would become of the two old men once the only world they'd ever known had been dismantled. What he couldn't say to her, even though he wanted to more than anything in the world, was that he might not be going back to Atlanta, either. He had no way of knowing what would happen when it was all over, but he couldn't burden her with his problems. It wouldn't be fair to ask her to keep that secret. If she felt estranged from her friends in town now, how would she feel then? ''I'll... They can... I don't know.''

He could feel her disappointment, he was certain of it.

''They can come to Atlanta with me.'' Being less than honest right now seemed justified. He could hardly explain to her that he might not be going back to Atlanta himself. Maybe she'd never have to know.

''Would they like that?''

He doubted it, but it was the only answer he could think of at the moment. ''Would you?''

She glanced back at him. ''Would I what?''

''Like to come to Atlanta?'' He drew a deep breath, but he still felt shaky inside. He couldn't do this. Shouldn't do this. What was he thinking? He'd just been reminding himself how uncertain his future was. He was crazy. "With me?"

Crazy about her.

She grew very still and lowered her eyes. "You know I can't do that. I have a son. I have...things I believe in."

"I'm sorry. That came out wrong." He took her in his arms, raised her chin and looked into her eyes. "I love you, Joella. I—"

"Don't say that. You can't mean that."

"Yes, I can. I do. I've never felt this way about anyone."

Then, just to make sure she understood what he was saying, he kissed her. He kissed her until he finally felt her melt against him. If he'd been asked, he would have traded the NFL deal for her, right at this moment. When he realized that, he released her. But letting her go didn't stop the way he felt inside.

"I love you, Joella."

"Love is more than wanting to drag me back to Atlanta with you."

He knew what she meant. For a woman like Joella, love was about commitment. Under the circumstances, that was the one thing he couldn't give her.

In fact, he couldn't be sure of his ability to commit even if everything suddenly straightened itself out. He wasn't the kind of man who could give the kind of things a woman like Joella needed. He wasn't good, solid husband material; he wasn't father material. Was he?

His silence seemed to tell her all she needed to know. She turned toward the car. "It's getting cold."

He wanted to call after her, to tell her what was in his heart. But he knew there was no point in it. If he really loved her, the best thing he could do for her was let her go. Leave her alone and let her get on with her life, instead of trying his best to tie her to him.

Because if she tied her life to his, then he ended up in prison, where would that leave her?

Nathan didn't know what to do about his discovery. Should he keep quiet and mind his own business, which was advice his mom gave him often enough? Should he tell someone? If so, who? The police? His mom?

A part of him figured that a shrewd businessman would use this information to increase his own fortune. That could mean blackmail, he supposed. Or selling the story to a newspaper.

Those ideas made his stomach kind of queasy. But he couldn't give up on them entirely.

He saw the memo on Venita's desk on a Thursday. By Sunday he had decided at least a quarter of a billion times exactly what to do about it. But he kept changing his mind. He wondered if this was what it was like to go crazy, when you couldn't even keep your own mind on one track for more than a few minutes at a time, no matter how hard you prayed for God to help you.

When Sunday school was over, he was so wrapped up in the problem that he didn't even realize when the other kids stampeded out for the church service. He was still sitting in the wooden chair, staring at the grape-juice stain on the floor, when his Sunday school teacher pulled her chair close.

"Nathan, is something wrong this morning?"

Oh, man. Mrs. Jerrill was pulling out the concerned grown-up voice. "Uh, no. Nothing."

"I couldn't help but notice that you hadn't prepared your lesson for this morning. That isn't like you, Nathan."

"No, ma'am."

"If you need to talk to someone…"

She paused, and he knew what she was getting at. He could talk to her. Grown-ups always seemed to think it should be so easy for kids just to spill their guts about whatever was on their mind. He looked at Mrs. Jerrill. She was a nice lady, a lot like his grandmother, except that he saw her more than he saw his grandmother. He imagined telling her that he'd just found out that every penny in the Scoville Mill retirement fund was missing and somebody might have to go to jail if it didn't turn up.

She'd probably drop her false teeth right into her lap.

That made him grin.

She smiled back. "You could talk to me, of course. But sometimes the best person to talk to is our own mother. You know you can tell your mother anything, don't you?"

Nathan wondered if this was what his mom meant by listening for God to speak through other people. He sighed. Probably so. And that meant he was going to have to tell his mom that Jordan Scoville might be a crook after all.

He couldn't wait to grow up. Life had to get easier.

Joella was so wrapped up in her own worries that her son's request for a family conference almost didn't sink in.

"Umm-hmm," she said, swirling another plate in hot, soapy water and wishing she could get Jordan Scoville's words out of her mind.

I love you.

The words were taking root in her heart, tempting her to search for a way to believe that things could work out. She knew that if things were supposed to work out with Jordan, God could handle that without any help from her.

But what if she could find a job in Atlanta instead of Spartanburg? What if—

"*Mom,* this is *serious.*"

Joella suddenly realized what she had been doing—ignoring her son for the sake of a foolish day-

dream. She set aside the plate, dried her hands and
sat down with Nathan at the kitchen table. He did
look serious, his big brown eyes troubled behind his
eyeglasses.

"Sorry, kiddo. I was distracted. But I'm all yours
now."

He nodded, but it still took him a few moments
to ready himself to speak. It occurred to Joella that
the subject of this particular family conference
might be more significant than Nathan's latest plans
to make his first million or thwart the second-grade
bully who sometimes made his life miserable.

"I know stuff I'm not supposed to know, Mom."

Joella's heart jumped. "What kind of stuff?"

"About Scoville Mill. But I wasn't snooping or
anything, I promise. I was there at Venita's desk and
there was this memo on top of her stuff and I just
glanced down and the words jumped right out at
me."

"Nathan, you know you aren't supposed to
be—"

"Mom, wait. Just wait, okay? I know all that.
And you can ground me for the rest of the second
grade if you want to. But…" His voice quavered.
"I gotta tell you before I get chicken. Okay?"

She put her hand on his. It felt so small. Sometimes she had trouble remembering that he was just
a kid. Only seven. That was the danger when they
were so smart. "Okay, Nathan. I'm sorry. You're
right. What did you want to tell me?"

"Somebody stole all the retirement money. It's all gone and the account is empty and somebody's going to have to go to jail if they can't find it."

Joella felt her lungs empty of air, suddenly and painfully. Her mind went momentarily blank and she simply stared at her son.

"It's true, Mom."

"You're sure?" she whispered.

"It said it right there in the memo."

Her blank mind began to fill up with consequences, with fears, with hurt. "Oh, no."

"Does that mean everybody in town's going to be broke and homeless, Mom?"

"I don't know, Nathan. I'm not sure what it means."

"You gonna tell anybody else?"

"I don't know." Confronting that question suddenly helped her see how tough it must have been for her son to decide what to do. She reached for him and wrapped him in a tight hug. For once he didn't squirm away. "All I know right now is that you were brave and strong to tell me."

"I don't have to tell anybody else, do I?" he muttered against her shoulder.

"No, sweetie. It would be better if you didn't. Can you keep this between us for now, until I figure out what to do?"

He nodded.

She went through the motions the rest of the evening, grateful to note that Nathan seemed unbur-

dened now that he had told her. He chattered about
his homework and what he planned to do when
school ended for the Christmas break. Joella barely
heard him. His revelation had stunned her. A part
of her wanted to feel betrayed, wanted to blame Jordan. But she simply couldn't believe that he was
responsible for the missing money, no matter how
badly he might need it for his own big business deal.

That left Mr. Mitchell or Mr. Truman, and that
was, if anything, even more unbelievable.

She felt sick and numb.

She thought about how much she had longed to
answer him when he'd said he loved her. *I love you,
too*. She was grateful she hadn't.

As she tucked Nathan into bed, she said, "The
memo… It didn't say *who* stole the money, did it?"

Nathan looked at her as if he knew exactly what
she was thinking. "No, Mom. But it couldn't have
been Jordan. I just know it couldn't."

Joella tried not to blame herself. She'd allowed
her son to spend time with Jordan. And if he turned
out to be as untrustworthy as her son's father, if he
ended up betraying her son, she would never forgive
herself.

Chapter Eleven

Joella had never had the courage—or a reason—to see either of the Scoville homes up close before. Just nights ago she had had a glimpse of the imposing Tudor estate on the outskirts of the village. And now she stood before the door of the gracious house in town where Jordan was staying.

This house, where Truman Scoville had lived in earlier years and now mostly went unoccupied, was a rambling two-story frame house with countless multipaned windows. Large enough to hold four or five mill houses, it nevertheless looked small beside the estate house she'd seen earlier.

Her hand trembled as she raised it to the polished brass knocker.

What was she doing here? How could she even consider doing this? That's what her fears wanted to know.

How could she not do this? That's what her conscience demanded of her.

She knocked and waited, her knees beginning to tremble in unison with her hands. Her mouth was dry and her heart was surely going to fly right out of her chest. And all that was before Jordan appeared in the doorway. He smiled when he saw her, his dark eyes lighting up. He wore a plush, plum-colored sweater and a pair of casual slacks that still held a knife-edged crease. He looked rich. Even more rich, somehow, now that she knew he didn't lounge around his house in old sweat clothes the way the rest of the world did.

Still, his hair was rumpled. His eyes looked tired. As sharp as his clothes still managed to look, his shoulders didn't seem quite as upright as usual. And all that made him seem human after all. Appealingly human.

Why did doing the right thing always have to be so hard?

"This is a surprise," he said, ushering her inside. "I hope nothing's wrong."

She entered hesitantly. The house was cluttered with antiques and expensive knickknacks—a beige rug as thick as a cloud beneath her feet, a grandfather clock carved with cherubs, a gilt-framed mirror, elegant vases and more. Looking around would have been like a day at the museum for Joella. But she couldn't make herself focus on the details.

"We have to talk," she said.

"Fine."

He took her by the hand. In spite of everything, his touch had the power to take her breath away. She gritted her teeth against her weakness and his concerned look. A fire crackled in the otherwise dark drawing room. A frozen dinner in a tray sat on a brocade ottoman, half-eaten.

"I've interrupted your dinner." A way out. She could leave. Come back later. Tomorrow. Next year.

"If you could call it that." He glanced at the tray and shoved the ottoman aside. He urged her into an armchair and squatted in front of her. "What's wrong, Joella?"

His eyes were so sincere, so concerned. As brown as Nathan's. That helped her remember how troubled her son had been, and that this man was responsible. That gave her courage.

"I know about the retirement fund." Her mouth was so dry she could barely form the words. Maybe he would deny it, explain everything away. But she saw the truth in the way his eyes changed. Concern turned to shame. She tried to swallow but couldn't. The truth was a crushing weight on her heart.

"What's going on, Jordan?"

"I'm sorry you had to find out, Joella."

A little anger sparked in her, fighting with the part of her that wanted to give him the benefit of the doubt. "I'm sure you are."

"I...I'm trying to set things right. I swear I am."

"Tell me what happened."

He stood and began to pace. His shoulders slumped even more than before; he looked completely defeated. The urge to comfort him, to take him in her arms, was overwhelming.

"I can't do that," he said.

"You have to."

He stopped and stared at her. The color seemed to drain out of his face. "Or you'll tell the others?"

She stood also, her strength to stand up to him fueled by anger at herself. How could she still be so susceptible to him? How could she still want to take him in her arms, knowing what she knew?

"Jordan, you don't leave me any choice."

"Give me time."

"Time to pay back millions of dollars?"

He took a step in her direction, his hands reaching for hers. She folded her arms across her chest, closing herself off from him. *God, please help me.*

"I know it's too much to ask," he said. "But trust me. Just a little longer."

Joella knew at that moment that the only smart thing to do was run out the front door and head for Hat Martin or Fred Roseforte, somebody who could take this dilemma out of her hands. Jordan was clearly at the end of his rope, and she was just heartsick fool enough to think she could save him, seduced by the pleading in his eyes and the memory of his kiss.

She loved him. And at all costs, she wanted to believe him.

"You're protecting somebody else, aren't you?" Hope stirred in her heart that he would accept this easy out she offered. Hope and dread. Would it really be any better?

"Don't, Joella. I'm... I'm responsible. I know how that makes me look, I know what you must think. But trust me. Just this once."

"I've trusted you all this time."

His face crumpled. Her softly spoken words appeared to have been the last straw. Could she have been so mistaken about him? Could everything her heart told her about him have been so wrong? Or had God simply shown her things that even Jordan didn't yet believe about himself?

She might be dreaming, she knew. Might be setting herself up to be played for a fool. But even Jordan Scoville deserved a chance to redeem himself.

"I'll give you more time," she said. "On one condition."

"Anything."

"I want you to pray." She saw his hope dissolve, as if she'd asked him to hoist the earth onto his shoulders. "Every day, until this is resolved."

He covered his face in his hands. "Joella, I can't pray. I don't know how. And no God in His right mind would listen if I did."

She was astounded to discover she could smile. "God always listens."

"But I—"

''Just ask for God's will to be done. That's all you have to pray for.''

He stared at her and she did her best to let him see only faith and hope in her eyes. Not the love she felt, or the dangerous, dizzying need for him that might be clouding her judgment. None of that could matter now. All that mattered was convincing him to let God help with his problem.

She saw him wavering, saw the emotions warring on his sad, beleaguered face. The longing to comfort him hadn't subsided but she was managing to resist it. If he had nowhere else to turn, maybe he would turn to the one place where he could truly find help.

''You're serious.''

She shoved her hands deep into her pockets and clinched her fists, the only way she could keep herself from touching him. ''Promise me.''

He hesitated. What if he said no?

''Okay. I…promise.''

Joella left quickly, not trusting herself with him any longer than was necessary. As she walked home, she wasn't shaking any longer. She wasn't plagued by doubts. She had the calm certainty that she had done the right thing. ''Thank you, God, for sending me the words.''

It never once occurred to her that Jordan wouldn't keep his promise.

Jordan had no intention of keeping such a ridiculous promise.

He told himself that over and over as he tossed out the rest of his frozen dinner and measured freshly ground beans into the coffeemaker. He stood by the machine as it gurgled and whirred and trickled hot coffee into the mug he set in place of the carafe.

"I can't pray," he said into the big, silent house as he doctored the coffee with cream.

But he'd had to agree; she'd left him with no other choice. Besides, he'd found himself completely unable to say no when he looked into her trusting brown eyes. So he'd promised. But that didn't mean he actually had to pray.

"But I am trying to do the right thing. That's all that really matters." His voice sounded hollow.

He sat in front of the fire and sipped his coffee. He couldn't banish Joella from his thoughts. The disappointment in her eyes had been harder to bear than he'd expected. His need for her had grown to an unbearable ache, as well. Even as he'd been asking her for time, he knew he had no right. But she'd given him time, given him the trust he'd asked for. Sure, there were strings attached. She'd set certain conditions. But she would have only his word that he'd kept his promise.

Even if there was a God up there expecting him to keep his promise to Joella, surely that God would understand that the only important thing here was that Jordan's intentions were good. Right?

Even with cream, the coffee was bitter.

The fire began to die, too, while the coffee grew cold. Jordan felt restless. Irritable. By the time he smothered the last burning coal in the fireplace and turned off the coffeemaker, he was in a thoroughly disagreeable mood. Sleep would help. Things would look better in the morning.

It came to him, as he crawled into bed, that this was the time when Joella probably intended for him to pray.

He pulled the covers up tightly under his chin. He lay stiffly on his back. He closed his eyes, but they popped open. God's will, indeed. He double-checked the alarm, to make sure it was set. He punched his pillows to fluff them up. He kept seeing the trust in Joella's eyes when he'd promised. He got up to close the tiny gap in the curtains that was allowing a sliver of moonlight to fall across the bed and distract him. That was the problem, of course. A promise was a promise. Sort of like a gentleman's agreement. Which wasn't a concept he'd been particularly bound to before now. He closed his eyes again, but saw only Joella's eyes.

At two in the morning he was no closer to sleep.

"Okay, okay," he grumbled. "But I don't have to get on my knees. I never promised that."

Then, in the demanding voice he used with the people who worked for him, he said, "Okay, this is for Joella's God. Work things out, how about it?"

He turned over on his side and pulled a pillow over his head.

"Amen."

Loving a woman like Joella had grown way too complicated.

He was asleep in two minutes.

Joella peeked through his open office door. He was ripping a sheet off a legal pad, wadding it up and hurling it toward a small pile that had accumulated beside a trash basket. But at least he hadn't hopped a plane for Rio de Janeiro. That meant something, didn't it?

She eased into the office. "Did you do it?"

He looked up. Shadows under his eyes said he hadn't slept any better than she had slept.

"I *promised,* didn't I?"

Somehow, his irritation assured her that he had kept that promise. She smiled. "This morning, too?"

"Nobody said anything about twice a day."

"You're right."

"You can't raise the stakes in the middle of blackmailing somebody."

"Of course you can."

She continued smiling, and the aggravation seemed to seep out of him. A small smile touched his lips, enough to gentle his expression but not enough to dissipate the worry in his eyes.

"Thanks," he said.

"For what?"

"For trusting me when you have no reason to."

"Fred Roseforte says I'm naive. I like to think I'm a good judge of character."

He fiddled with his pen. "How did you find out?"

She'd expected this question the night before. She didn't want her son dragged into this, but she doubted if she was practiced enough to hide the truth. "I'm the only one you have to worry about."

He looked relieved. He also looked at her in a way she might have described as longingly. She felt an answering longing within herself and brushed it aside.

"So," he said, "do you plan to check up on me every day?"

"Do I need to?"

He smiled again. "No. But I'd like it if you did."

She did check up on him every day, but it began to seem like a private game between them. Jordan liked that. He liked seeing her every day.

His nightly prayer was less grudging as the days went by. It was sometimes followed by moments of a feeling that was hard to label, until he heard one of the unavoidable Christmas carols on the radio one day. One of the ones that mentioned peace. That's how he felt sometimes. Peaceful, even in the middle of all this turmoil over the mill and his own precarious business dealings.

Once, he even thought of doing as Joella suggested and starting his day with a prayer, as well.

He resisted going that far.

One day, as she was leaving, he asked if he could take her and Nathan to buy a Christmas tree. She agreed, but when he arrived that Saturday afternoon, she wouldn't let him take her to any of the lots in the next city. They ended up on Lyle Exley's farm, ax and saw in hand.

"This is crazy," he said as they tramped through the woods. Crazy as it was, compelled as he was to protest, he was exhilarated by being here with Joella and Nathan. "They have trees ready to decorate not twenty minutes from here."

"They're expensive," she protested.

"I have money."

"You have two good hands and a strong pair of shoulders, too."

"You noticed." He felt elated.

She glanced at him. Her cheeks grew pinker. "Besides, this is more fun."

He thought about telling her that he still loved her, even if she didn't want to hear it. He thought about telling her how he felt sometimes after he prayed, but he couldn't talk about it. Not even to Joella. All he could do was look at her in her soft, faded jeans and her corduroy coat and her baseball cap and realize that he'd come to think of her as the most beautiful woman in the world.

He couldn't talk about that, either.

"Hey, Mom! Look at this one!"

Nathan waved them toward a clearing. His nose was red from the cold, and no matter how often

Joella pulled his stocking cap back over his unruly brown hair, it always ended up stuffed into the back pocket of his jeans.

"This one's perfect," he said, pointing to a big, round twelve-foot tree that would require moving every bit of furniture out of their tiny living room.

"That's way too big for our house, Nathan."

"Aw, Mom."

"How about this one?" She pointed instead to a slim tree with tiny little cones on the ends of its branches. "It'll fit perfectly in the corner by the window."

"But, Mom, this is the only Christmas tree we'll have this year, cause there won't be one on Main Street. So it's gotta be a big one. It's just *gotta* be."

"First you've *gotta* have a room big enough for it, son. And I don't know of a house in Bethlehem big enough to hold that tree." She glanced at Jordan. "Well, I do know of one house big enough."

And that's how Jordan found himself chopping down two evergreens, a slim one with tiny cones for the living room at the Ratchford house and a big, round one with a trunk that should have required a lumberjack's license for his own living room. The smile on Nathan's face would be worth the sore shoulders.

What he hadn't counted on was Nathan's insistence that he get to help decorate the tree at Jordan's house.

In fact, Jordan hadn't actually intended to decorate the tree at all. He'd envisioned propping the tree against the gardener's shed behind the house. He'd never had a Christmas tree. He didn't intend to start this year. But he hadn't counted on the persuasiveness of a seven-year-old.

The only way out of having a Christmas tree twinkling merrily in the corner of his own living room was a compromise that ended up delighting Nathan.

"How about this instead?" he said as they set up one of the trees in the corner of Joella's living room. "We'll set up the big tree on Main Street. We could decorate it for the entire town."

Nathan looked skeptical. "But we got it for you."

"Let me do this," Jordan said. "To make it up to everybody in town."

As Nathan mulled over the proposition, Jordan realized that he meant it, too. It wasn't just a way to get Nathan to give in, it was what he wanted to do, deep in his heart. That kind of unprovoked altruism gave him pause, almost made him want to back down.

But Nathan agreed and that afternoon, after he'd dragged a dusty box of decorations down from the attic, bought holiday sugar cookies from the supermarket and made up a thermos of mulled cider the way Grace always had when he was a child, he met Joella and Nathan back on Main Street.

"This is so cool," Nathan was saying as they unboxed the strings of lights that Jordan remembered from his childhood. "It'll be almost like we're having Christmas in town after all."

Jordan glanced at Joella. She looked so grateful for her son's enthusiasm.

By the time they had the lights wound around the tree—a strategic operation masterminded by Nathan, who knew far more about tree decorating than Jordan did—they had attracted a crowd.

Claire and her sons brought a box of glittery bells to hang on the tree. "Mind if we join you?" she asked.

Jordan felt awkward at first, but her bright smile assured him that this friend of Joella wasn't holding any grudges. At least at the moment.

"Christmas trees work wonders," Joella whispered as he stepped back to watch the family now swarming around the evergreen with Nathan.

Hat Martin came next, an angel wrapped in tissue in his hands. "This usually goes on top of the tree at the church," he said. "But I thought more people would enjoy it this way. If that's all right with you folks."

As the sun went down, someone opened the diner and started dispensing hot chocolate, its sweet aroma filling the air. A garland of popcorn and cranberries contributed by the manager of the pharmacy was laced around the branches.

As the crowd grew from a half dozen to half the town, Jordan slipped off to the side. Surely someone would point a finger and protest Scrooge's right to join in the festivities. He didn't want to spoil things with his presence. But he couldn't quite bring himself to leave. He told himself they wouldn't notice him. He hung on the fringes of the crowd, feeling left out and certain he deserved it.

Even from the sidelines, he began to enjoy the look of pleasure on the faces of the townspeople, the sounds of their laughter. No one said a cross word to him, even when Randy, the Down's syndrome worker from the mill, came up and took him by the hand.

"You have to help, too," Randy said, tugging him back into the center of the festive group. "Everybody has to help."

"You're right, Randy," Joella said, thrusting a silver star into Jordan's hand.

Jordan stared at the shiny ornament. With a sense of awe that these people were still willing to welcome him to their festivities, he found the perfect spot on the tree for the silver star.

And when someone started a spirited version of "The First Noel," he discovered that their voices touched him, bringing out that peace he'd experienced in fits and snatches over the past few days. By the time they joined hands in "O Little Town of Bethlehem," he willingly, gladly, took Joella's hand in his left and Hat Martin's hand in his right and became part of the circle.

He couldn't sing, for there was a tightness in his throat that wouldn't go away. But the spirit of community and the singing filled him nevertheless and he found his heart whispering a silent "Thank you"—to whom, he wasn't certain.

Jordan rode that spirit the rest of the weekend. He took Joella and Nathan to Sunday dinner at a nice restaurant in Columbus. They window-shopped at the mall afterward and Jordan spotted the computer Nathan coveted, and had visions of his own about the night before Christmas.

"I could help," he said to Joella as they went back to the car, Nathan flying ahead of them as usual. "With his Christmas, I mean. The computer. He really should—"

"Absolutely not." She shook her head with determination.

"But..."

"You're wasting your breath, Jordan."

He decided not to waste his breath, but he didn't give up the idea.

Before they got in the car, while Nathan wasn't looking, Jordan took Joella's hand in his and kissed her fingers. She grew very still and her eyes closed momentarily. She slipped her hand out of his and stuck it in her pocket, but Jordan carried the warmth with him all the way home.

The spirit didn't leave him until he arrived at work on Monday morning and saw Venita's face. She was hanging up the phone, slowly. She looked like someone who had just heard the news of a death.

"That was the state auditor's office," she said. "If we can't account for the retirement money, they'll file charges. We've got until December 24."

Chapter Twelve

While the rest of the town counted the days until Christmas, Jordan ticked off the hours until Christmas Eve. Qualms mushroomed into foreboding with each new sunrise.

"You're worried," Joella said to him one night a week before Christmas.

They were walking to the elementary school for the annual Christmas pageant. Nathan was a shepherd, and greatly miffed because no one had been able to see that he was so clearly better suited to play one of the Three Wise Men.

"Everything's under control," Jordan lied, and felt uneasy with the deception. Deception was as much a part of big business as cell phones in the circles in which he ran. But he couldn't seem to handle it anymore. He was losing his edge.

"*Your* control, I suppose?"

"Who else?"

She smiled. "Aren't you asking every day for God to work things out?"

He frowned. He wanted to tell her that God hadn't come up with a single extra penny in the week he'd been praying. Neither had God given him any brilliant ideas for saving his father and his uncle. The only stroke of inspiration he'd had was the bit of creative bookkeeping he'd finally figured out that would dictate who the auditors would find naughty or nice.

Of course, his choices for where to point the finger were limited. There was himself. Or…himself.

Ever since the day he'd doctored the books, he'd barely been able to breathe.

"I'm asking," he said tightly. "But I'm not getting any answers."

And in the meantime, harsh reality drew closer every day. The closer the day of reckoning came, the more shape the idea of prison took on. The fuzzy edges of his nightmares were coming into focus and he could barely stomach what he was seeing. In the abstract, doing the right thing had a noble ring to it. But in living, breathing color…

Jordan's stomach took a nasty turn.

He had no choice. He breathed deeply against the churning inside him. After all, what was the alternative? Could he for one minute let it come out that his father and his uncle had taken the company's retirement money? Could he let them fall from grace in a town where they were so loved? Of course not. So for once in his life, he had to do something noble.

And who knows. Maybe it was his just deserts. After all, over the past decade he'd done plenty in the name of profit that could have landed him in hot water, and never once been caught.

If justice was God's idea of a solution, Jordan wasn't crazy about it.

"Are you okay?" Joella put a hand on his arm. "You look a little pale."

Her touch calmed him. He closed his eyes for a moment and tried not to think of the other payoff for doing the right thing. Not only would he be in prison, but Joella and her son would believe, as everyone else would, the worst about him. That hurt.

"I'm great," he said. "Just great."

"Be patient," Joella said as they slipped into seats near the front of the stage.

"If you're getting ready to tell me God works in mysterious ways, you can save your breath," Jordan said.

Joella laughed. He liked that about her. He'd somehow had the impression that people who believed in God had checked their sense of humor at the door of the church. Not Joella. And for all Jordan knew, God was laughing right now, too. At Jordan, who was sitting pretty for his comeuppance.

The Christmas pageant was delightful, charming enough even to dispel Jordan's pessimistic mood.

He'd seen Broadway musicals and Shakespeare performed at the newly reconstructed Globe Theatre in London. But nothing had caught him up and transported him the way these pint-size herald angels and a Virgin Mary missing her front tooth did.

"You were right," he told Nathan as the three of them walked home. "You were wasted as a shepherd."

"Yeah. You know they got Samantha Fletcher to carry the frankincense. A *girl*." He had clearly never been so outraged in his life. "The Bible didn't call them the Three Wise *People,* you know."

Nathan groused all the way home and Jordan marveled at the gentle way his mother both soothed him and reminded him that he wasn't the center of everyone's life. "Maybe God wanted you to learn a little humility," she suggested.

The loving admonition struck a nerve with Jordan. Maybe Joella's God had the same thing in mind for him. It also occurred to him that this God he'd been praying to might be more than Joella's God.

This might be Jordan's God, too.

The notion shook him. He missed most of the rest of the conversation between mother and son, absorbed in the awesome idea that the God Joella and Nathan and so many others prayed to might have room for Jordan, as well .

Nevertheless, by the time they scooted through the front door of the Ratchford home, Nathan was laughing and telling them stories about the funny mishaps that had gone on backstage during the pageant. While Nathan got ready for bed, Jordan wanted to take Joella's hand and tell her what a wonderful mother she was. He wanted to hold her close. He wanted to kiss her good-night. But he didn't do any of those things.

"He's a good boy," he said, accepting the cup of cider she handed him. Its warmth was a poor substitute for what he wanted, needed. But keeping a physical distance from Joella was surely one more thing he could do just because he knew it was right.

"He's the best." Her eyes clouded, something he rarely saw.

"What's wrong?"

She shook her head. "Nothing. Sometimes I think I'll never be able to keep up with him. I worry that he won't have everything he needs because…"

The lights from the Christmas tree in the corner blinked on and off, casting light on her dark hair. He longed to touch her hair where it glimmered, went dark again, then shone again. He longed to kiss the lower lip she bit into in the midst of her worry. He made himself listen to her worries instead. "You think he needs advantages."

She nodded. "He's so bright," Joella said. "He should go to good schools and have plenty of books to read and…everything."

He thought about the computer he'd bought. He hadn't yet figured out how he was going to get her to take it. If it came directly from him, she might turn it down.

Maybe he could enlist Venita's help.

"He has you for a mother," he said. "That puts him light-years ahead of all the other kids."

"I'm immune to flattery, Jordan Scoville."

She was immune to everything he had to offer, he thought as he made his way home, and he ought to be glad. When Bethlehem shut down, she would move on, get a better job, find a good man. Good husband material. Good stepfather material. Nathan would have brothers and sisters and plenty of presents under the tree in years to come.

The very idea made him miserable because he knew he wasn't part of that happy picture. More miserable than the idea that he might be spending those same years behind bars.

Still, better him than Mitchell and Truman. Prison would kill them.

Seeing him in prison might kill them, too.

Sometimes he was almost glad to leave this in the hands of God; it was too much for him to go around and around with, too much for him to try to figure out. God was welcome to it.

By the next day, things had gone from bad to worse.

The state auditors had sent a list of the documents they wanted to see prior to their December 24 visit.

Venita looked at him with sympathy and foreboding as she passed the list to him.

"We're sunk, aren't we?" he asked.

"Unless you've got a few spare millions stashed under your mattress."

That was blow number one. Next, his partner called with another message of gloom and doom. Their deal with the NFL was going sour.

"They're looking at Omaha, if you can believe that," Les said. "And we're looking at a thousand acres of red clay and kudzu, unless we wise up."

Jordan could see it coming. The NFL would pick the frozen Midwest, and all his capital would be tied up in south Georgia farmland. He would lose everything, including the chance to leave his father and his uncle living comfortably while he made license plates. He wouldn't even have a company for Venita to run. Another wish thrown in his face. The worst of it was, even if everything worked out perfectly and nobody ended up in prison and Jordan didn't lose his shirt, the upshot would be that he would soon be back in his familiar old world.

Alone.

No Joella, no Nathan. But alone. He couldn't imagine leaving them behind, but he knew good and well that Joella had no intention of living in, raising her son in, Jordan's familiar old world. Who could blame her?

Work it out, God. Isn't it time for You to get in gear?

Finding himself talking to God in the middle of the day irritated him further.

He reminded himself he was talking to his partner, not the man upstairs. He repeated Les's last words. "Wise up?"

Les then brought up his usual solution to a tricky business problem that couldn't be resolved any other way. "It's time to oil the machinery a little, wouldn't you say?"

Jordan knew exactly what Les meant. The two of them had been doing business this way for years. Courting clients with booze and friendly women. Spending money freely to generate goodwill, and when goodwill alone wouldn't do it, cold hard cash often turned out to be the best lubricant of all.

Smart business, Jordan had always said.

Today it sounded like bribery.

So this was who he'd really been all these years when he'd thought he was so important. He tried to imagine explaining all this to Joella, asking her to accept that life-style. His stomach felt queasy. Oh, well, he was going to have worse than that to explain to Joella and to the state auditors and to everyone else in Bethlehem.

"I don't think so," he heard himself say to Les.

"What? What do you mean, you don't think so?"

Jordan didn't know what he meant. This wasn't what he'd intended to say, but it was what was coming out of his mouth. "I mean, if this is supposed to work out, it'll work out without paying anybody off.''

Was this God kicking in? he wondered. If so, this wasn't exactly what Jordan had in mind. It was becoming clear that God's will had something to do with Jordan Scoville taking a big tumble.

Merry Christmas, Jordie. There'll be a pair of handcuffs under the tree for you this year.

He tried to imagine the look on his father's face, on Uncle Truman's. On Nathan's face. At least Nathan would have his computer. Venita had agreed to take care of that, no matter what.

That still left Joella. He wondered what kind of presents she would find under the tree on Christmas morning, and knew somehow that she was counting on him to deliver what she really wanted. The security of her hometown, with a happy ending for everybody.

He would have to disappoint her.

Joella tried to be content with the way things were working out.

She sat on the floor in the living room with brightly colored paper and bows and a jumbo roll of tape spread around her knees. Nathan was in Spartanburg at the movies with Claire and her kids, so she could play Santa undisturbed.

She had the radio tuned to a station playing Christmas carols, but she couldn't quite work up the enthusiasm to sing along. She hadn't even plugged in the lights on the tree.

Christmas was less than a week away. Her meager shopping was done. She just had to finish wrapping things for her mother, her brother and for Nathan. She stared at the largest box. She still didn't feel quite right about the offer Venita had made to her the day before. If Scoville Mill had an extra computer, shouldn't it be sold along with everything else instead of ending up under her tree for her son? Venita had said it was too outdated to sell and Joella had no reason to doubt that.

But the box it was in looked so new.

She wrapped the box anyway, in a roll of bright red foil she'd found for a quarter at a yard sale last April, and hoped she wasn't being selfish in wanting her son to have something special.

His last Christmas in Bethlehem would be a good one, as she'd promised herself it would.

And things were working out for after Christmas, as well. She'd done as Claire suggested and spent a day in Spartanburg looking for work. She could start in January in a real estate office, answering the phone. She'd never done that kind of work before and she didn't have the right clothes for it, but everyone assured her she could do it. And the woman who owned the company said she might want to take the real estate course at the local technical college. She could get her license, the woman said.

A tear trickled down her cheek, falling with a soft splat onto the package she wrapped. She blotted up the tear and stuck a bow over the damp spot. All of it sounded scary. So she did what she always told Nathan to do about things that sounded scary.

"God," she said, pausing to gain control of her voice. "I know I'm in Your hands. I know *all* of it's in Your hands. Please help me to live in faith today instead of fear. Help me to remember that it's all going to work out."

All of it except what was in her heart.

What was really dragging her down, what was really keeping the spirit of Christmas out of her heart, was the way she kept worrying about Jordan. What would happen to him if the missing retirement money didn't make a reappearance? Would he, as Nathan had said, end up in prison?

Even if all that worked out, wouldn't he just go back to Atlanta and be the same unhappy man who had driven into Bethlehem a month ago?

She stowed the wrapped presents under her bed, except for the computer, which was too big even for her closet and had to go into the laundry room on top of the dryer. She locked the laundry-room door, tidied up the scraps of paper and bows and ribbon on the floor and plugged in the tree in preparation for Nathan's return. She stared at it halfheartedly as the lights began to twinkle.

She remembered the fun the three of them had had, decorating the tree. Jordan had never strung cranberries and popcorn and Nathan had felt so important showing him how it was done, correcting his technique and giving him advice on how to work faster. Jordan had taken it all with a smile. If she could trust the look on his face, he thought almost as much of her son as she did.

If she could trust his face. Wasn't that the key to the whole thing? Wasn't she making the same mistake all over again, trusting a man with a bankbook where his heart should have been?

If only trusting him were her only crime.

Sometimes Joella feared she cared about him too much. Sometimes...

She couldn't let herself go there. She'd been that route with Andrew and look where it had gotten her. If God was testing her to see if she'd learned anything from her experiences with Andrew, she was certainly failing the test.

Glancing at the clock, she realized Nathan wasn't due home for another hour. An hour she didn't really want to be here alone with her thoughts. She grabbed her parka and headed out for a walk. The day had been sunny, although the sun was about to dip below the trees. But the weather was still mild enough for a walk, and anything was better than sitting home and brooding.

The streets of Bethlehem already had a deserted look to them, although she supposed that had to do with the fact that very few families had decorated for the holidays. So with the bare trees, the lowering darkness and the sparsity of festivity, Bethlehem seemed barren. Still, she took comfort in the familiar houses, in the occasional wreath on a front door, in the Christmas-tree lights that blinked at her from windows up and down the streets.

As she turned onto Main Street, she heard voices raised in song and smiled.

Since the tree had gone up on Main Street, people had started gathering around it at dusk to sing carols. No one had organized it. But the community spirit that had been generated that night had apparently felt so special, so powerful that people couldn't stay away. Each night as the sun went down, people trickled in. Songs were sung. Some nights, coffee or cider or hot chocolate were passed around.

Joella walked in that direction. Tonight's crowd was a big one. They were singing ''Silent Night.'' She began to hum as she approached. She was about to sing when she noticed Jordan, standing on the fringes of the circle. She hesitated, then walked up to him.

''We could join them,'' she said.

He looked reluctant. ''You belong. I don't.''

''You're the only one who doesn't think you belong.''

He seemed to think about that, then extended a hand to her in invitation. She wanted to take his hand so badly that she held back, but only a moment. She let him enfold her hand in his and they walked to the edge of the group.

His hand was big and warm and his hesitant baritone made her feel breathless. Why did she have to like his presence so terribly much? Of all men, why him?

They sang until it was fully dark. Then the townspeople headed back to their homes, the visitors back across the highway to their tents and campers. Joella's heart was full by the time the group dispersed, with shouts of "Merry Christmas" ringing in the air. She ignored the talk she heard in passing, more fanciful discussion of the villagers buying the mill. She didn't want to hear it, didn't want her mood spoiled. The villagers buying the mill was as much a daydream as her living happily ever after with Jordan Scoville. And Joella had to keep her feet on the ground.

"This is nice," she said to Jordan, who didn't leave her side as the crowd broke up. "Maybe nicer than all the big, elaborate stuff we've done in the past."

"You always do that, don't you? See the best in everything."

"Not always," she admitted. "But I try. Isn't it better than only seeing the worst?"

"I don't know, I—"

"Joella!"

She turned toward the sound of Claire's voice. Her friend was walking toward her, her two sons in tow. Where was Nathan?

"We got back just in time for the singing," Claire said.

"Was the movie good?" Joella asked, looking over Claire's shoulder.

"Well, they loved it." Claire nodded toward her sons. "Too bad Nathan couldn't go this time."

Joella felt the warmth around her heart turn to a cold chill. "What?"

Claire gave her an odd look. "I said— Joella, what is it? You didn't think Nathan was with us, did you?" She clutched Joella's arm. "Please say you didn't think that."

Jordan moved closer. "Joella?"

Joella put her hand over her mouth to hold in the cry that threatened to spill out. She tried to remember what time her son had left the house. How many hours had it been? How long had her son been missing?

Chapter Thirteen

The officers from the county sheriff's department kept telling them that there was little point in trying to search for a small boy in the dark.

"Wait till daylight," the sheriff had urged the people of Bethlehem. "Let's take time to get this thing organized and we'll go out at first light."

Nobody had paid attention but his deputies, and for that Joella was grateful. A massive search was underway.

She sat on the bench in front of the laundromat on Main Street, trembling and wondering why she couldn't get warm even wearing Jordan's cashmere overcoat over her parka. Claire kept telling her she should go home, she should get in out of the cold. But Joella couldn't move.

"I have to stay here," she murmured to her worried friend. "He'll be back soon and I want to see him as soon as he gets to town. I have to be here."

As soon as the crowd of carolers realized that Nathan had been missing since noon, they rallied around to see how they could help. And somehow word spread and the crowd had doubled, tripled in size. Townspeople and visitors came with flashlights and hot coffee and words of encouragement.

"We all know Nathan," one of the visitors said softly, patting Joella's hand. "He's a fine boy and we're not about to let anything happen to him. We'll find him. Don't you doubt that."

Joella had nodded, numbness overtaking her little by little. She racked her mind for words to pray, but she couldn't think. Her entire being was made up of fear. There was room for nothing else, not awareness of the cold, not faith, not even a coherent thought. All she knew was Nathan's face and the ice-cold dread that filled her.

Bethlehem's Main Street hadn't been so busy at this time of night in longer than she could remember. Even Mr. Mitchell and Mr. Truman came out to make sure that the sheriff understood the importance of this small boy. Venita came back after two hours, so hoarse from calling his name that she could barely talk.

"He'll turn up, Joella," Venita said, sitting close to her on the bench and draping an arm around her slumped shoulders. "Don't give up hope. Don't ever do that."

Joella shivered. Something had to be wrong. He would come if Venita called him. She knew he would.

Claire came to hover again. She tried, but couldn't hide the fact that her eyes were as wildly frantic as if the missing boy were one of her own. "What can I get you?"

My son. "Jordan. Where's Jordan?"

"I'll find out."

He was by her side in minutes. His shoes were caked with mud. Joella stared up at him, beseeching him wordlessly, barely noticing when Venita relinquished her place on the bench. Jordan slipped into place beside her. His arm around her shoulders imparted more comfort than Venita's had, and Joella didn't even have the wherewithal to feel guilty about that.

"I just made the rounds of all the checkpoints," he said. "We've got people stationed along the highway, at the edge of the woods, by the river."

"By the river." She hadn't thought of the river. She closed her eyes and choked back the sob of terror that rose in her chest. "He can't swim, you know."

"Then he's not likely to go to the river, is he? He's a smart boy, Joella. He—"

"That's my fault. I'm afraid of the water."

"I didn't know you were afraid of anything," he murmured, pulling her cheek against his chest.

She whimpered and was grateful there was no one

but Jordan to hear her. "I'm afraid of losing my boy." Her voice cracked.

"You're not going to lose Nathan. I promise."

She liked hearing the promise, even though the part of her brain that could still work knew that Jordan had no more control over what happened to her son than she did for the moment. "Jordan, I can't... I can't think...can't remember how to pray for him. I want to, but...it's like I'm afraid to even say the words out loud, even to God."

There was a long silence and Joella listened to the crackle of scanners from the sheriff's patrol cars and the hum of people.

"I could do it for you," Jordan said softly.

Joella thought she might cry. "Could you do that?"

"Sure." Then he took her hands in his and prayed for her son, the way she'd taught him to, asking for God's will.

"God, please take care of Nathan tonight. We all love him and we're—" His voice broke. There was a pause, then he started again. "We're scared for him and we'll all feel better knowing You're with him, keeping an eye on him doing Your will. And please help us be strong while we look for Nathan. Amen."

His voice was deep and commanding, surely a voice God would hear no matter how many other voices were clamoring for attention, Joella thought, even though his voice had trembled when he'd spoken her son's name. The tears she'd been able to contain so far began to spill down her cheeks as she heard this man who barely believed asking God to help her son.

Surely that was a miracle in itself. And if God could work that miracle...

When Jordan finished asking God for help, Joella opened her eyes and saw a big gunmetal gray car gliding down Main Street and stopping at the knot of people. Joella held her breath. The passenger door opened and Nathan stepped out, looking discouraged and tired.

"Nathan!"

Joella found her legs then. She ran to her son and wrapped him in her arms. She'd never noticed how frail a seven-year-old felt. He didn't even squirm in her embrace. He slumped against her and wrapped his arms around her neck. Joella whispered a prayer of thanks, but couldn't let go of her son.

What a chump. That's what everybody had to be thinking, Nathan told himself as he walked home, his mom on one side and Jordan on the other. What a major league dope ol' Nathan must be.

Things in Charlotte hadn't turned out exactly the way he'd had them planned. He'd ridden the bus in just the way he'd planned. No problemo. But once he'd stepped off the bus in Charlotte, things started getting short-circuited.

He had his map, of course. And the bus station

wasn't too far from Deadbeat Dad's office. But Nathan had learned that what looked like a pretty short distance on a map could take a little longer to negotiate on foot. And some of the streets around the bus station were a little scary. Guys that didn't smell so hot gave him funny looks. One followed him for a block, mumbling stuff Nathan couldn't understand. That's when Nathan started wondering what would happen to his mom if he didn't make it home. Then she'd have nobody to move to Spartanburg with. She'd be all alone.

Swell.

Anyway, when he finally found the building, things didn't go so hot there, either. There was a guard in the lobby, wearing a gun and everything, and he wouldn't even let Nathan on the elevator until Nathan told him who he was going to see.

Nathan knew then that he might run into some problems. If the old Deadbeat Dad wouldn't answer his son's E-mail, why would he let him come up on the elevator, either?

But even his old man apparently had that much conscience. He'd told Barney Fife to send Nathan up. The elevator was all chrome and mirrors inside, and it made Nathan feel just a little bit throw-uppy when it zoomed up to the forty-second floor.

It was nothing compared to how throw-uppy he felt when the elevator door whooshed open and this man in a pin-striped suit stood there staring at Nathan with the baddest-to-the-bone expression Nathan had ever seen in his life.

"Dad?"

The man put his hand on Nathan's shoulder and dragged him away from the lobby, where people were staring, into a private office so he could chew him out without any witnesses. By that time, Nathan had figured out there would be no mushy, tearful reunion between clever son and remorseful father.

And he was right. There wasn't.

The worst of it, though, was that his own father had tickets for something called *The Nutcracker* and he refused to have his life disrupted by a youngster who needed more supervision than he was getting. So he sent Nathan—his very own kid that he ought to be touched and heartbroken to see, if you could trust made-for-TV movies, which you obviously couldn't—home in a company car driven by one of his flunkies.

Nathan hoped he never saw his father again.

Jordan stood outside Nathan's bedroom, watching as Joella tucked her son into bed. She'd seemed so fragile earlier, as if she might collapse any moment. She'd looked stronger the minute Nathan stepped out of the car, but before he left her alone he wanted to assure himself that she was okay.

He kept thinking of the way she'd asked him to pray for her son, when she couldn't, and how Nathan had materialized the minute he'd finished his awkward appeal. It was enough to make him believe that somebody was up there looking out for him. Or, if not for him, at least for people like Joella and Nathan Ratchford.

He felt his heart swell, that he'd been given the gift of knowing them, of being taken into their hearts.

"He's a real creep," Nathan was mumbling. "And he's fat, too. He wasn't fat before, was he, Mom?"

Jordan smiled. Maybe there was some justice in the world.

"No, Nathan, he wasn't overweight."

"I bet he was still a creep, though, wasn't he?"

Jordan watched, fascinated, as Joella brushed Nathan's hair off his forehead. The touch was soft, gentle, a whisper of motherly love.

"We can't always understand what's in another person's heart, Nathan," she said. "He must be a sad, miserable person if he can't even find joy in his own son. Just think how sad and miserable we'd be if we didn't have each other to love, how much happiness we'd be missing."

"He yelled at me and his face got all red and bulged out over his tie and I thought maybe he'd have a heart attack." Nathan's voice grew very small. "For one minute I *hoped* he'd have a heart attack."

"But you know it will only make you cold and

sad inside if you start to hate him. Then you'd be just like him. You know that, don't you?''

Jordan felt the weight of that insight. That's exactly what he'd been like, cold and sad inside because he'd allowed himself to hate this town. He wondered if the way he felt right now meant he was no longer that cold, sad person. If it was true, if he'd changed, he owed it all to Joella and Nathan.

And to God, came a quiet voice in his heart.

Nathan sounded skeptical when he spoke again. ''You think we ought to feel sorry for him?''

''I think we ought to try not to judge him or hate him or let him hurt us. Because we still have each other, and he doesn't have anything but money and power. And it doesn't seem to be making him very happy.''

At that, Jordan flinched. Put that way, he and the man Nathan had labeled a creep had a lot in common. In fact, a month ago, Jordan would probably have handled the situation exactly the way Andrew Ratchford had. The realization made him feel very small, and very lucky that he didn't have to be that way again.

He listened as Joella urged her son to pray for his father, to ask God to hold him and care for him. Then she kissed him good-night and turned off the bedroom light. Jordan walked with her out to the living room. He put an arm around her shoulders. He questioned his right to do so, but he felt her trembling and knew she needed the support.

''I don't know how you can be that charitable,''

he said, looking into her eyes. "I'm ready to kill the sorry—"

She smiled and put her finger to his lips. "It isn't that I'm charitable. It's just that I don't want Nathan growing up feeling bitter, or thinking that it's him, that somehow he's lacking."

He pulled her close and held her tightly against him; her head tucked perfectly under his chin. He thought nothing could go wrong if he could just manage to hold her like this for a while. A very long while. "You're very wise with him."

"I'm not so wise," she said. "I just ask God for the right words and then trust that I'll be given what I need."

He kissed her forehead, then the corner of each eye, followed by each cheek. He wanted to cover her soft, sweet lips with his. But he knew sweet kisses weren't what she needed right now, when she was already confused and distressed.

On his walk home, Jordan thought about what she'd said, about asking God for the right words to help her son. He found himself wishing that God could work through him the way God could apparently work through Joella to comfort a little boy like Nathan. If God could work through him, maybe he could save his father and his uncle from ruin and shame. Maybe, if there was a God to help him, he could save this town.

Maybe, with that kind of help, he could even save himself from ending up like Nathan's father.

* * *

Joella wrapped a newspaper page around one of Claire's plates and nestled it into the box with the rest. Claire planned to move the day after Christmas—now just days away—and they were finishing the last of the packing. The boys were at the school playground playing ball.

"Don't look so gloomy, Jo." Claire was passing glasses down from the cabinet so they could be packed next. "It's a new beginning. That can be exciting. That's how I'm trying to look at it."

Joella set the glasses in a neat row on the empty countertop. "I know. I know I have a lot to be grateful for."

She thought about the way God had brought Nathan safely home from Charlotte and knew it was true.

"Sure we do. We're young. We've got our kids. And you've got a great job waiting for you. Real estate. Do you know how much money you could make in real estate?"

"I don't care how much money I can make. Money can't—"

"Buy happiness," Claire finished for her, jumping off the counter after clearing out the top cabinet shelf. "I know. You've told me. Look at Jordan Scoville. See, I've got it memorized."

Joella turned away, shuffled through the stack of newspapers to give herself time to compose her expression. Claire was studying her when she turned back.

"What is it, Jo?"

Joella felt her lower lip tremble, but it was too late to turn her back on her friend again. Claire dropped her section of newspaper and put a hand on Joella's wrist.

"Come on, tell."

With the palm of her hand Joella blotted the tears gathering in her eyes. "Oh, Claire, I've messed up something awful."

Claire led them to the kitchen chairs and clasped Joella's hands across the table. "I'm listening."

"I thought I was too smart for this. And now I've made the same mistake all over again."

"You're scaring me, girl. What are you talking about?"

Joella steadied herself with a long, deep breath. "I've let myself fall in love with Jordan Scoville."

"Oh, honey."

The tone of her best friend's voice said it all. *You poor sap.*

"I don't know how this happened to me. It's just like Andrew all over again."

"Is it?"

"Well, sure it is. He's rich. He's heartless." Even as she said it, she knew that wasn't true. "He's got a credit limit in place of his soul."

"Does he?"

Joella jumped up and reached for a paper towel to wipe away the tears that were flowing freely now. "You've seen what he's done since he's been here."

"But you said—"

"I'm a dope. I fell for it all. Just the way I did with Andrew. He's going to bleed this town dry, then hotfoot it back to Atlanta and I'll never see him again and Nathan's going to be hurt all over again and… And it's all my fault."

"Now, Jo, you don't know any of that, do you?"

"Don't I?" She gave Claire a challenging look and felt justified when her friend shrugged.

"Well, sure, the odds are good that's exactly the way it's going to happen."

"Umm-hmm."

"But you don't know for sure what God has in mind, now, do you?"

Joella didn't want to be encouraged in that kind of wishful thinking. Wishful thinking had gotten her and Nathan where they were, which was about one week away from heartbreak. "I'm not looking for any miracles, Claire."

It was nothing short of a miracle.

That's all Jordan could think as he sat at the desk in the familiar old office at Scoville Mill and stared at the old inkwell he knew his mother had given his father for their first wedding anniversary.

A miracle.

"You're sure about this?" he said to his partner.

"Am I sure?" Les laughed. "Get yourself here. Tonight. We've got papers to sign. And celebrating to do."

The line went dead and Jordan replaced the receiver gently, as if afraid of waking himself from a dream. Two days ago the widow had signed. All the land was theirs. This morning—months earlier than expected—the National Football League had announced it would expand into south Georgia. Jordan Scoville was part owner of the land where a new NFL stadium—not to mention a minivillage of restaurants and hotels and nightspots and an amusement park—would spring up over the next two years before the first kickoff.

Jordan Scoville would soon be a multimillionaire. Right now he was still cash poor, his money tied up in land. Sure, he could convert the land to cash in a heartbeat. Les no doubt knew plenty of people who would like to buy into this sweet deal. But if Jordan held on, the land would be a gold mine over the next two years.

He would soon be rich beyond his wildest dreams.

And all of it had fallen into place in a matter of hours. Almost as if, Jordan thought, some guardian angel had decided to take a hand in working things out.

Not that God cared whether Jordan Scoville was filthy rich or not. Not that God had any notions about using a professional football team to achieve anything good in the world. No, prayers or no prayers, God had no hand in any of this.

Did He?

Chapter Fourteen

Jordan let his fingers trail along the edges of the picture frames on the library table in the parlor of the big, dark house where he'd grown up.

"What are you going to do, Jordie?" Venita's voice demanded an answer, and the right answer, now.

The house was empty today, and Jordan wasn't entirely sure why he'd come. He had this foolish notion about connecting with his mother, as if that might make the decisions he had to make easier. He'd wanted to be here alone and had known that would be possible because Mitchell and Truman were at the holiday luncheon at their club, a luncheon they'd invited him to attend. He could still see their disappointed faces when he'd held fast to his refusal.

He wasn't feeling festive.

He'd signed all the papers. He'd put on a good show of celebrating with his partner two nights earlier. But he hadn't felt festive then and he wasn't feeling festive now. He was feeling hollow. Empty. Disgruntled.

This wasn't the way you were supposed to feel when your dreams came true. He knew that.

Even Les had noticed his strange mood. When he'd prodded, Les had been stunned by Jordan's response.

"Do I know anybody who'd buy your share? Are you nuts! You don't want to bail out *now!*"

"Just asking," Jordan had said testily, refusing to meet Les's eyes.

"Sure, you could get a few million for your share now—easily. But in a few years we'll be worth more than a few million. You'd be crazy to bail out now. You know that, don't you, Scoville?"

"Sure, Les. Of course."

At this moment, Jordan wished he hadn't even voiced the question out loud. It made it real. The idea of selling out—and using his investment elsewhere—wouldn't let go of him. And it wasn't making him happy.

Venita cleared her throat, reminding him of her presence and her need for an answer. She had come looking for him with news that the auditors would be delayed until the afternoon of the twenty-fourth. But they hoped—insisted, really—that Jordan would call before then to explain why the documents they'd requested hadn't been delivered. They wanted answers. The only answer Jordan had was that he hadn't yet had the courage to deliver the documents that would implicate him once and for all.

"What can I do, Venita?" He turned it back to her.

Her silence screamed at him. He stiffened his back. He shouldn't have told her about his deal going through. She didn't understand that he didn't have any ready cash on hand. Besides, he could hardly take his own money to cover somebody else's mistakes. Could he? Nobody would expect him to do that. Would they?

Even God couldn't have had that in mind.

"Is the money that important, Jordie?"

"I'd be broke. Ruined."

"Like Mr. Mitchell and Mr. Truman, you mean?"

The dry disapproval in her voice ate at him. Guilt raised nagging questions in his mind. What would Eugenia do? What would Joella do? It was clear what Venita would do. At least, theoretically. Thinking theoretically was a lot easier than getting down to brass tacks, he'd discovered.

"Listen," he said, hoping to appeal to Venita's reasonable nature, "I've been talking to my attorney. He says nobody's going to lock up anybody their age. The worst that will happen is that everything will be liquidated to—"

"The worst that will happen is that two dear, kind

men will end their lives in disgrace, when all they've ever wanted was to do right by everyone.''

What was it Nathan had called his father? A creep? If the shoe fits… ''Venita—''

''I thought they'd taught you that, too. I was obviously mistaken.''

She leveled one final, searing look on him and left. The heavy front door closed with a hollow echo. Or maybe that was simply the echo of her accusing words in his head, in his heart, in his soul. His empty heart, his empty soul. She was right, he knew that without question. But this was everything he'd worked for, everything…

Everything you schemed for, he corrected himself.

He turned back to the photos. Heavy, gilt-trimmed wood framed portraits of his mother, his father, his uncle, his ancestors, his childhood. They all looked different to him now than they had when he'd arrived more than a month ago. Then, the portraits had looked forbidding and cold, so formal there was no room left for emotion. The photographs from his childhood—birthday parties and vacations at the beach—had looked equally empty.

Jordan realized now that the only thing empty in the Scoville family was him. Even the promise of eight figures in his bank account wasn't enough to fill him up.

In fact, only one thing in his life had come close to filling him up. Joella. Joella and her son. And he would soon be going back to Atlanta without them.

It came to him then. This is why God had let his deal go through. So he would have something to offer Joella and Nathan. Of course! That had to be it! With the money he now had, he could give them anything, everything. He could make it up to them for every hard knock life had given them, for everything they'd ever lacked thanks to Scoville Mill. He could see it all so clearly now.

He put the image of his father and his uncle out of his mind as he headed out the door.

Joella's ritual for December 22 was always the same. This was the day she made cornbread for her Southern cornbread dressing for Christmas Day. Big, crusty batches of the bread would be mixed with celery and sage and onion and turkey broth. That was her contribution to the family meal, which this year would take place in her brother's apartment.

She looked around her little house, where she'd packed a few boxes but not nearly enough, given the fact that she planned to move the last day of the year. She knew she was just stalling, hating to face the inevitable. She also knew she hated the idea of not having one last family Christmas here in Bethlehem with her whole family. But maybe it was just as well. Maybe knowing it would be the last would be too hard, too emotional. This town was her life, her family.

How could this be the end? she wondered.

She turned on the oven to preheat it and took eggs out of the refrigerator. Before she could break the eggs into her bowl full of cornmeal, she heard the knock on the front door. Wiping her hands on the gingham kitchen towel she'd tucked into her jeans for an apron, she went to the door. It would be the Reverend Martin, she supposed. Or Claire.

Jordan stood in the doorway, his eyes bright and his hair windblown. He reminded her of Nathan, full of something he could barely contain, about to burst with the effort. She didn't think she'd ever seen him look so boyish. It twisted her heart. She wanted to close the door in his face, because it was the only way she could imagine protecting herself. Looking at him like that and not listening to her heart was almost more than she could manage.

"Jordan."

He came in, brushing past her, and she knew her voice must have held a soft invitation that she couldn't hold back. *Hang tough,* she told herself. *Whatever he's got to say, you don't have to fall for it. You don't have to get drawn in by it.*

He took her by the hands. She felt the tension in his body, and steeled herself.

"Marry me, Joella."

Her head took a momentary spin. Marry him? He was asking her to marry him? It took every bit of determination she had to remind herself there was no glass slipper. He was no prince. There was no happily ever after.

She pulled away from his touch and yanked the blue-checked towel loose from the waist of her jeans. "What?"

"I want you to marry me. We'll go to Atlanta, the three of us. I'll take care of you. I'll make you forget you ever had to live like this."

"I don't want to forget it," she said, feeling anger well up in her. "This is the way I've always lived. This is—"

"But you don't have to. Don't you see? I love you, Joella. I love Nathan. I want to give you everything you deserve."

He'd said he loved her. She fought not to hear those words. "And everybody else in Bethlehem? What about them, Jordan?"

Some of his boyish enthusiasm faded. "I can't save everybody. But—"

"I don't need saving, not the way you mean it," she said, jerking beyond his reach, rejecting the tempting warmth and comfort. "You know, the Bible is right. It would be easier for a camel to pass through the eye of a needle than it would be for somebody like you to realize that money can't buy the things I really want for Nathan."

"But—"

"I want community for him, the kind of hometown I grew up in." Joella plowed ahead. "I want a father who'll be devoted to him, but money only got in the way of that before. You know, all you've ever seen me wearing is blue jeans and flannel shirts.

That's not because I can't afford glittery dresses and diamond earrings. It's because I don't need them. I don't want them. I want more important things than that. And you've got so much money you'll never be able to see that.''

"But Joella, I..."

He looked crushed. She wished she hadn't had to say all those things, wished there was some way she could take them all back. But they were true and they had to be said. They were the words that would cut her free of Jordan Scoville, the words that would keep her from making the same mistake all over again.

"I don't want a rich man, Jordan," she said softly, her anger gone.

"But Joella, that's what I am. That's what I have to offer you."

She smiled, her heart breaking for him. "You have much more than that. You just haven't figured it out yet. And with all that money, you probably never will."

Nathan's arms hurt. And so did his head.

He walked down Main Street, his empty wagon rattling along behind him, kicking at piles of dead leaves and loose rocks as he went.

His arms hurt because he'd been hauling so much stuff down to the tent village in the days since school closed for the holiday. Wagonful after wagonful. His pockets were stuffed with money from their tips, but he didn't really care now. He wasn't saving for something special anymore, now that he'd already gone to Charlotte and found out that being an ambitious and enterprising young man didn't impress his dad.

His head hurt because of everything else.

His head was full of all the stuff that was going on around him. Like the people in the tent village, who were so happy and laughing all the time, like they had a special secret nobody else knew. Like everybody in Bethlehem packing up to leave, even his mom and him, which meant he'd be at a new school in January where he wouldn't know anybody and where he wouldn't have Venita's computer to work on and he might actually have to go through junior and senior high before he could get to Duke University.

Then there was the worst thing of all, and that was what he'd overheard his mom telling Reverend Martin after choir rehearsal the night before.

Jordan Scoville had asked her to marry him.

Nathan's tummy felt icky thinking about it. Not that he didn't like Jordan, which he did. Not that he wanted Jordan to go away and never see them again, which he didn't. But he wasn't sure it was the right thing for his mom to marry Jordan. In fact, he was sure it *wasn't* the right thing.

He might have felt differently a few weeks ago, before he went to Charlotte and saw firsthand what kind of man his own dad was. But he'd seen how mean and unfeeling his dad was, and it was clear to Nathan that, no matter how Jordan acted, the two men were just alike. They dressed the same, didn't they? They were both rich, weren't they? And his mom had been so softhearted that she'd fallen for both of them, hadn't she?

Well, he couldn't let his mom's heart get broken again.

His wagon hit a root growing up out of the sidewalk and nearly toppled over sideways. Nathan turned and looked at the wagon. It was making him rich.

He left it on the sidewalk and headed for the offices of Scoville Mill.

Somebody had to save his mom, and it looked as if he was elected.

Jordan didn't sleep much the night Joella told him his money didn't necessarily make him very good husband material. So when the sun rose on December 23, he needed the hottest shower he could stand and the strongest coffee he could stomach to get himself moving.

He still didn't feel ready to face Nathan Ratchford when he opened his front door and found the boy sitting on his front steps.

Seeing the boy brought up all the feelings he'd been trying so hard to bury under work. He wanted this boy in his life; he wanted to watch him grow and teach him things. But Joella had made it clear she didn't want her son learning anything he had to teach.

She was right, too.

But that didn't keep him from wanting it. Didn't keep him from wanting her, too. Facing the reality that he wouldn't have either of them left a raw, yawning ache deep inside him.

"Can we have a conference?" Nathan asked, his expression as stern as it was possible for a seven-year-old with unruly brown hair and big, round glasses to be.

Jordan tamped down the ache. "Here?"

Nathan peered around him and into the house. "Will we be by ourselves?"

Jordan nodded. Maybe this was good. Maybe Nathan was here to help him get Joella to change her mind. "Everything will be confidential. I promise."

Nathan walked in, heading for the parlor. He sat in the biggest of the two armchairs and drew his legs up, crossing them at the ankles. Jordan sat across from him.

"You can't marry my mom."

The words cut. Jordan felt his final shred of hope unravel. He supposed he should tell the kid there was very little danger of that. "Oh?"

"'Cause I know what you did."

"And what is that?"

"About stealing the retirement money. I'm the one who found out and told Mom."

Jordan wanted to look away. Seeing the condem-

nation in Nathan's eyes was harder than he had
imagined. "I see."

"But I figure Mom's pretty softhearted and she
decided to forgive you."

"And you're not as forgiving?"

"If you're a crook, you'll just break her heart.
Sooner or later."

"And if I'm not a crook?"

"But you are."

Nathan sat back, arms folded across his chest. His
gaze was unwavering, unyielding.

"I don't think you have anything to worry about,
Nathan. I'm not going to marry your mom."

Nathan blinked. "But you already asked her."

"She said no."

"Oh." Nathan flicked one of his shoelaces, considering that. "I suppose you'll keep trying to get
her to change her mind, huh?"

"Your mom doesn't strike me as the kind who
changes her mind very easily."

Nathan sat back and folded his arms across his
chest. "No. Not usually."

"Then it seems you're in no danger of picking up
a crook for a stepdad anytime soon." Surprisingly,
the comment hurt.

"Good." Nathan unfolded his legs and nudged
toward the edge of the seat. "But just in case, I think
you ought to tell her you changed *your* mind. 'Cause
if you don't, I can see to it that everybody in town,

maybe in the whole state, will know that you're a crook and you stole all our retirement money.''

Jordan nodded. ''I see.''

''They'd probably lynch you or something.''

''You think?''

''Yep. So, is it a deal?''

Jordan looked at this boy who was willing to do whatever it took to protect his mother from the kind of man who had already hurt her once. It occurred to him that Joella was right. Nathan deserved the best in a father, just as she deserved the best in a husband. And money couldn't buy that. In fact, money might just stand in the way. After all, as good-hearted as his parents had been, all the money had made it impossible for Jordan to feel that in his heart when he was growing up. The money always got in the way.

Jordan took a deep breath. One more step in this direction and there was no going back. Not once he'd opened the possibility to Nathan. He let the breath out, slowly, waiting for some sign that the old Jordan Scoville was still around to protest.

Not a peep.

''What if I had another plan?'' asked the new Jordan.

''What kind of plan?''

''If I had a plan—a plan for paying back all the retirement money—would you help me?''

''Maybe,'' Nathan said warily.

"We'd have to move fast," Jordan said. "We've got approximately thirty-six hours. Are you game?"

"Is this crooked, too?"

"Nope. I can promise you, Nathan, this isn't crooked. In fact, what if I told you this is probably, maybe, something in the neighborhood of being God's will?"

Chapter Fifteen

Christmas Eve dawned drizzly and cold, the kind of day that always made Joella feel like pulling the covers up around her ears and burrowing in for a long winter's rest.

Unfortunately, the day before Christmas held too many tasks for lying around in bed. There was work, of course, followed by last-minute gift wrapping and a stop by the supermarket for the cranberries she'd forgotten the day before. She had to call her brother to double-check the time of their mother's flight on Christmas morning, so they could all meet in time for the trip to the airport. And, of course, the annual walk-around to neighbors' homes to deliver little gifts—some fudge, some cookies, a beribboned jar of homemade potpourri—winding up this evening with the Christmas program at the church.

The eyes she hadn't yet opened began to fill as

she thought of the walk-around, a tradition she remembered from childhood. Tonight would be the last.

She yanked back the covers and jumped up. No wallowing around in sadness today. It was Christmas Eve. A day of miracles and merriment. She wasn't going to ruin it by focusing on the things she didn't have. She knelt by the bed and focused her morning prayers on gratitude.

"Good morning, God. Please take care of me today and please take care of the people I love, helping us to do our best to live in Your will this day. Help me especially stay focused on all the blessings You've brought me." She swept right past that moment when she wanted instead to consider all the hardships she'd been handed. "Thank You for this season, when You remind us that Your love is so deep and abiding that You gave us the gift of Your son. Thank You for warm homes, good food, the love of family and friends." She wouldn't think, either, of the love she resented having to walk away from. "Thank You for providing everything Nathan and I need for a new start. Thank You for all the gifts and blessings in my life."

She kept her eyes closed and her hands clasped for a moment, resisting the urge to ask for the things her heart desired. She knew by now that God had better things in mind than anything her heart might desire. Some days it was easier than others to accept that. But she would try. Especially today.

Forcing herself to hum a carol, Joella dressed quickly. As she ran a brush through her hair, she noticed that her eyes were still puffy. A woman might find the courage to turn down a marriage proposal from a man who looked like Prince Charming, but that didn't mean she wouldn't cry herself to sleep over it two nights in a row.

"Thank goodness I'm too busy to worry about that today," she said to her reflection, hoping to convince herself, hoping God would heal her heart and dry her tears before too much longer.

Her hurt over losing Jordan was as deep as her hurt over losing Bethlehem, a physical ache that throbbed away beneath the smile she forced herself to present the world. She felt lonely and afraid, but she knew better than to believe that clamoring voice in her head that insisted Jordan Scoville could make it all better.

She listened instead to the still, quiet voice that warned her that Jordan had some changing to do before he could do anything but bring her misery.

She stuck her head in Nathan's bedroom on her way to the kitchen, but his rumpled bed was already empty. She found him in the kitchen, wolfing down a bowl of cereal. He looked guilty when she came in.

"I would've made you oatmeal this morning," she said, ruffling his hair. "With honey and raisins."

He jumped up, his spoon clattering against the bowl. "I'm late."

retirement money they'd all counted on. The secret gnawed at her, setting her on edge, stirring up fear and insecurity and the anguish of being alone with what she knew.

"My husband says they're going to get the truth out of the Scovilles before the day is up, or know the reason why," said the clerk in the next line.

"Oh, dear," said a little old lady whose son worked at the mill. "My Jerry is so angry. You know, he's as likely to start swinging his fist as listen to what people have to say when he gets like that. I told him he ought to just stay home today. But he's that much like his father was. A hothead."

Clutching her bag from the supermarket, Joella stood under the awning, troubled by the talk. She watched the drizzle and wondered what she should do. The dreary weather hadn't slowed down the hustle-bustle of last-minute holiday preparations a bit. Like her, everyone seemed to have purpose this afternoon. Townspeople scurried about, none of them seeming touched by the spirit of the season. A small knot of campers clustered together under the awning in front of the barbershop, which was already closed for the day. The campers were the only ones Joella saw who looked the least bit festive. They laughed and gestured, growing quiet only when townspeople passed, then putting their heads back together as soon as the locals had passed. The two government employees in suits and overcoats checked their watches, glanced toward the mill offices, nodded grimly and went into the bank.

Everyone, it seemed to Joella, was acting strangely today.

She started for home, gazing up at the mill offices before she turned off Main Street. Golden light glowed from the window of the reception area and the office where Jordan had been working. The rest of the windows were dark. She thought of going for Nathan. She wanted him home with her for Christmas Eve. They could sing carols or he could read the Christmas story to her while she finished her wrapping. Besides, what if Fred and the supermarket clerk were right? What if people were angry enough to plan a confrontation with Jordan this afternoon? She shivered and veered off toward the office.

As she approached, Venita was walking out the front door, her yellow rain slicker the only bright spot on the street. "Merry Christmas!" Venita called out. Her face was the happiest one Joella had seen so far today.

"Merry Christmas to you." Joella did her best to match Venita's spirited greeting. "Is Nathan still here?"

Venita glanced over her shoulder. "I'm afraid so. They have their heads together over the computer."

"I was hoping he'd come home with me," she said, wondering if she should warn Venita what she'd heard. No, that was alarmist. Nothing was going to happen. Not in Bethlehem. Not on Christmas Eve.

"You can try. But I wouldn't count on it," Venita said.

Venita headed for her car and Joella walked toward the door of the office building. But as she approached, the door flew open. Nathan dashed out, almost plowing into her in his haste.

"Whoa, young man. Slow down and watch where you're going."

He evaded her grasp and ran backward a few steps. "Sorry, Mom. Gotta run."

"But, Nathan—"

"See ya!"

And he was off like a streak, darting clumsily between people before he skidded through the door of the dime store. Joella contemplated going after him, collaring him and ordering him home. But he'd looked so excited, so happy. Happier than anyone she'd seen today, except maybe Venita. Well, at least she could go in and talk to Jordan, urge him to wind things up and send her son home.

And go home early himself, just in case Fred Roseforte and hotheaded Jerry and some others like them decided that Bethlehem should not lie still on Christmas Eve.

Jordan was hunched over the computer at Venita's desk, a frown etched deeply into his forehead, pecking at the keys with his two index fingers. "Nathan, good boy. That was fast. Listen, I can't do this as fast as you can. So why don't you..."

He looked up then and grew silent.

"Joella."

He spoke her name like a caress, soft and intimate. She felt it like a touch, deep inside her. He looked different, she thought. Despite the frown, there was something peaceful about his gaze today.

"Merry Christmas," she said, barely remembering why she'd come in, knowing it was only an excuse. She'd come to see him. She knew that now. Why else would she have come in after seeing her son dash off? For Jordan. Only for Jordan.

He stood and took her hands in his. "Merry Christmas to you, Joella."

She thought he might kiss her. She could almost read the intention in his eyes. She grew still inside, and wished he would, despite all her best intentions. Just one kiss.

He dropped her hands.

"You shouldn't be here," he said. "I mean, you probably have a million things to do."

He wouldn't kiss her. He didn't even want her here. "I came after Nathan."

"Ah, Nathan. Yes. Well, he's not here right now."

"I'll wait for him to get back."

"Oh. I see. Well, why don't I send him home? Soon. How would that be?"

He looked like a small boy caught at something,

a look she knew very well. She didn't know what he was up to with her son, but she knew she couldn't trust him because of the look in his eyes. That knowledge hurt. And she'd thought he looked different. Changed.

Changed by her love. That's what she'd thought, wasn't it? That she could change him, show him the way. Would she never change her foolish ways?

"Some of the men might come by today. They want some answers. They're angry."

He nodded. Understanding seemed to sink in. "Don't worry, Joella. Nothing's going to happen to Nathan. I promise."

It made her sad to realize that his promise meant nothing to her at that moment. Her heart might be broken over that, but she also knew that she would be okay. Because she could rely on God's promises. God could mend broken hearts. He would mend hers.

"You'll send him home, then?"

"I'll take care of him. I promise."

And he would. He promised her that again in his heart as he watched her walk across Main Street toward home. He just couldn't promise to send her son home right away. He and the boy had too much to accomplish before the end of the day and he couldn't do it alone—Nathan was a computer whiz and Jordan was barely computer literate. Besides, Jordan had to make a run to the bank in Greenville and then—

The door opened and Nathan was back, his arms overloaded with a box from the dime store.

"Got 'em. Got every single gift bag they had, and every one at the drugstore and the supermarket."

"Good boy. We can do this, can't we? In time, I mean?"

With the confidence of youth that the impossible could always be accomplished, Nathan nodded. "Sure."

"Okay, you keep on here. I'll run to Greenville. And…one other stop."

"Where?"

"Ah…"

"No more secrets."

"Right. No more secrets. I'm going to talk to Hat Martin."

"Oh. Okay." Nathan nodded, as if a visit to the town's minister made perfect sense in the middle of a crisis in which they were running short of time. "He could probably put in a good word for us."

"Right. Exactly."

The trip to the bank went without a hitch, which was to be expected, since the small Greenville bank probably hadn't seen so much money at one time in its entire operating history. Say what you like about money, it did oil the machinery, Jordan thought. And this time it felt right.

Then he sped back to Bethlehem, slowing down

only when the drizzle began to mix with a light snowfall.

He braked to a halt in front of the church and paused a moment to look around him. The snow was dusting the ground and casting a magic haze over the little town. Jordan felt his heart stir. He remembered only one other snowfall at Christmas in all the years he'd been in Bethlehem. He'd been seven, just like Nathan. And he'd asked for snow for Christmas, a wish that always prompted his parents to share a bemused glance. No matter how they encouraged him to ask for something else, he'd held fast to his one wish for snow.

He hadn't been surprised when the snow had arrived on time, although everyone else had been astonished. It never snowed in December in South Carolina.

"I guess You were trying to tell me something," he said softly. "Too bad I wasn't listening."

"Beg pardon?"

Jordan started and turned to find the Reverend Martin a few feet away.

"Reverend Martin, hello. I was just..." He hesitated. This wasn't the kind of thing he would normally be able to admit. Actually, it wasn't the kind of thing he would have been doing a month ago. If he was a changed man, he might as well go for broke. The irony of that thought made him smile. "Just talking to the One in charge."

Hat Martin smiled. "Always a good idea, my boy."

"But I came by to talk to you. If you have a minute."

"Certainly, certainly. In my office?"

Jordan looked around at the light snow swirling through the air. "I kind of like it out here, if it's not too raw for you."

"This is God's office. Better than mine any time. Now, what can I do for you today, Jordan?"

"Well, I had this plan, you see. And I decided...all by myself...that it must be God's will. Since I'd been praying for God's will, you understand. So it made sense to me.... Anyway, it's occurred to me that maybe I ought to check it out with somebody else. Somebody who has more experience in figuring out God's will. Since my track record isn't too good in that regard. If you know what I mean."

Hat Martin's smile had grown broader with every word. He put his hand on Jordan's shoulder. "An excellent idea, son, excellent. Let's hear what God's been telling you, why don't we?"

Dusk was falling and Nathan still hadn't come home. Joella's nervousness grew. She kept peering out the window, watching the snow accumulate on the ground and in the corners of the window. It wasn't much—the streets and sidewalks were still clear—but it was enough to give the little town the look of a greeting card.

But Joella remembered the feeling in town that afternoon and knew that Bethlehem was sorely lacking in holiday spirit.

Why wasn't her son home yet?

She bundled up and started after him. As she turned the corner onto Main Street, her heart began to pound uncomfortably. A crowd had gathered on Main Street, in front of the offices of Scoville Mill. Fear clutched her. She ran the last block.

The murmur of the crowd sounded angry, hostile, to her ears. She looked around and saw, in addition to the campers and the auditors, the faces of people she'd known all her life and told herself there was nothing to fear. But the words wouldn't sink into her heart.

"They've locked us out," someone said angrily.

"They'll have to come out sometime," came the reply.

"A lock can't keep us out!"

"We've got a right to answers!"

Then hotheaded Jerry leapt onto the front steps. "Those windows are no match for a tire iron. I can tell you that right now."

Joella cried out, "No!" But no one seemed to hear her.

"Don't worry, my dear."

She looked around at the sound of Hat Martin's gentle voice.

"Nathan," she said. "He's in there."

"So he is," the minister said. "Why, I believe that's him now, with Mr. Scoville."

"Oh, no."

The front door had opened and Nathan had indeed walked out, with Jordan at his side and his little red wagon behind him. Joella began to push through to the front of the crowd, determined to get her son out of the way before anything started.

"Hey, Jerry. Merry Christmas." That was Nathan, greeting the angry mill worker as if there was nothing out of the ordinary in finding an enraged mob collecting on the streets of Bethlehem.

Jerry mumbled a return greeting and backed away just as Joella reached the front of the crowd. The auditors reached the front about the same time, asking questions that were drowned out by the questions being shouted from the townspeople.

"If you'll clear the way," Jordan was calling out, "Nathan's got a few deliveries to make. Could you just make room for him, please?"

The crowd shifted around, their grumbles growing muffled as Nathan began passing out holiday gift bags from his wagon. He seemed to have one for every family in town, including Joella. She stared at the bag, which he'd given her with a wink. Everyone seemed as stunned as Joella. They were all staring at the bags. Even the state auditors got bags. Gifts, when their world was falling apart?

"Probably delivering our pink slips in time for Christmas," Fred Roseforte grumbled.

Joella looked up at Jordan, who was looking down at her. Despite the angry crowd that faced him, he didn't look one bit worried.

Then the first gasp sounded as someone finally opened a gift bag. Astonished cries began to ripple through the crowd. A stunned laugh. Joella peeked inside her own bag, where a little blue book was nestled in tissue.

"A bankbook!" someone cried.

"And look at all those zeroes."

With trembling fingers Joella took the book out of the bag. It had her name on the inside page. And it was indeed a bankbook. A savings account in her name. And the total deposit listed was more money than she had ever expected to see in her lifetime.

"What's the meaning of this?" demanded one of the auditors, who was waving a bankbook, as well. "If this is a bribe, I'll—"

Jordan laughed and waved the crowd to silence. He looked almost giddy, Joella thought. What in the world was going on here? "What you have is the retirement account for Scoville Mill. Four-point-six million, I think, is what it holds. So the future of everyone here is secure, even after we close the doors. I believe that was your concern today, gentlemen."

The two men in cheap suits looked at one another, frowned into the bankbook. "Well, yes, but—"

"Then I wish you a Merry Christmas. I think you still have time to get home for the holiday, gentlemen."

Then Jordan turned his attention to the crowd. Or, more to the point, he turned his attention to Joella.

"And what the rest of you have is a savings passbook," he said. "Think of it as a Christmas bonus. You can use it to relocate. Or you could buy the houses you live in and stay here in Bethlehem. Or some of you have talked about buying out Scoville Mill, which goes on the auction block the day after Christmas."

Joella's eyes grew wide. He was smiling right at her.

"And with a new contract to manufacture souvenir T-shirts and caps for the new NFL team in south Georgia, I'd say the future looks pretty good for whoever becomes the new owner of Scoville Mill."

After a moment of stunned silence, cheers went up in the crowd. Everyone began talking at once. Joella heard them talking about buying the mill where they'd worked all their lives. But her focus was on Jordan, who stood uncertainly on the steps until Nathan prodded him forward.

"You're not exactly rich," he said. "But you'll be comfortable."

"But Jordan, how—"

"So you don't need a rich husband anymore. But I was hoping you might… That is, I've been thinking about what you said and... Will you marry me?''

"Oh, Jordan, I—"

"No, wait. Before you answer, you have to know, I don't have a penny to my name."

"Not a p-penny?"

He shook his head. But before he could speak, Nathan jumped in. "He had all this land, Mom, to build a football stadium. And the NFL decided to put a team where he had his land, so he was going to be a billionaire—"

"Well..." Jordan said.

Nathan refused to be dissuaded. "A billionaire. But he sold it all so he could save the town 'cause Mr. Mitchell and Mr. Truman—"

"That's enough, Nathan." Jordan's voice was firm.

And his eyes were clear. Joella felt she could see straight to his heart. She understood it all now. His silence had been necessary to protect two old men who were dear to him. She also understood the human frailty that had made him pause over the idea of giving up billions for the sake of a town where he'd never felt welcome.

"That's a wonderful story," she said softly.

He touched the back of her hand, almost shyly. "I'll be starting over. But I have...faith...that I'll be led to the right work."

"Faith?"

"That's right."

She thought for a moment of the simple perfection of God's plan, and her own human frailty in doubting it. "I know where you might find a position."

"You do?"

"There's a little mill in a little town in South Carolina. They might be looking for a new CEO."

"Well, that's a possibility. But I think they'll probably be looking for a family man."

Tears filled Joella's eyes. "Then you might be just the man for the job."

As he swept her into his arms, another cry went up from the crowd. Joella looked up in time to see a million lights go on all over town, more magical and spectacular than the lights had ever been in Christmas Town, U.S.A.

And as they began to twinkle, the visitors who had been given so much Christmas spirit over the years by the people of Bethlehem cried out, "Merry Christmas!"

Joella looked around for her son. He stood on the top step of Scoville Mill, jumping up and down, laughing. If he was like her, he would always remember this as the best Christmas ever, just as his mother had promised. Then she looked into Jordan's eyes. They, too, were filled with wonder, the eyes of someone seeing the light for the first time in his life.

*   *   *   *   *

Dear Reader,

Some people, I suppose, come to faith easily. Others of us arrive at our faith by reaching out while lost in the darkness and finding only one thing to guide us: God. We learn the hard way that God is all we need, all we'll ever need.

I'm one of the ones who came to my faith the hard way. Only when death, disease and family problems all came crashing down on me at once was I able to see the truth—that I couldn't handle any of it alone. And I became one of those people who now expresses gratitude for all the difficulties life has brought.

This is my first inspirational romance and I'm so excited to be starting down this path. For more than a decade, I've enjoyed writing about the power of love. What could be more powerful than adding the dimension of faith to stories of men and women finding strength and healing in love? I hope you have enjoyed visiting *Christmas Town* with me.

Wishing you all the best,

Peggy Gilchrist

Take 2 inspirational love stories FREE!

PLUS get a FREE surprise gift!

Special Limited-Time Offer

Mail to Steeple Hill Reader Service™
3010 Walden Avenue
P.O. Box 1867
Buffalo, N.Y. 14240-1867

YES! Please send me 2 free Love Inspired™ novels and my free surprise gift. Then send me 3 brand-new novels every month, which I will receive months before they appear in bookstores. Bill me at the low price of $3.19 each plus 25¢ delivery and applicable sales tax, if any*. That's the complete price and a saving of over 10% off the cover prices—quite a bargain! I understand that accepting the books and gift places me under no obligation ever to buy any books. I can always return a shipment and cancel at any time. Even if I never buy another book from Steeple Hill, the 2 free books and the surprise gift are mine to keep forever.

103 IEN CM6G

Name	(PLEASE PRINT)	
Address		Apt. No.
City	State	Zip

This offer is limited to one order per household and not valid to present Love Inspired™ subscribers. *Terms and prices are subject to change without notice. Sales tax applicable in New York.

ULI-199   ©1998 Steeple Hill

A HOLIDAY PRAYER

by Debra Kastner

Available in December 1998 from
Love Inspired®

Handsome Rory March tenderly soothed widow
Maddie Carlton's aching heart and filled the void
in her impressionable son's life, until Maddie
began to believe in the miracle of love again.
But would her most precious holiday
prayer be answered when
she discovered Rory's
shocking secret?

Available at your favorite retail outlet.

 Love Inspired®

ILIHP

Available in January 1999 from
Love Inspired®...

A HOME,
A HEART,
A HUSBAND

by *Lois Richer*

Maggie McCarthy has her hands full with two twin girls and a family farm to run, so she gladly accepts Grady O'Toole's offer of help. However, she loses her life's focus and her faith when she is forced to sell her farm and move to the city. Is it too late for Grady to prove to her the importance of family, faith and love?

**Watch for A HOME, A HEART, A HUSBAND
in January 1999 from**

 Love Inspired®

Available at your favorite retail outlet.

ILIAHHH